I0793028

IMAGES
of America

LOS ALAMOS VALLEY

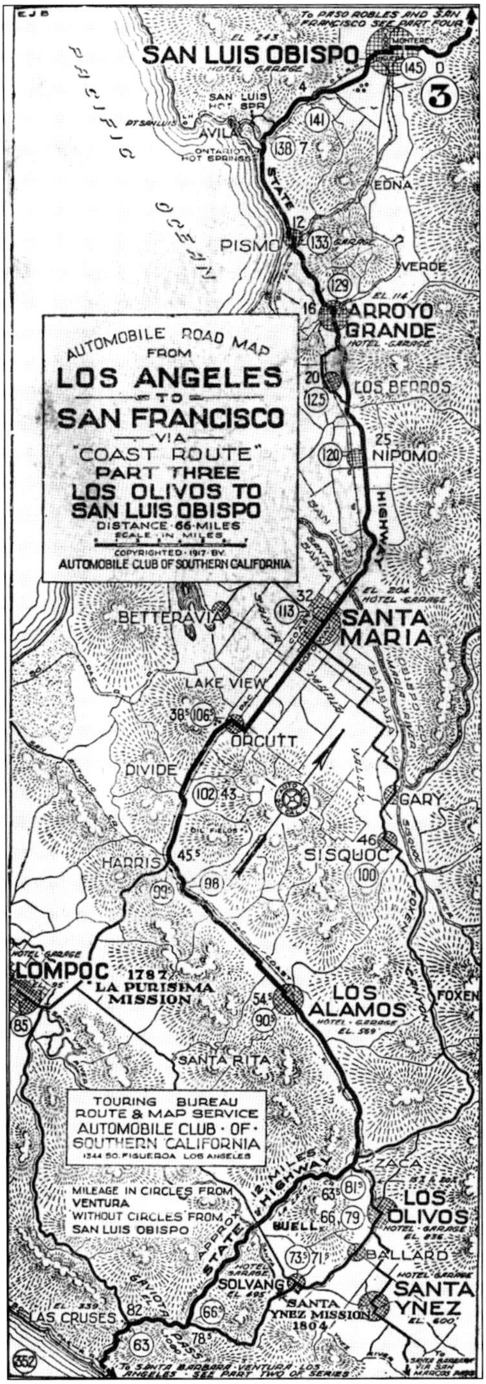

The Southern California Automobile Club published this map in 1917, one of a series of four detailing the route between Los Angeles and San Francisco. This section shows the route from Ventura to San Luis Obispo. The mileage from Ventura is shown in circles. Los Alamos offers hotels and garages. The Pacific Coast Railroad, still in existence at this time, parallels the state highway. Los Alamos is shown larger than Solvang, and Buell had not yet become Buellton. There are oil fields in Orcutt, but not yet in Careaga Canyon (west of Los Alamos) or Cat Canyon (north of Los Alamos). The communities of Las Cruces, Santa Rita, and Divide shown on this map no longer exist. Santa Rita Road, west of Los Alamos, is no longer in use by the public. (Courtesy of Santa Ynez Valley Historical Society.)

On the Cover: Unidentified young women wave farewell from a caboose at the Los Alamos station in anticipation of a ride on the Pacific Coast Railroad headed north from Los Alamos. The ladies' dress and the railroad ties missing in the foreground suggest they may have been greeting a new railroad as well as bidding adieu to their friends. The line was extended south of Los Alamos to Los Olivos in 1887. (Courtesy of the Santa Ynez Valley Historical Society.)

IMAGES
of America

LOS ALAMOS VALLEY

R. Lawson Gamble

ARCADIA
PUBLISHING

ISBN 978-1-4671-3331-9

Published by Arcadia Publishing
Charleston, South Carolina

Printed in the United States of America

Library of Congress Control Number: 2014954866

For all general information, please contact Arcadia Publishing:
Telephone 843-853-2070
Fax 843-853-0044
E-mail sales@arcadiapublishing.com
For customer service and orders:
Toll-Free 1-888-313-2665

Visit us on the Internet at www.arcadiapublishing.com

To Laura Abeloe, Jeanette Sainz, and all who labored to preserve Los Alamos memories, and to Dorothea Gamble, who encouraged a love of history.

Contents

ACKNOWLEDGMENTS

It takes a village to compile a community history with images, and that is how this book came about. This work is meant to represent those whose life threads are woven into the fabric of Los Alamos—their cultures, races, work, play, dreams, disappointments, and joys. We have done our best, assisted by the people of town and valley, all of whom demonstrated willingness to share their stories and photographs and offered unending encouragement for this project. We relied on some souls more heavily than others, and they deserve special recognition. Chris Bashforth and the staff of the Santa Ynez Valley Historical Museum made their resources and historical images available to us. Curt Cragg, author of two Images of America books, contributed photographs and expertise. Jeanette Sainz shared her family photographs and artifact collection as well as stories of ranch, oil, and town life. Joe Carrari contributed insights into the beginning of viticulture in the valley and the growth of the Los Alamos Rancho. Kathy Christoferson was coordinator extraordinaire, introducing us to town and valley people. We relied heavily on the 1996 "Tour of Los Alamos Historic District" commemorative booklet by historian Jim Norris and other booklets from *Los Alamos Old Days*, published by the Men's Club of Los Alamos. Joe Dana and the Olga Reed School opened their archives to us. Mike Farris of the Santa Maria Valley Historical Society contributed images and special knowledge of the area. Madeleine Jex, John Morley, Charlie Gonzales, and others also supported this project. We wish to acknowledge everyone whose assistance in this effort came too late to include here. Unless otherwise noted, all images appear courtesy of the Santa Ynez Valley Historical Society.

Many of the citizens of town and valley who experienced the historic lives and events in Los Alamos are gone now, and the town is poorer for it. Some threads lost from the Los Alamos fabric may never be recovered. It is fortunate that a few individuals and groups have made great efforts to preserve this important history.

INTRODUCTION

J.D. Mason wrote in *A History of Santa Barbara and Ventura Counties*: "It is hardly possible to conceive the existence of a pleasanter location than the Los Alamos Valley, or one combining more valuable resources with natural beauty. The valley is rather tortuous in its course so that the sea breeze, which usually sweeps too strongly for comfort through the coast valleys generally, here gets baffled and confused, bringing only a gentle reminder of its origin, although there is health and vigor in its freshness and purity. . . . If there is a pleasanter and better spot in the world, I have never seen it."

Because the surrounding hills offered protection from the hot, drying breezes, the Los Alamos Valley was the first of the surrounding valleys to feel the plow. An ample supply of groundwater lay just beneath the valley floor. The richness of the soil and the beneficial conditions supplied by cool, damp mornings and plentiful afternoon sunshine assured that virtually any crop could thrive here.

At one time, a great inland lake covered the entire Los Alamos Valley. Sea levels were lower than present, as much of the earth's waters were frozen into ice. The vast weight of thicker ice near the center of the continent lifted the western edge to expose valleys of the coastal ranges and more of the Channel Islands. When the earth began to warm, the ice melted, the sea levels rose, the continent's western edge settled, and the inland lakes slowly drained. The lake that covered the Los Alamos Valley subsided more slowly than others, depositing copious amounts of rich soil and minerals along the way. At last, only San Antonio Creek remained, carving its way the length of the valley from its upper reaches near Los Olivos to its union with the Pacific Ocean south of the Sal Point Headland.

The Paleo-Indians came during the first warming that followed the last ice age and settled along the coast in the estuaries. These Indians would not have ventured far inland. The interior was inhospitable, a "predator hell hole" according to paleozoologist Valerius Geist. It was inhabited by such formidable creatures as three short-faced bear species (two of them super carnivores), lions twice as large as African lions, saber-toothed cats, jaguars, a cheetah-like cat, and large dire wolves. It was a good place to avoid altogether. The grizzly bear, a formidable predator in its own right, came later, possibly by way of the Bering land bridge.

The Chumash Indians appeared in Los Alamos Valley over 13,000 years ago. For a people whose tenure in the valley prior to the intrusion of the first Europeans is far longer than the subsequent habitation by all other peoples combined, proportionally little has been written about them. In pre-contact times, four Purisimeño Indian villages existed along San Antonio Creek. West of Los Alamos were Step (meaning "flea") and Saxpilil. East of Los Alamos was Cuaslui (meaning "sliding place"). The village of Saqsiyol (or Socciol) was located nearest the present location of the town. An alternate name, Mas'iwik, meant "jug basket," referring to the Chumash twined water basket sealed with tar, and may possibly refer to Laguna Seca, a small lake in Cañada Laguna Seca. The village may have been located at the mouth of that canyon, just west of Los Alamos.

The peace and relative prosperity of the indigenous population was disrupted forever by the arrival of the Spanish and their fortlike missions. Mission La Purisima Concepcion was built nearest the Los Alamos Valley and influenced it most. During its early years, the native inhabitants of the valley were enticed or otherwise brought to the mission grounds. By 1805, the native villages of the valley were abandoned as places of permanent residence, leaving only an adobe or two for the Indians who guarded the mission's enormous horse herd. These horse-tending Chumash became highly skilled horsemen with a hands-free riding technique that earned them the special name "vaqueros."

As elsewhere on the South Coast, the Chumash suffered greatly from newly introduced diseases, against which they had no resistance. A smallpox outbreak in the mid-1840s dealt an especially severe blow. By the mid-1850s, only eight natives were left in the valley.

As with much of California, the first privatization of the land began with Spanish land grants, authorized first by Spain and later by Mexican governors. The Americans readjusted these grants when they assumed power. The Los Alamos Valley was comprised of two large grants: Rancho Los Alamos and Rancho La Laguna. In the 1870s, Dr. J.B. Shaw purchased 14,000 acres of Rancho Los Alamos for his boss, financier Thomas Bell, and 14,000 acres of Rancho La Laguna for himself. From these contiguous ranchos they platted the town of Los Alamos and named the street that divided the two properties Centennial Street, for the recent 100th birthday of the United States.

The economic engine that would drive the valley and town of Los Alamos over the years was fueled first by cattle, then by agriculture, oil, and, finally, wine and tourism. While each resource superseded the next, all still play a part to this day.

The town itself was born of a change made in the routing of the stagecoach from the northern Foxen Canyon route to the Los Alamos Valley. The town grew further with the arrival of the Central Coast Railroad and prospered from the routing of State Route 101 (and later the freeway) through the valley. The surge of automobile travel in the first decades of the 20th century offered additional economic opportunity.

The town today is not as large as it was in the heyday of the automobile—there are fewer hotels, gas stations, and restaurants. There is no longer a jail, a police station, or a bank. But the folks who live here prefer it this way.

A quote in the Old Days souvenir program of 1978 expresses the feeling poignantly: "Los Alamos is a wide spot in the road, comfortably out of range of any beer can tossed from a passing car on the 101 Freeway. And Los Alamos is determined to remain just that—a tranquil rural settlement located in one of the last of California's unspoiled pastoral valleys."

One

Then and Now
A Drive Down Bell Street

History is visible everywhere in Los Alamos. Old buildings house new enterprises. Many buildings appear much as they did in earlier days. A traveler approaching Los Alamos along El Camino Real (Route 101) will see hills blanketed with wheat-colored grasses and dotted with picturesque oak trees. These are the Golden Hills. Nearer town is a weathered, wooden sign with "Los Alamos" painted on a background of a stagecoach and six. The sign features the dates for Los Alamos Old Days, a fall weekend celebration of the rich history of this town of 1,000 residents. The Skyview Hotel soon comes into view high on a hill, with its long, curved drive lined with palm trees. The off-ramp for northbound traffic winds under the highway bridge to a stop sign at Bell Street, named for Thomas Bell, one of two founders of Los Alamos. Directly across the intersection is Main Street. Originally intended as the town's business center, Main Street took on a residential character, and Bell Street developed into the commercial zone in its stead. At this intersection 100 years ago was a railroad crossing. On the right, the glistening rails of the Pacific Coast Railroad approached from the depot, curving gently away to the south toward the end of the line, Los Olivos. This chapter shows the buildings of Los Alamos as they appeared in the past, contrasted with recent images. The reader will travel across the tracks (look both ways!), turn right on Bell Street, and enter the town. Here begins the journey into Los Alamos history.

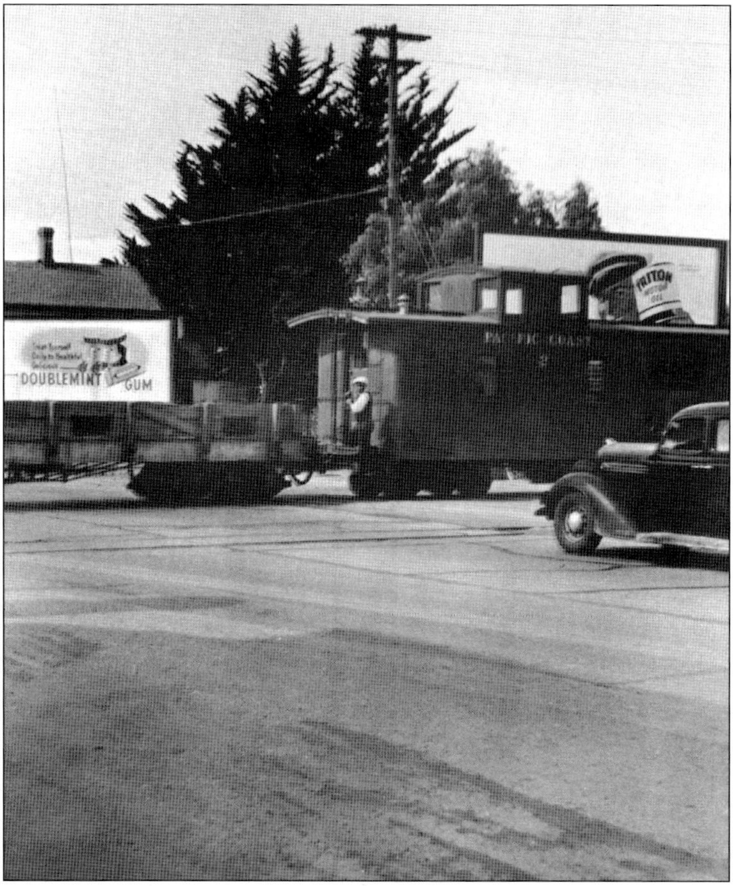

A car waits at the crossing for the Pacific Coast Steam Railway caboose to pass in the early 1940s. The Doublemint Gum advertisement on the billboard across the tracks dates this photograph to 1940 or 1941. The narrow-gauge railroad arrived in Los Alamos in 1882, and the suddenly unconstrained citizens of Los Alamos immediately embarked on a multitude of excursions. (Courtesy of Los Alamos Men's Club [LAMC].)

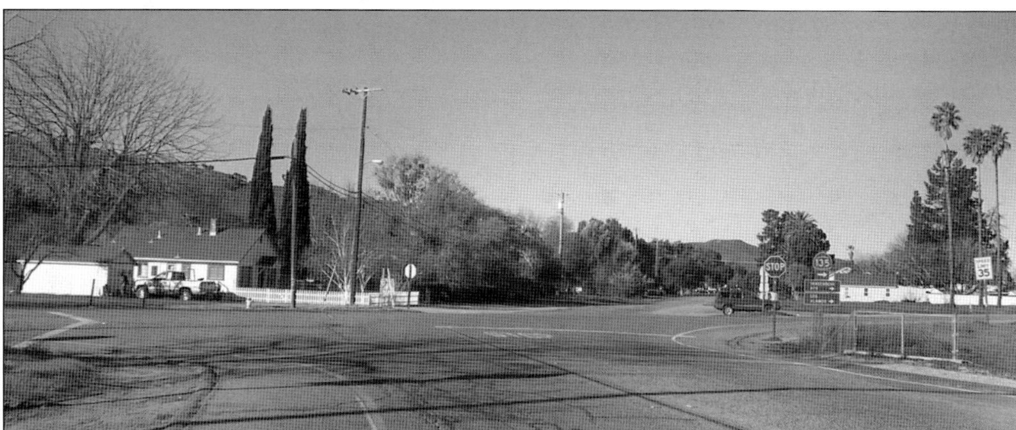

This photograph was taken soon after the construction of the freeway to the town of Los Alamos in the 1960s. The ramps appear to be new. The triangle of land where the gas station, café, and motel stand is empty today, and the trees are gone. The railroad track would have crossed this intersection leading to the depot, the building with the long roof to the left. Today when the traveler exits the Route 101 Freeway at the south Los Alamos exit, the ramp terminates at a stop sign. The railroad tracks are gone. Across the intersection, Main Street angles obliquely away. Yesterday's traveler would have approached Los Alamos along Bell Street from left to right.

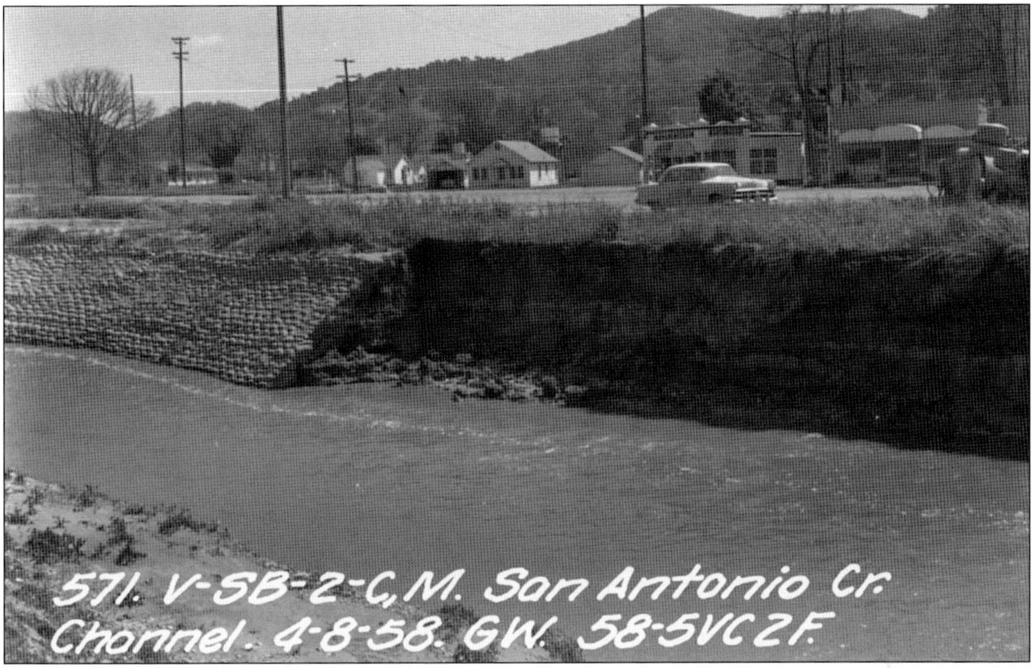

This photograph was taken from the north bank of San Antonio Creek on August 4, 1958. The Standard gasoline service station and the café beyond the Ford coupe were located at the south end of Los Alamos on Bell Street. There was a motel behind the café and a shaded picnic area just to the west of it. The house to the left of the station is on Main Street.

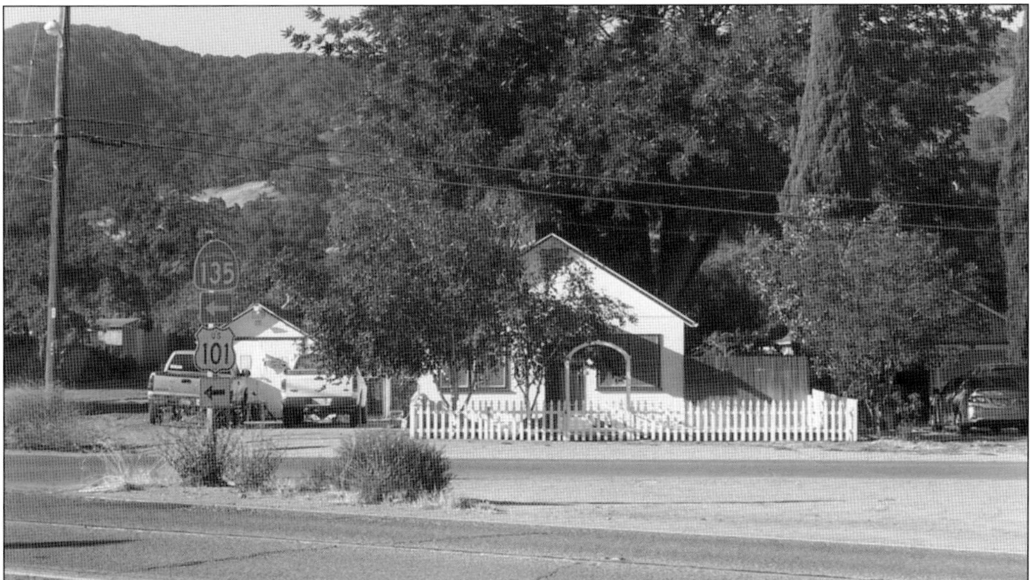

The same house stands on Main Street today. The service station and motel complex are now gone. Old Route 101, which ran along Bell Street in the 1950s, became Route 135 after the new highway was constructed. In the foreground, Bell Street angles away from Main Street toward the town center. The barn and garages to either side of the house are essentially unchanged. (Photograph by author.)

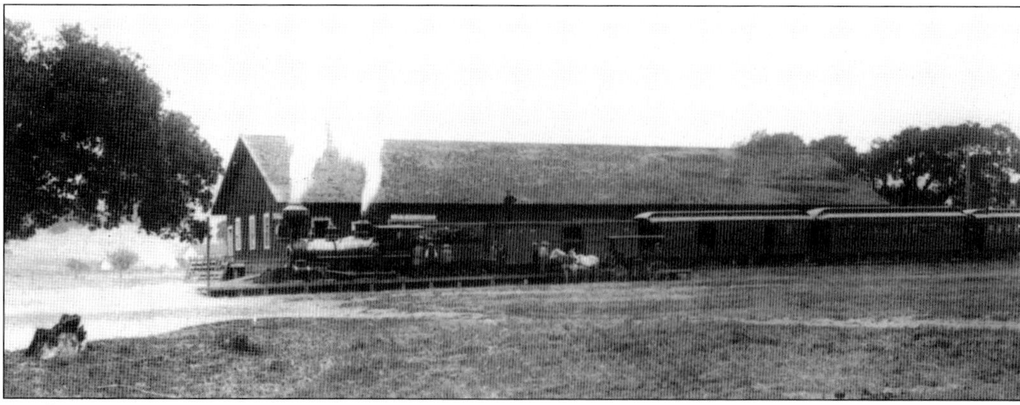

A train waits for baggage to be off-loaded at the Pacific Coast Railway station in Los Alamos. This train, consisting primarily of passenger cars, is headed north toward San Luis Obispo. This photograph was taken after the station was built in 1882 but before a two-story addition was made following a fire in 1901. A carriage waits to transport a passenger to a nearby hotel.

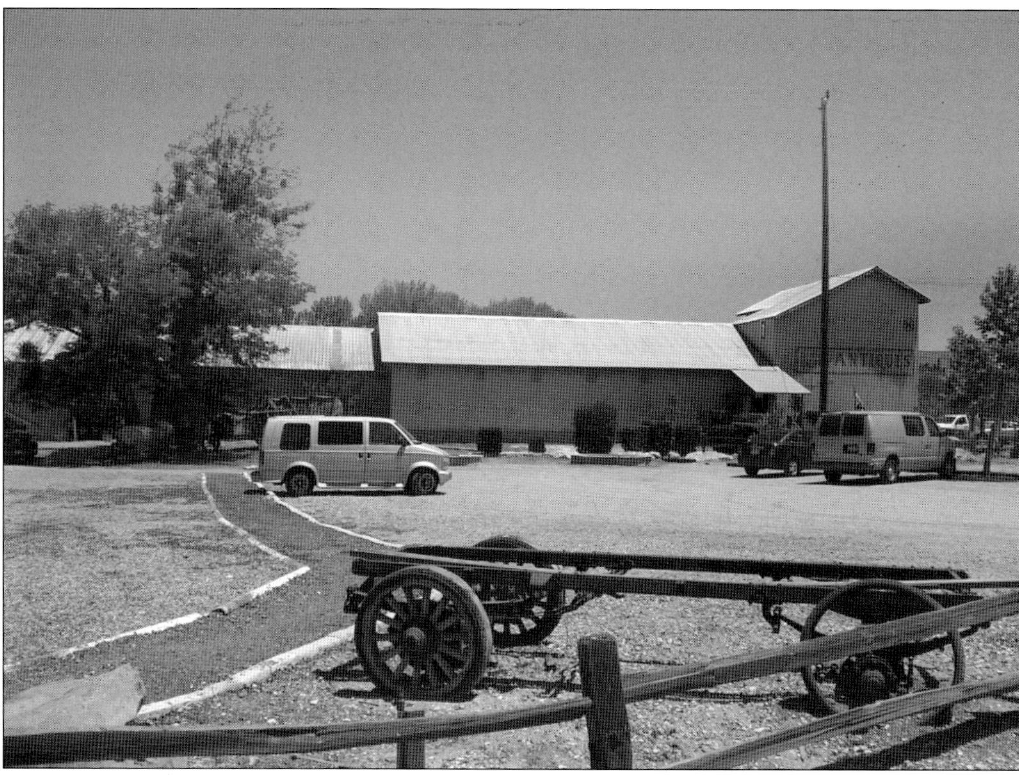

The Los Alamos depot served the Pacific Coast Railway until the line was abandoned in 1941. It is the only depot for that line still standing. The original depot burned down in 1890 and was then rebuilt. Today, the building is home to Los Alamos Depot Mall Antiques. The store is a major attraction for tourists, boasting a large inventory supplied by over 60 antiques vendors. (Photograph by author.)

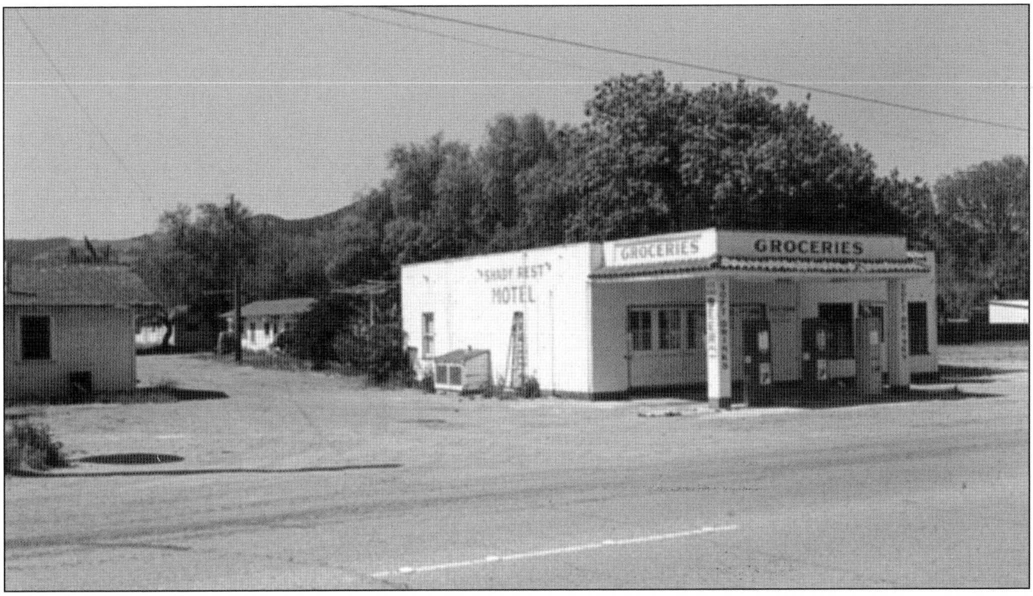

The Shady Rest service station and grocery store was originally constructed as the Shady Rest Motel in 1923, with eight individual cabins. By the 1960s, the motel was abandoned, but the service station continued to exist in various forms. Among the building's many reincarnations was the Pool Hall, Waterhole, Drum General Store, Taylor's Place, Cindy's Place, Maxine's Tavern, Steel Horse Saloon, Los Alamos Tavern, and the Ghostriders Tavern.

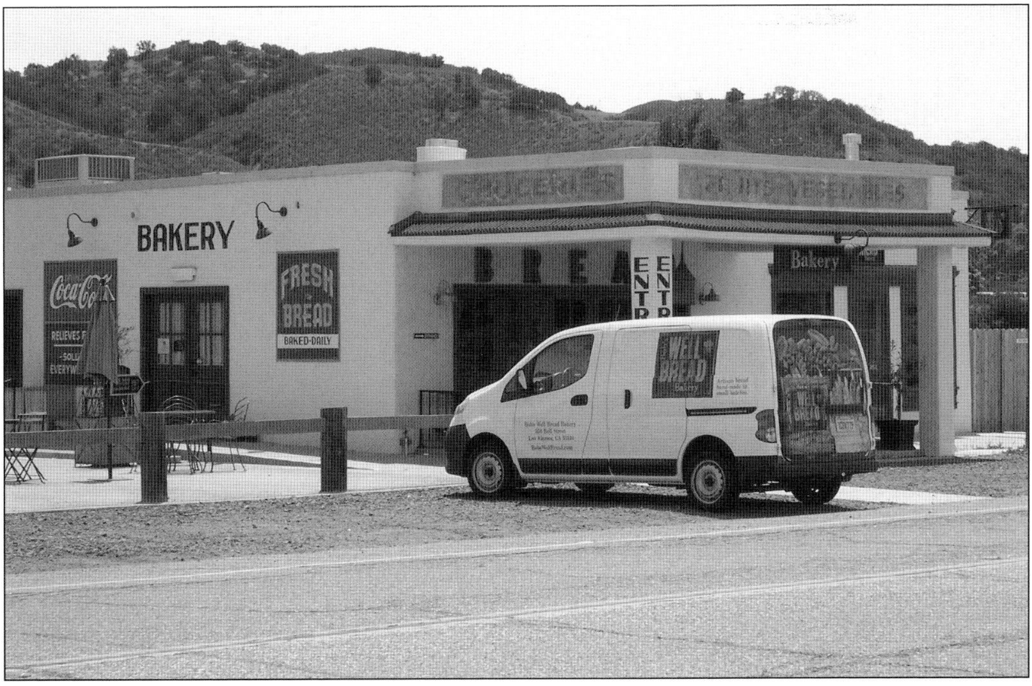

The latest incarnation of the Shady Rest Motel is the Well Bread Bakery, where fresh bread and pastries are sold. The gas pumps are gone, but, otherwise, the building's exterior has changed very little. A cabin from the original motel still exists behind the bakery. It is now a private residence. (Photograph by author.)

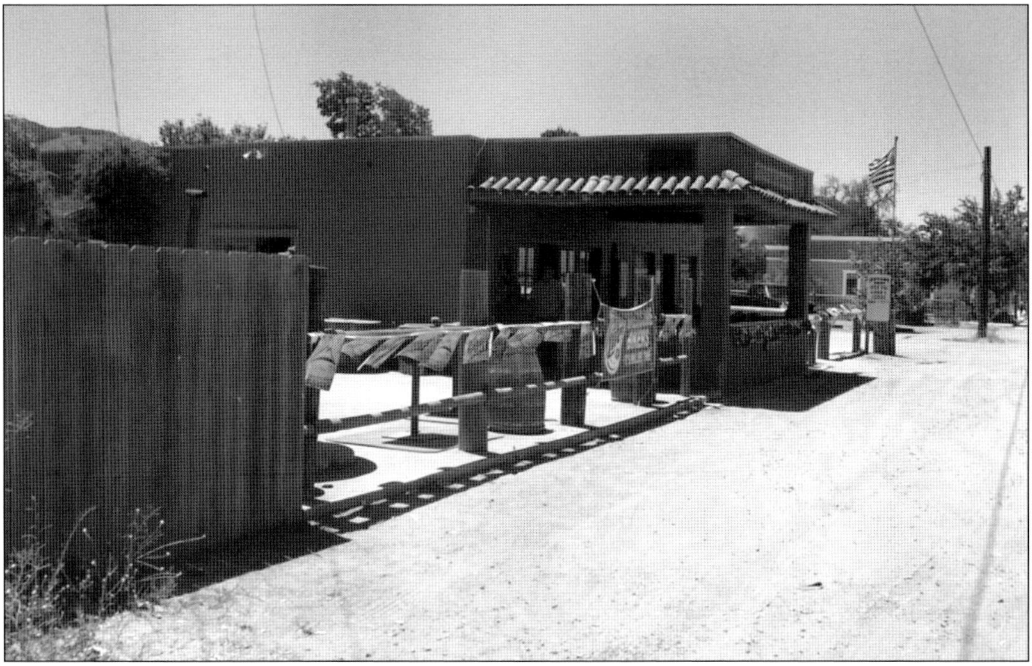

Ghostriders Tavern was another of the stores that occupied the Shady Rest building in the past. The tavern would move to the building visible just beyond, at far right. The tavern, with preferred motorcycle parking, was primarily a biker establishment. It was named in honor of those bikers who are departed.

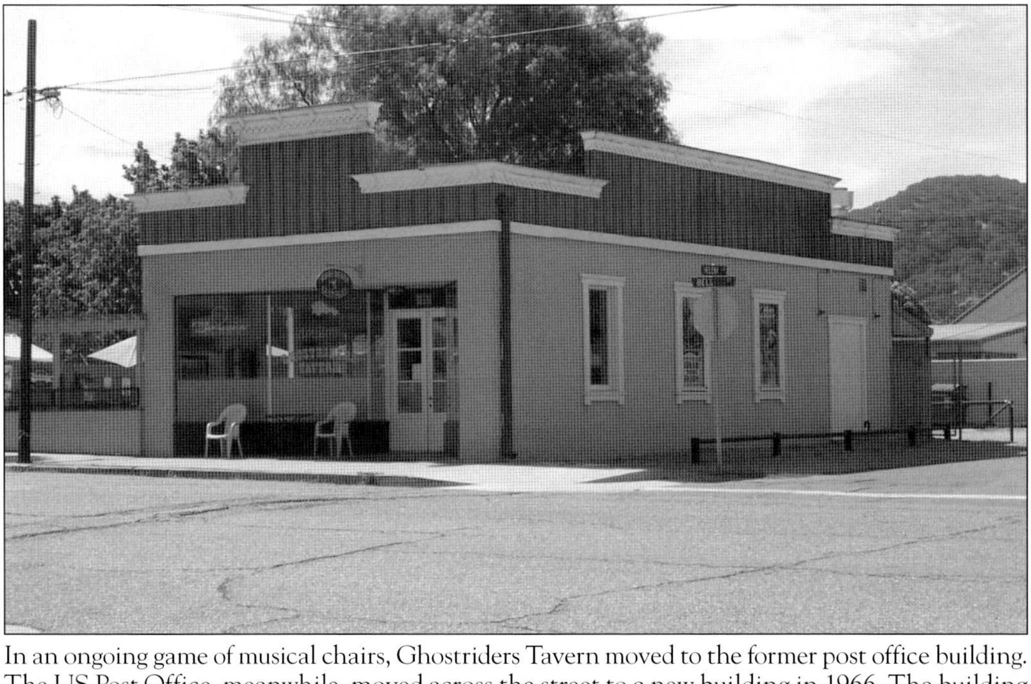

In an ongoing game of musical chairs, Ghostriders Tavern moved to the former post office building. The US Post Office, meanwhile, moved across the street to a new building in 1966. The building pictured here has also been a liquor store, a senior outlet store, the Los Alamos Trading Company, the Last Frontier Hardware, an antiques store, and Stewart's Market. (Photograph by author.)

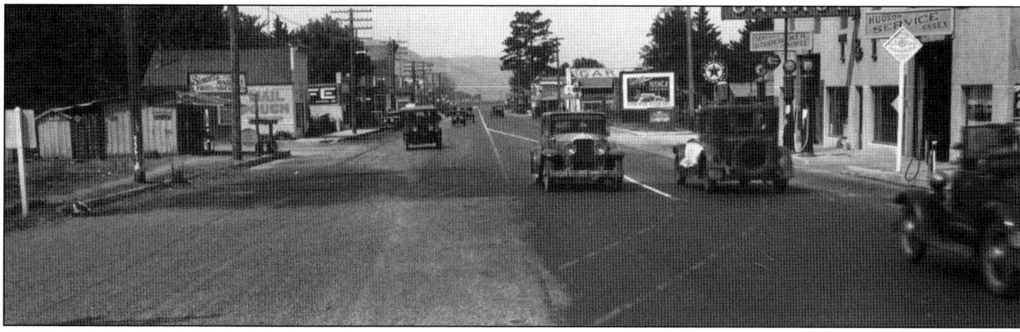

The T&T Garage (right), located on the corner of Bell and Helena Streets, was operated by Harold Ties. The garage sold Texaco products. Built in 1922, it boasted a large interior space for servicing many automobiles at the same time. The family kept a private residence on the second floor. Across the street (left), Stewart's Market occupies the site of the current Ghostriders Tavern.

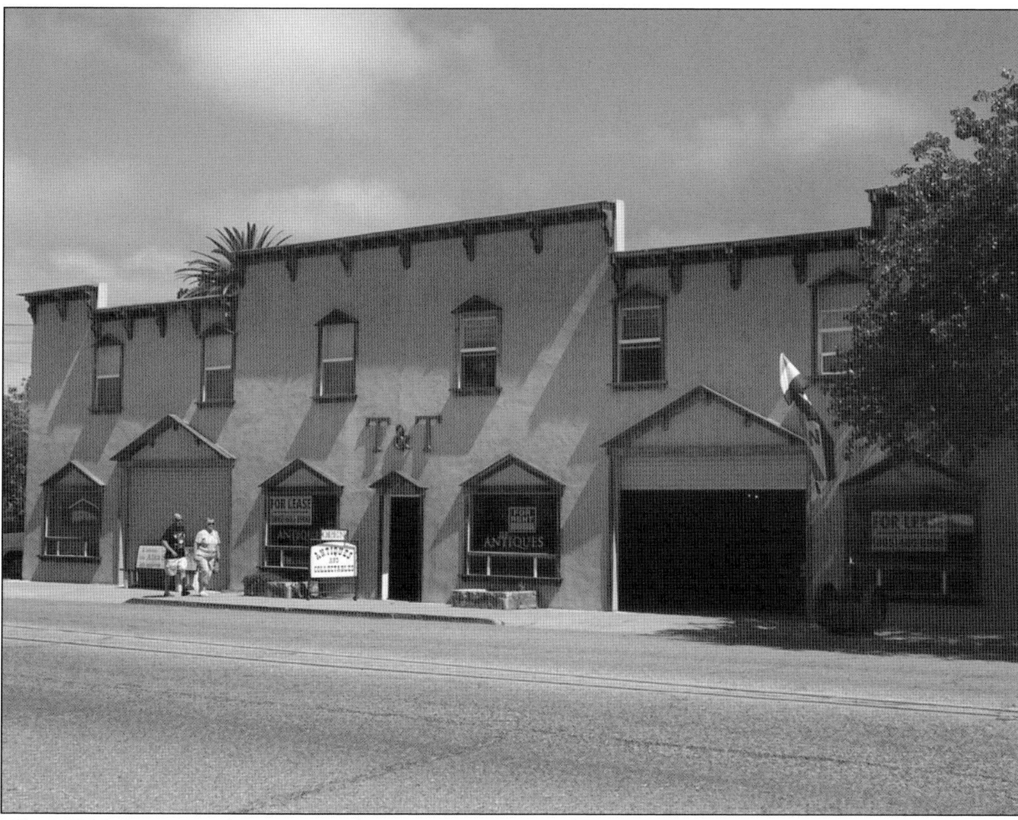

The T&T Garage today is named T&T Antiques and Museum. In the museum is a display that illustrates the history of Los Alamos. It is a joint effort between the Santa Ynez Valley Historical Society and the Thompson family. The facade of the building is unaltered. The store maintains a large inventory of antiques, from dinnerware to old automobiles. (Photograph by author.)

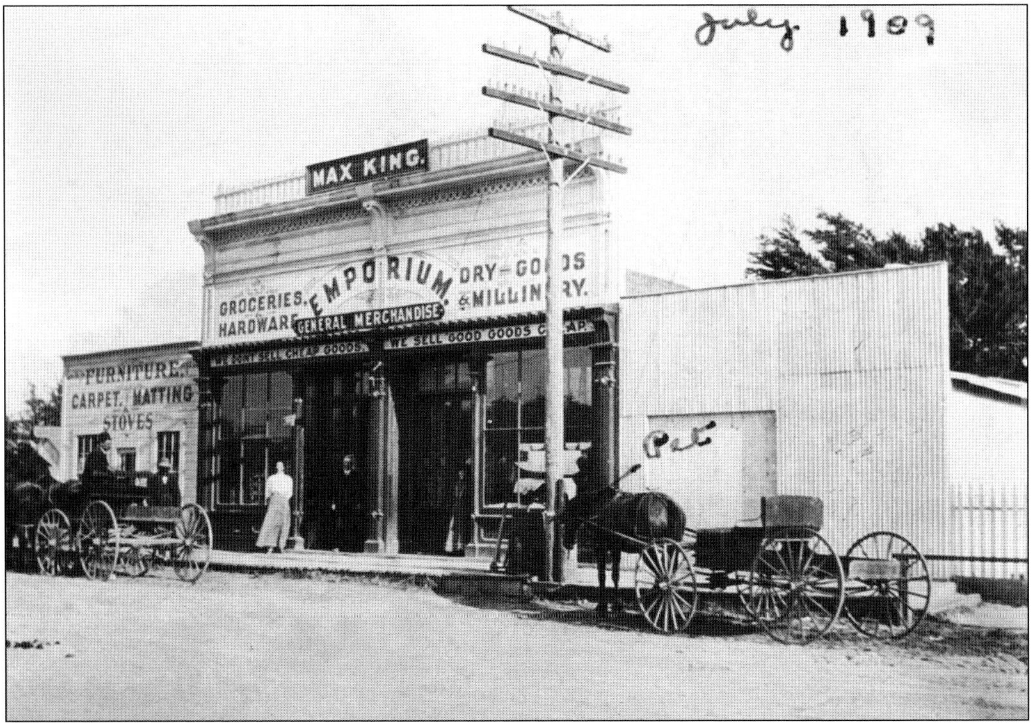

Max King's Emporium is seen here in 1909. Prior to that, in the 1880s, the building housed Alfred Newman's grocery and Mrs. Fred Newman's millinery. There have been many proprietors since Max King, but the building has always remained a store, a proviso established in its terms of sale. The annex on the left no longer exists. The general store is now a national historic site.

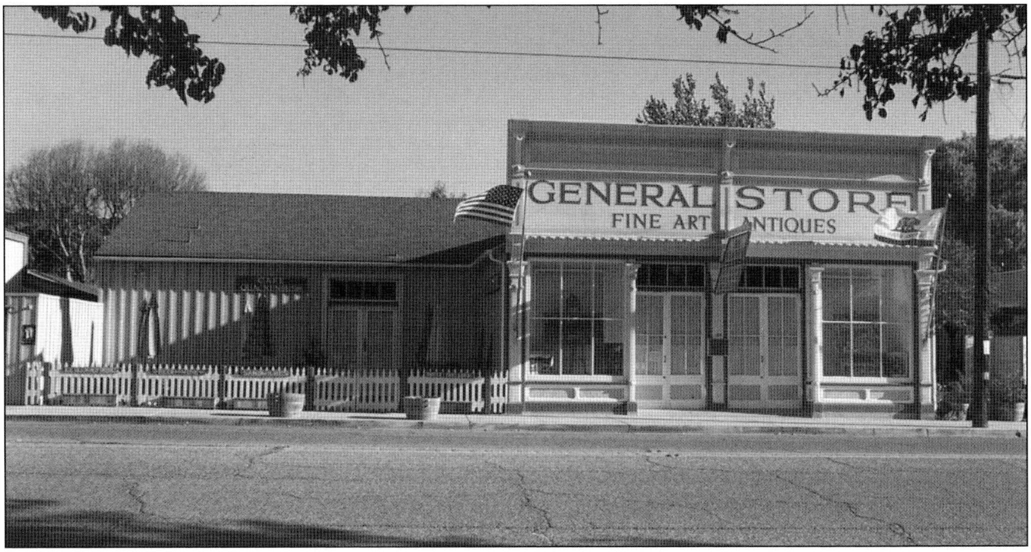

The building today is the General Store, home to the Art Brut Gallery, which displays the work of contemporary plein air artists. The establishment also sells antique furniture and collectables. Ralph Quackenbush further refurbished the building's interior after he purchased it for an art gallery in 1998. A popular part of the store is Café Quackenbush, where local residents often enjoy breakfast or lunch on the outdoor patio. (Photograph by author.)

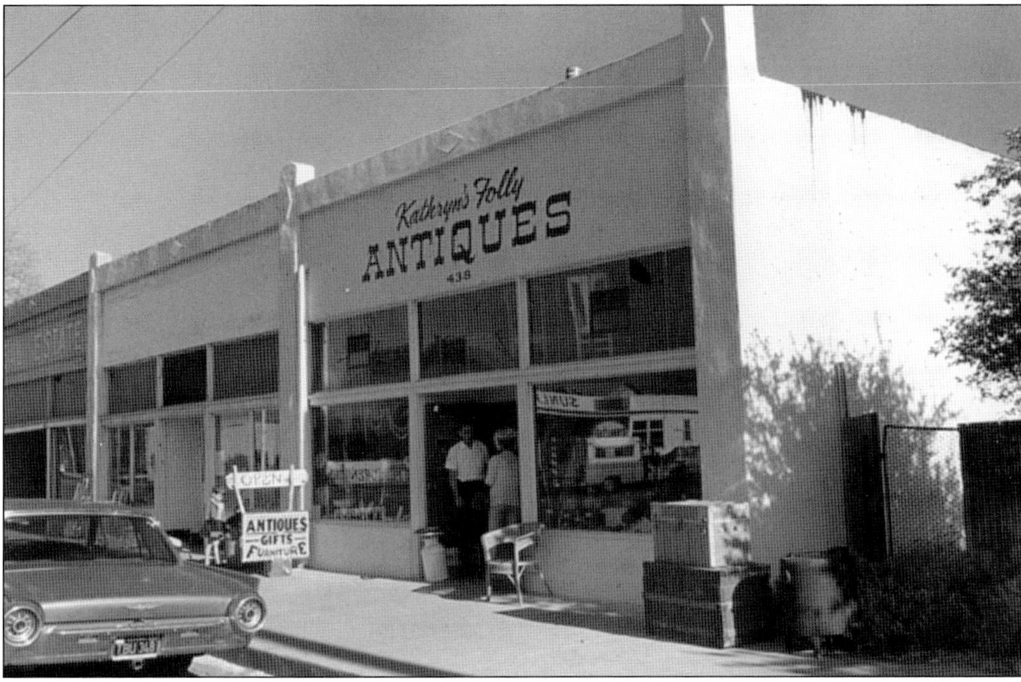

There have been many businesses located in this building over the years. Built in the 1930s, it may be as close to a strip mall as will ever exist in Los Alamos. It has been home to the post office, a real estate office, a video store, a butcher shop, a meat market, a liquor store, an ice cream parlor, and even a museum.

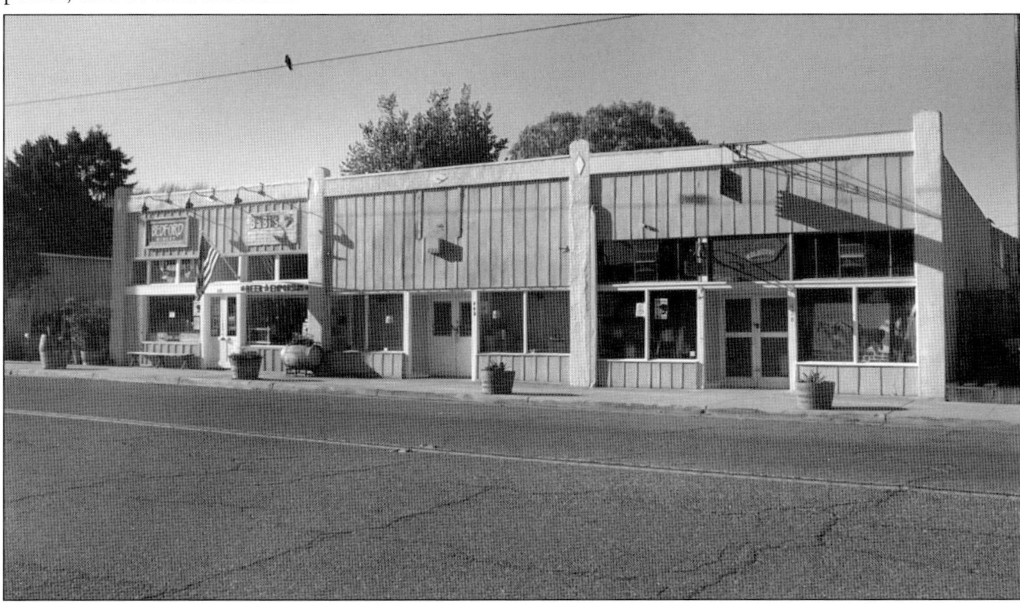

Today, the building is as busy as ever. The Bedford Winery tasting room occupies the space at far left, with an attractive outdoor patio next to it. The Thompson-Bedford Vineyards are located east of town on Alisos Canyon Road. Other businesses are currently moving into the middle spaces. Keane's Eclectic Antiques, at far right, has called this space home for several years. (Photograph by author.)

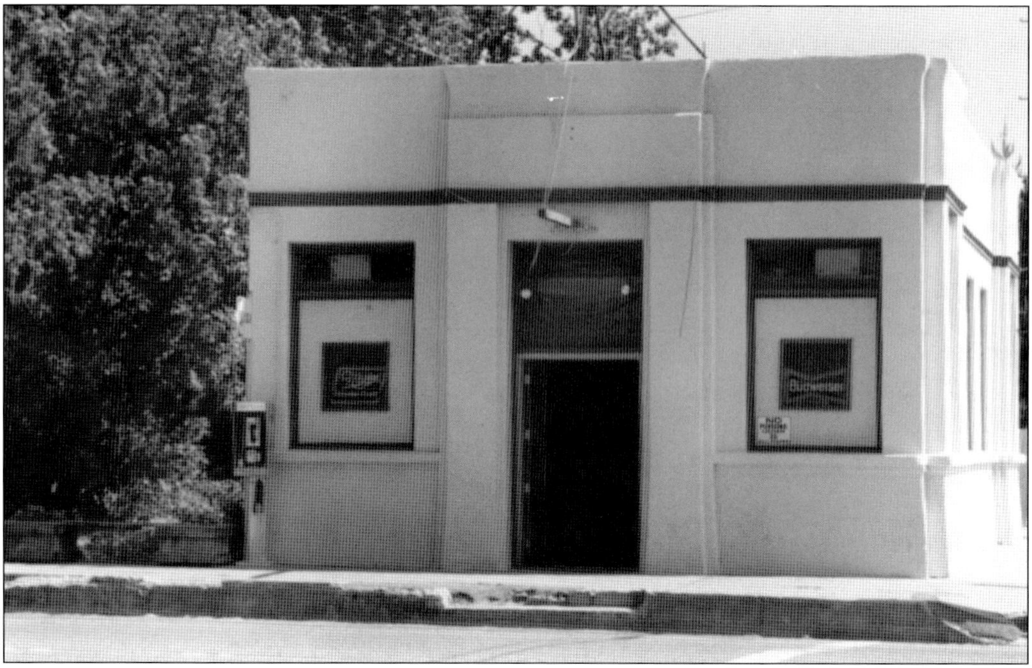

Early structures on this site, housing a drugstore, barbershop, post office, and general store, were torn down, and this building was constructed for the Bank of Santa Maria in 1916. The Los Angeles Trust & Savings Company and the Pacific Southwest Trust & Savings Bank followed. The Lariat Saloon (pictured) was located here until 2010.

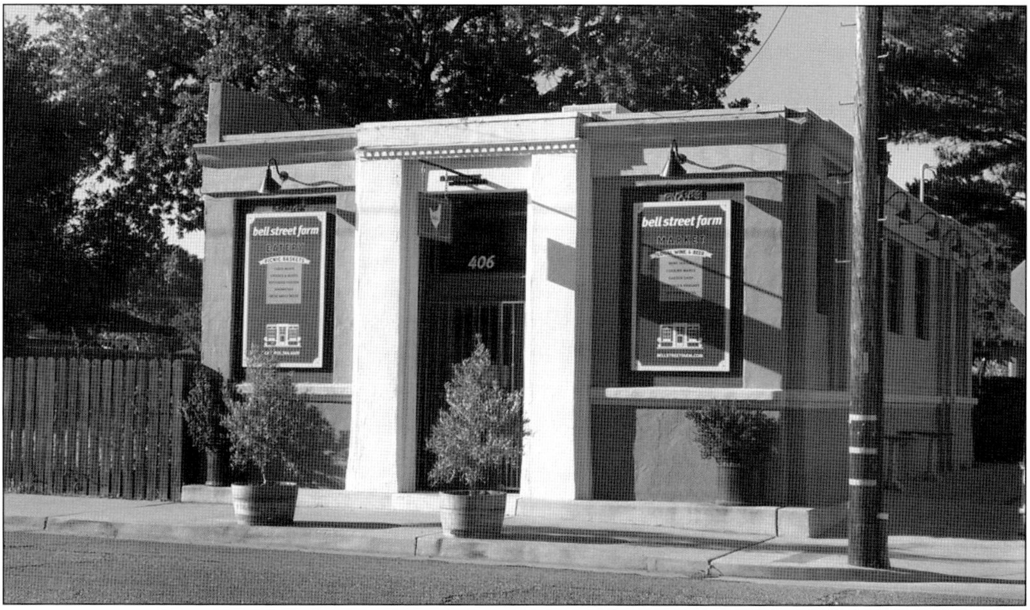

Bell Street Farm Eatery & Market, a cozy restaurant/delicatessen, is the current occupant of this former bank building. The market showcases assemble-your-own picnic baskets and accessories for creating a portable meal, as well as gifts and merchandise from local artisans. Bell Street Farm is a popular destination for tourists. This building has never been a jail, as some have surmised. (Photograph by author.)

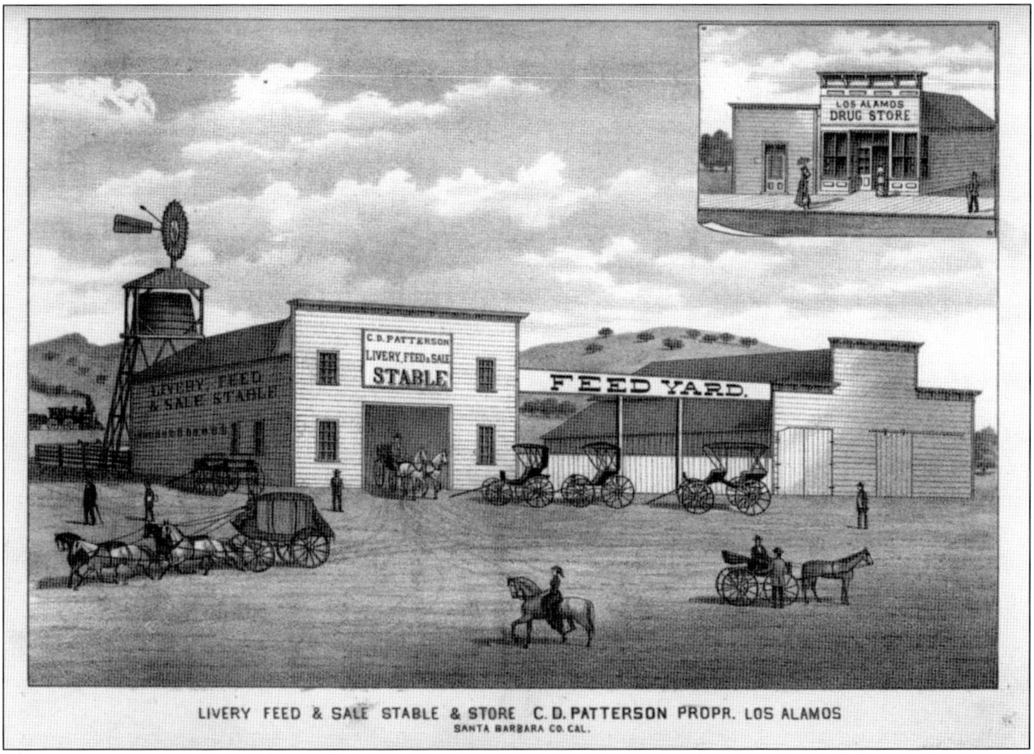

C.D. Patterson's Livery & Feed Stable occupied much of the block on the north side of Bell Street west of Centennial Street in 1880. The livery housed the local stagecoach. Owner Charlie Patterson was also a stage driver and had a regular route. It is said that he was so nearsighted he could not see the leaders' ears from his perch on the hurricane deck of the Concord Coach.

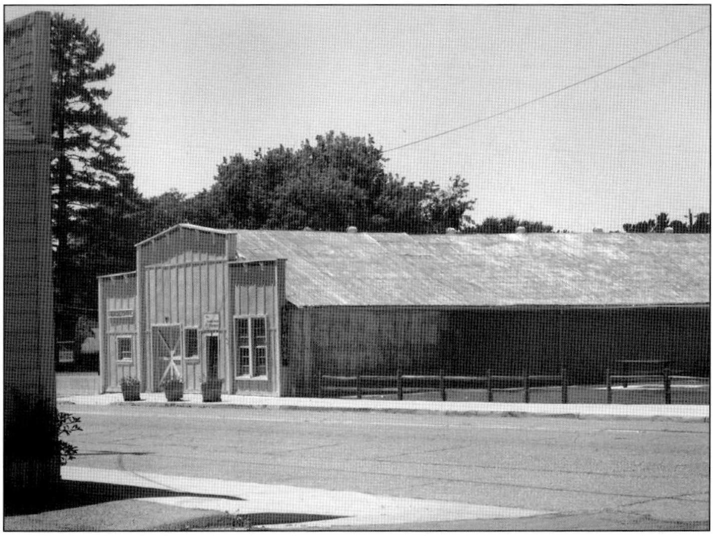

One of the buildings from C.D. Patterson's Livery & Feed Stable is the home of the Gentleman Farmer antiques store and of WB Delachutz Lighting, a distributor of lighting for stage and set. The Gentleman Farmer specializes in country, canine, and English sporting equine gifts and art. Owner Madeleine Jex follows trade shows during the first half of the week and then returns to open her shop. (Photograph by author.)

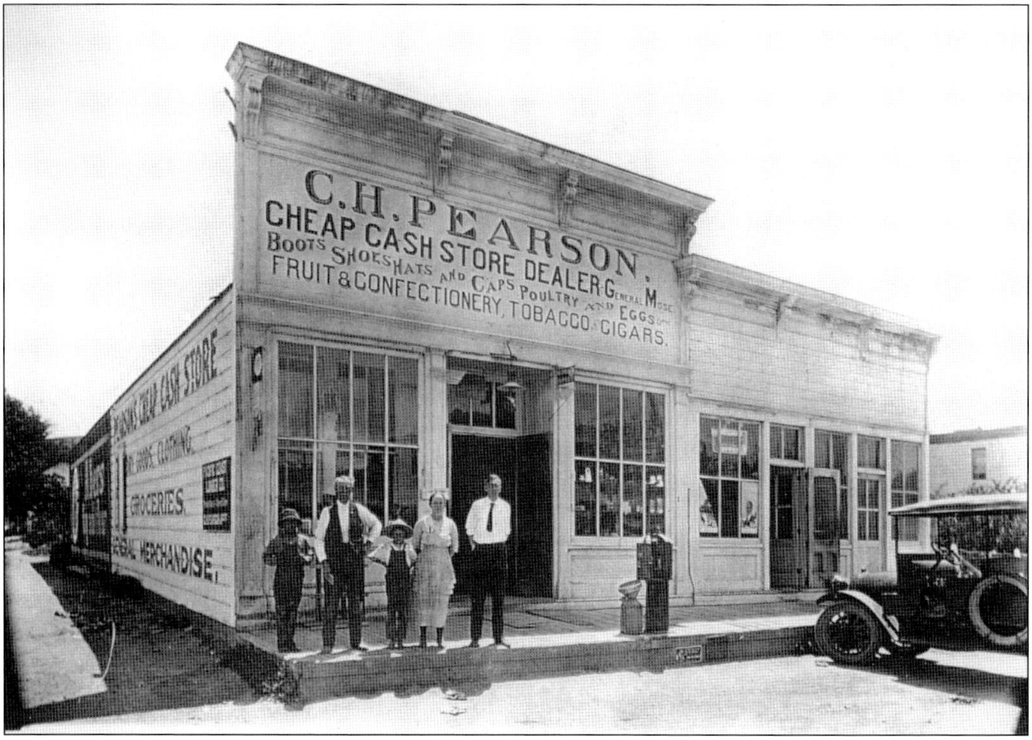

C.H. Pearson was a true opportunist. In his Cheap Cash Store, he sold whatever was needed, from coffee to coffins. Posing here are, from left to right, an unidentified boy, C.H. Pearson, Robert de Rieux, Mary de Rieux, and Mr. Clarke. Note the spittoon on the boardwalk (yes, Pearson sold chewing tobacco). After Pearson died, the store's entire interior was purchased by Knott's Berry Farm and is on display there.

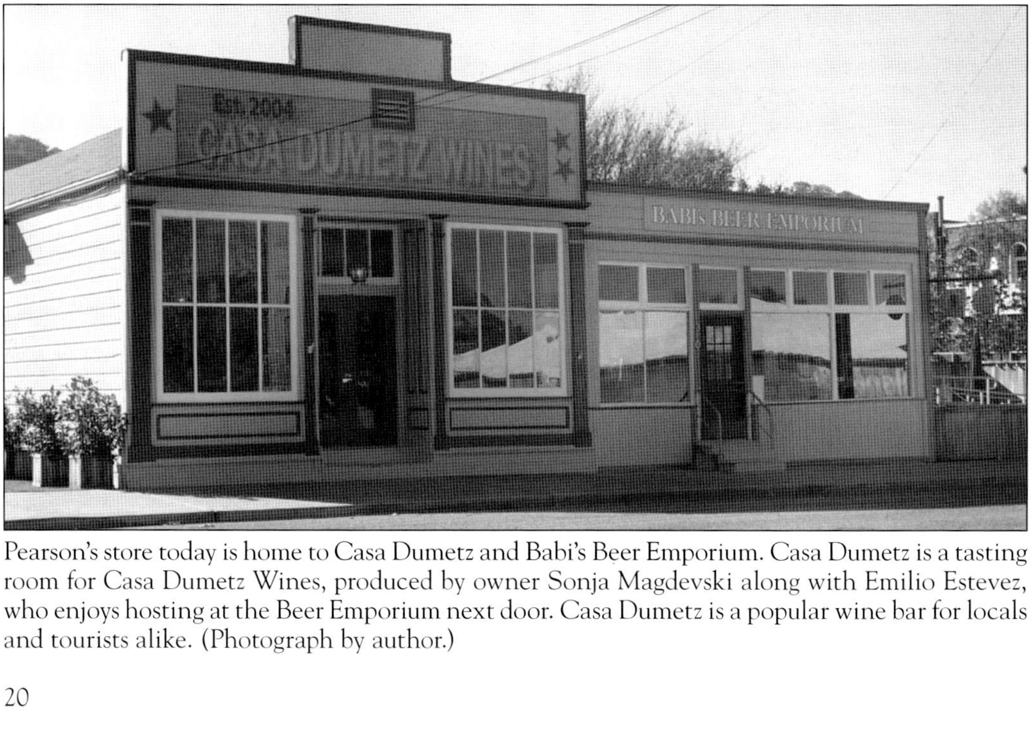

Pearson's store today is home to Casa Dumetz and Babi's Beer Emporium. Casa Dumetz is a tasting room for Casa Dumetz Wines, produced by owner Sonja Magdevski along with Emilio Estevez, who enjoys hosting at the Beer Emporium next door. Casa Dumetz is a popular wine bar for locals and tourists alike. (Photograph by author.)

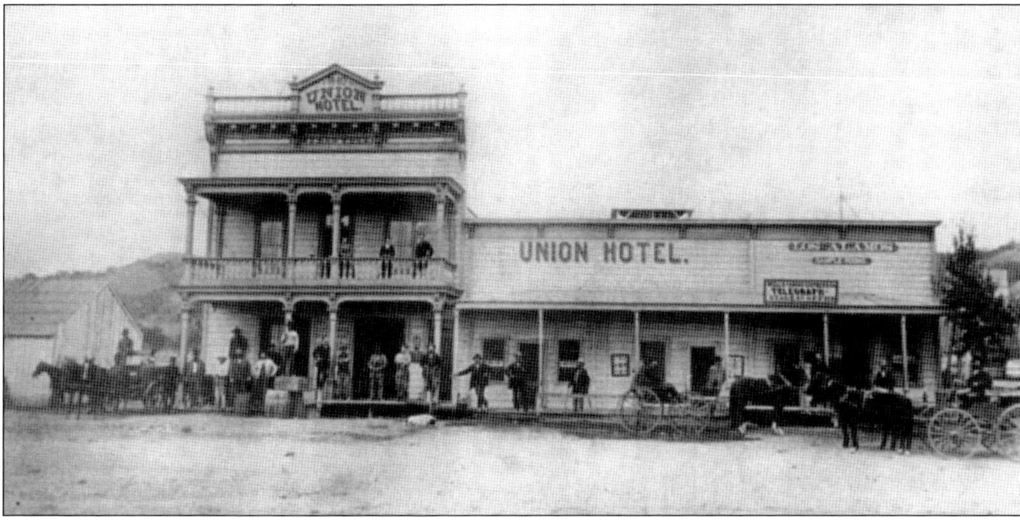

The men, horses, carriages, and the sleeping dog were carefully arranged for this photograph of the 1880 Union Hotel. The hotel, under the proprietorship of J.D. Snyder, offered food and lodging and housed the Wells Fargo Express Agency, the telegraph office, and the stage office. The original hotel burned down in 1886. The Los Alamos Hotel was built on the site in 1915.

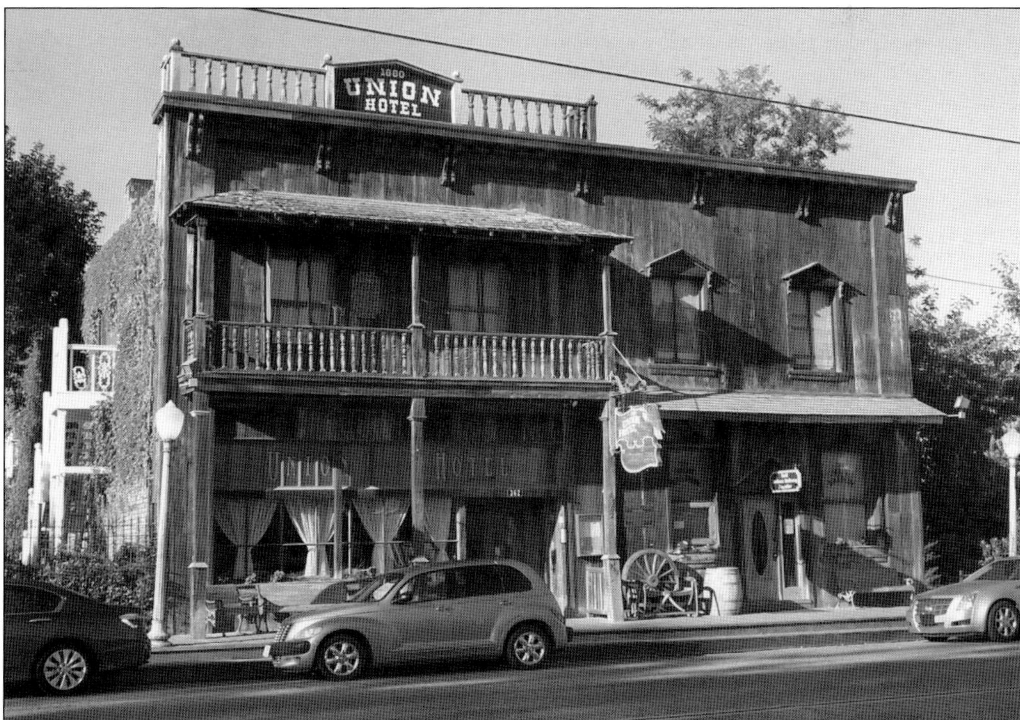

The Union Hotel today looks much as it did when it was first built. It was restored by Dick Langdon in 1972. The facade was built over the existing Los Alamos Hotel. Rooms are furnished with Victorian antiques, and two chandeliers from the movie *Gone with the Wind* adorn the dining room. The Wine Bar, newly opened by Kurt Russell and featuring Gogi and Hudson-Bellamy wines, occupies the bar room. (Photograph by author.)

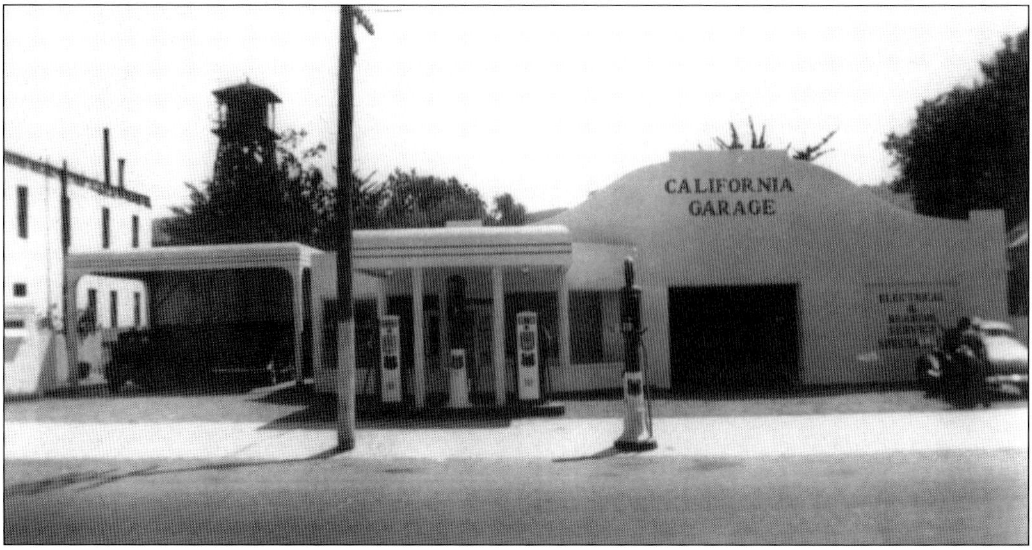

The Scolari California Garage was built by brothers Alfonso and Pietro Scolari from the ground up in 1926. It sold Union Oil products. Al worked in the station along with his wife, Dora, well into the 1980s. The garage offered a complete service line, including fuel, oil, and repairs for automobiles. The garage also helped keep the local tractors running.

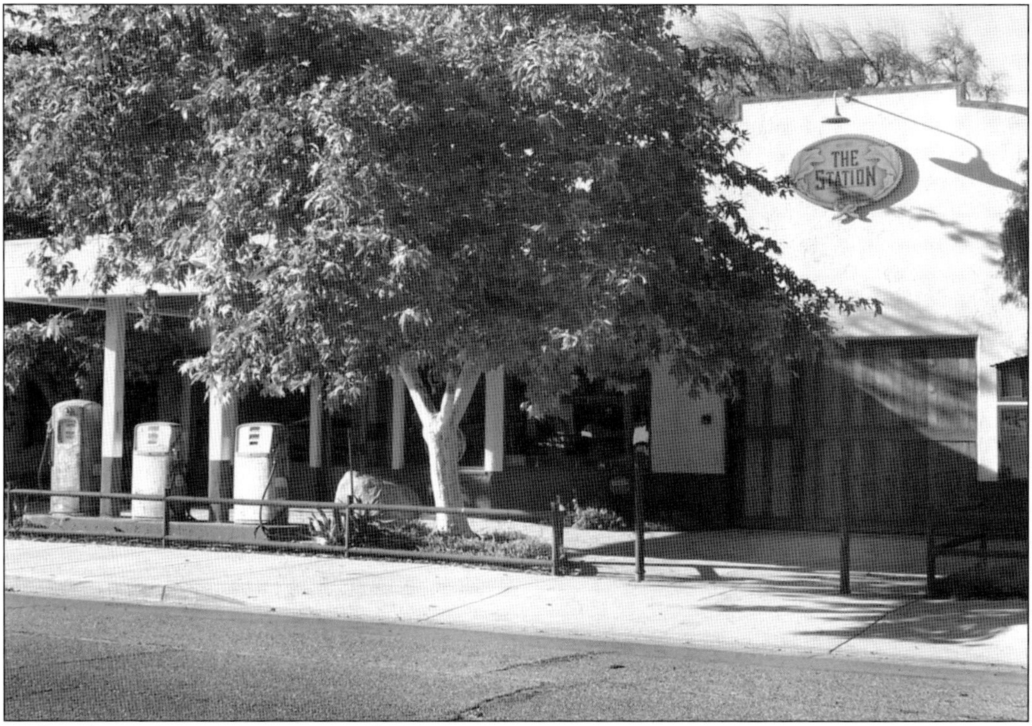

Today, the California Garage is called the Station and serves foie gras rather than gasoline. The interior of the station was renovated and caters to large groups for wedding receptions and other special events. Manicured and beautifully landscaped lawns and patios surround the building. The Station was the result of a collaboration between owner Sean McGrath and designer Tony Cano. (Photograph by author.)

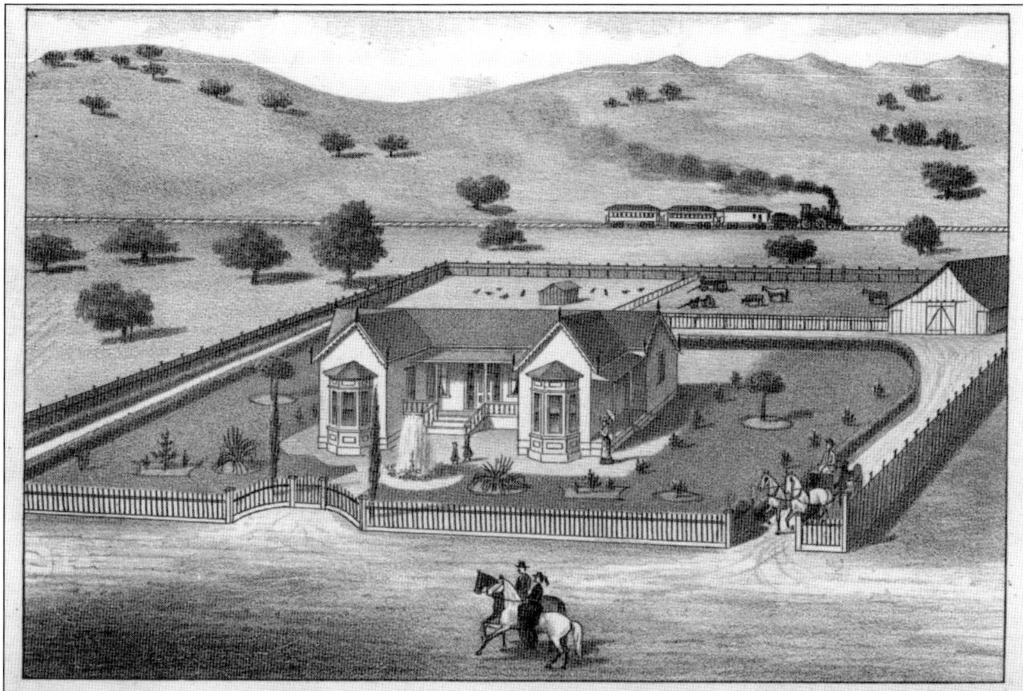

RESIDENCE OF A. LESLIE, LOS ALAMOS, SANTA BARBARA CO. CAL.

This is a drawing of the Alexander Leslie residence, built in 1880. People spoke of Leslie as the mayor of Los Alamos because of his active involvement in the progress of the town. The Leslie family was large, and every child played an instrument. In the evenings, the family would sit on the front porch and entertain the town with their music.

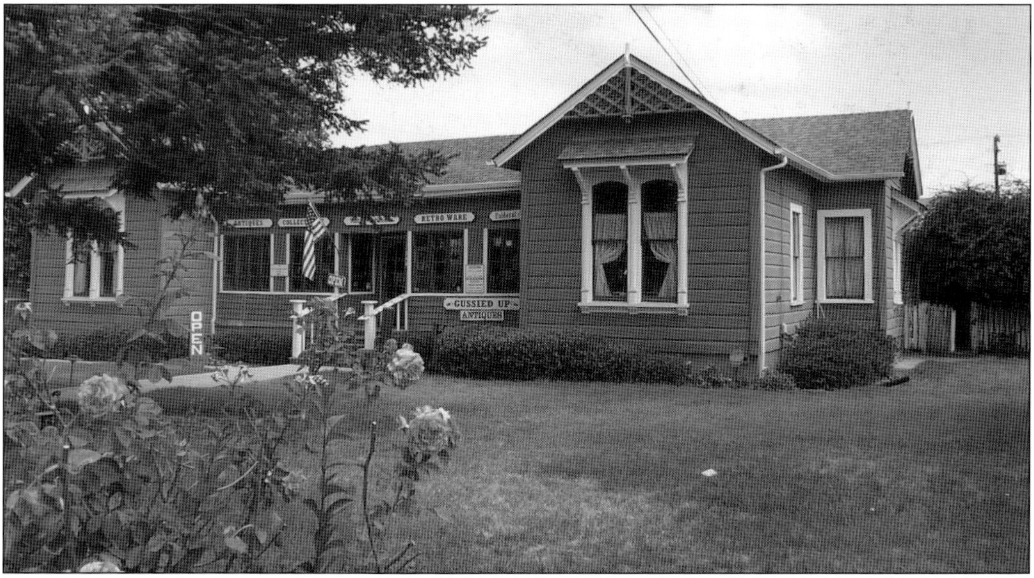

The Leslie residence today is home to Gussied Up Antiques. The exterior and interior of the house are well preserved. The shopper can browse from room to room and gain a true sense of the history of the home while viewing antiques for sale. The proprietors in many cases have selected antique furniture to suggest the look and purpose of each room. (Photograph by author.)

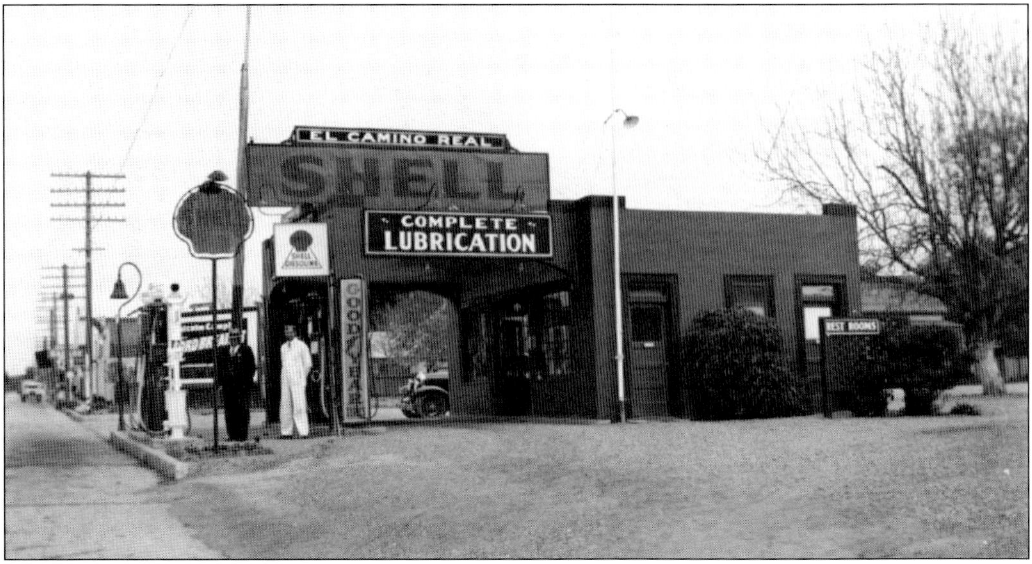

C.H. Pearson, and then Henry Gewe, ran a blacksmith shop on this site until 1912. A.E. Robbins (left) purchased the shop from A.B. Wurtz in 1923 for his Shell station. Route 101 passed directly in front of the Robbins Shell station. The bell suspended from a crook (left) symbolizes the old mission road route. Robbins ran the El Camino service station for the next 40 years.

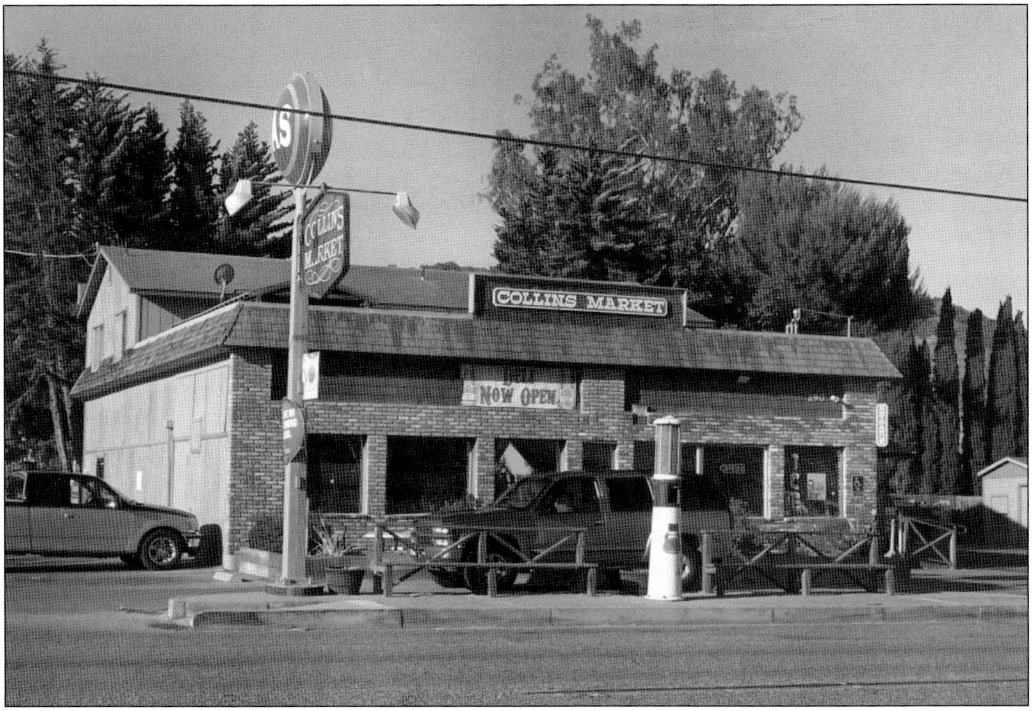

Gasoline is still sold here today, but the old pump in front of the building is no longer functional (the modern pumps are out of sight to the right). Ed and Pauline Collins bought the business from Alvin Robbins in 1979, and their daughter and son-in-law purchased it in 2007. Collins Market is also a full-service convenience store, selling everything from work gloves to hot burritos. (Photograph by author.)

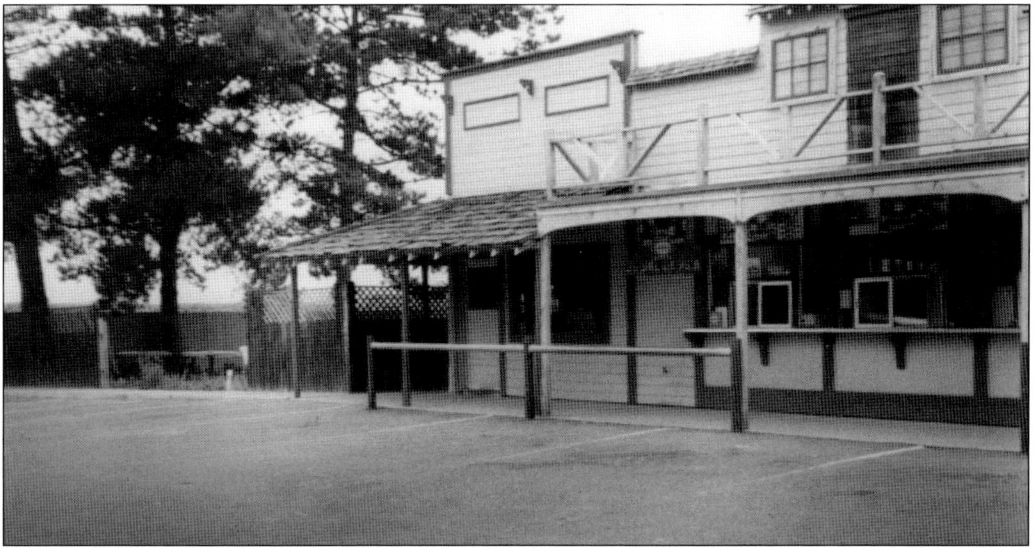

Bill King and Carl Jensen built the Broken Wheel Restaurant in 1966 and served Italian food. It was popular for many years. Carl Jensen sold it to Charlie Gonzales in 1978. According to Gonzales, Jensen made him an offer he could not refuse. The building is seen here shortly after the sale took place. (Courtesy of Charlie Gonzales.)

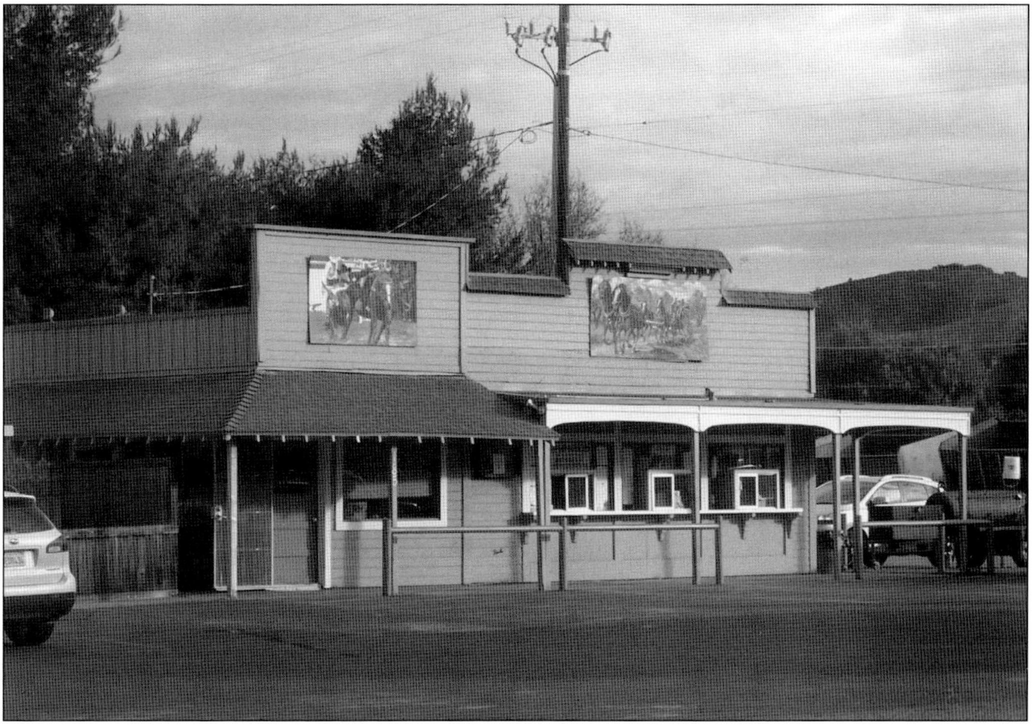

Charlie's Place is popular with locals, truckers, and travelers. Charlie's experience working in the food business with his parents, Jessie and Henry Gonzales, stood him in good stead. At first, the restaurant was not successful, according to Charlie. But once he added a steam table and began to serve Mexican food and tri-tip sandwiches, he soon had a loyal customer base. (Photograph by author.)

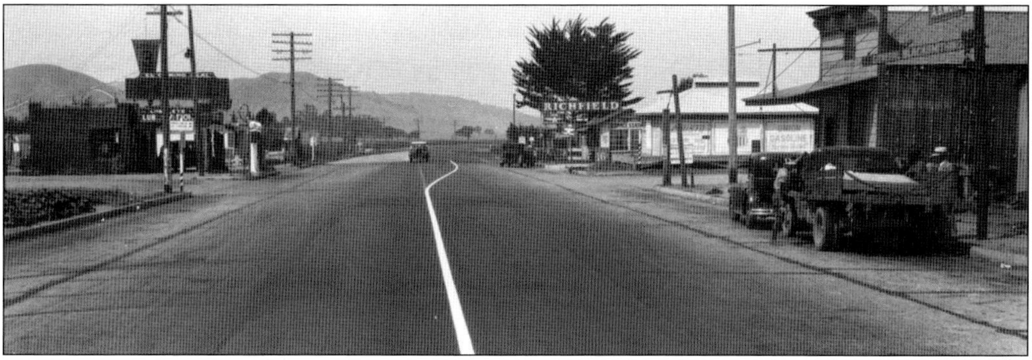

Gasoline stations and blacksmith shops stood side-by-side in the early days of the automobile. Here at the edge of town, the Richfield Oil Flying A service station enticed drivers as they headed west. The Pioneer service station, owned by Frank "Dad" Knox, was one of the first gasoline service stations in Los Alamos. Knox lived in a residence situated behind the house. The service station boasts sanitary restrooms.

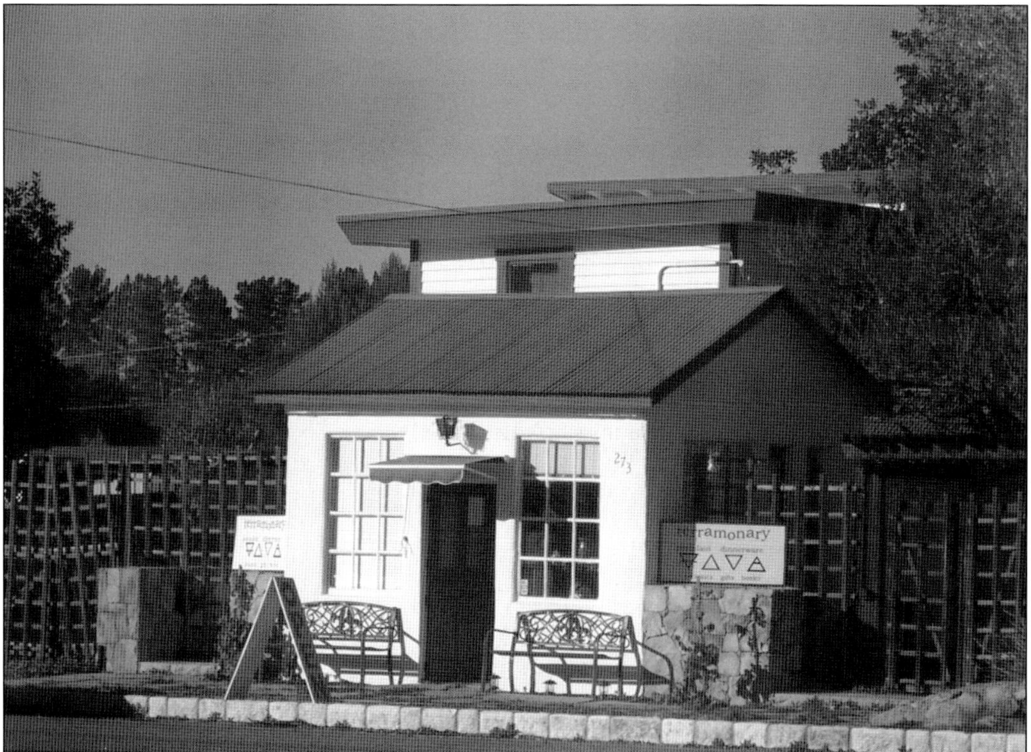

The building today is about the same size, but it looks quite different. With a new, skylighted roof, it is home to Terramonary Porcelain Dinnerware, a ceramics store featuring handcrafted pottery by Ramona Clayton and original novels by Terry Row of Clifton Edwin Publishing. Row writes his books and sells Ramona's pottery in the small building in front, while Ramona creates more pottery in the residence. (Photograph by author.)

Two

Los Alamos Valley
They Came First

The town of Los Alamos was born of Los Alamos the valley, itself created from the residue of a subsiding lake bordered by the low-lying Solomon Hills to the north and Purisima Hills to the south. The uplifted ledge where the valley narrows at its western end slowed the outflow of water to the Pacific Ocean and caused the rich soil and minerals washed down from the hills and mountains to deepen on the valley floor. The Chumash Indians established villages along San Antonio Creek and took advantage of this rich environment, competing with the California grizzly for seeds, grains, and acorns. Then came the Spanish. The Franciscan fathers established La Purisima Mission and moved the Chumash there. They used the valley's rich grasslands and plentiful water supply to support the mission's herd of cattle and horses, appointing a handful of Indians to become herders. These Indians lived in a pueblo called a rancheria and developed into skilled vaqueros. The first land grant in the valley was an 1839 parcel of 48,803 acres gifted to Don Jose Antonio de la Guerra y Carrillo, son of the former commandant of the Presidio of Santa Barbara. A parcel of 13,000 acres east of Los Alamos was granted to Don Octaviano Gutierrez in 1845 and named Rancho La Laguna. When the missions were secularized, the horse herd disappeared, and the few remaining Indians brought their vaquero skills to the ranchos. Chumash Indians built the Los Alamos adobe under the direction of Jose de la Guerra. Despite the political changes in California, life in the Los Alamos Valley in the next decades would be about grazing cattle, rodeos, cattle buyers, stagecoaches, and bandits.

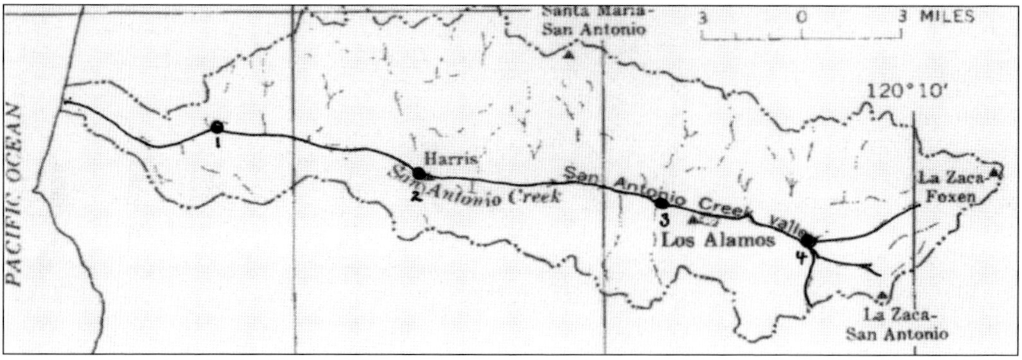

The author compiled the map shown above, with notes from Chester D. King and John Harrington. The latter spent many years among the Chumash. It shows the watershed of San Antonio Creek and the likely location of the Chumash villages along it. The creek, which defines Los Alamos Valley, is located between two principal river systems, the Santa Maria River and the Santa Ynez River (not shown). Along San Antonio Creek are the villages Saxpilil (1), Step (2), Saqsiyol (3), and Cuaslui Creek (4). The village of Saqsiyol was likely located just west of Los Alamos, at the mouth of Cañada Laguna Seca. Below, the standard shelter used by the Chumash Indians was the tule hut. The frames were built of native willow and thatched with tule, which grew in the wetlands. Ropes of fibrous plants held the form together. This hut was constructed at nearby Purisima Mission. (Below, photograph by the author.)

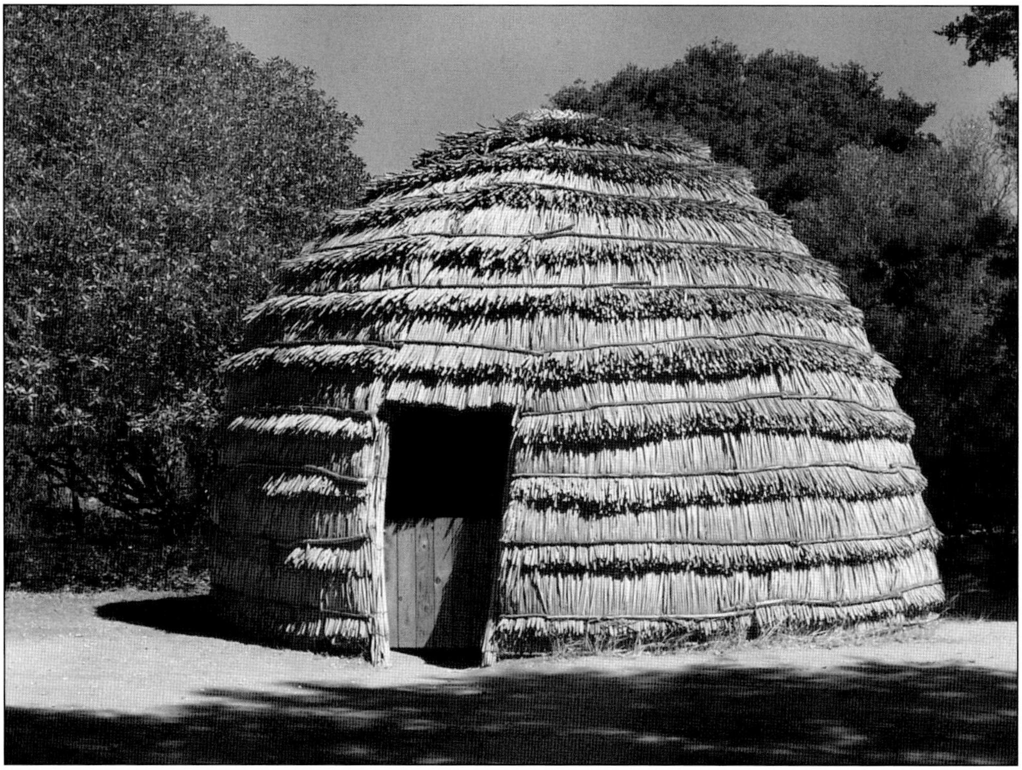

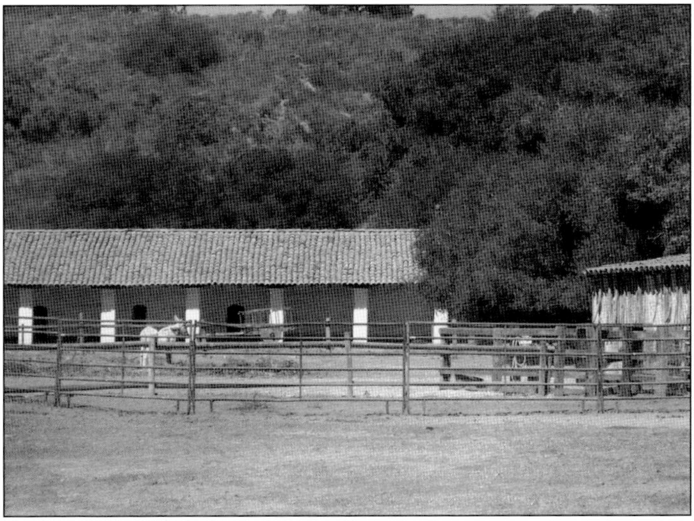

Left to decay, the La Purisima Mission was restored and is kept as a living museum. This photograph shows a portion of the mission and its corral. Both the mule and the *carreta* were ubiquitous tools indispensable to mission life. The mission affected the Los Alamos Valley deeply. The fathers relocated the Chumash from the valley to the mission, leaving only enough Indians to tend to their horse herds. (Photograph by author.)

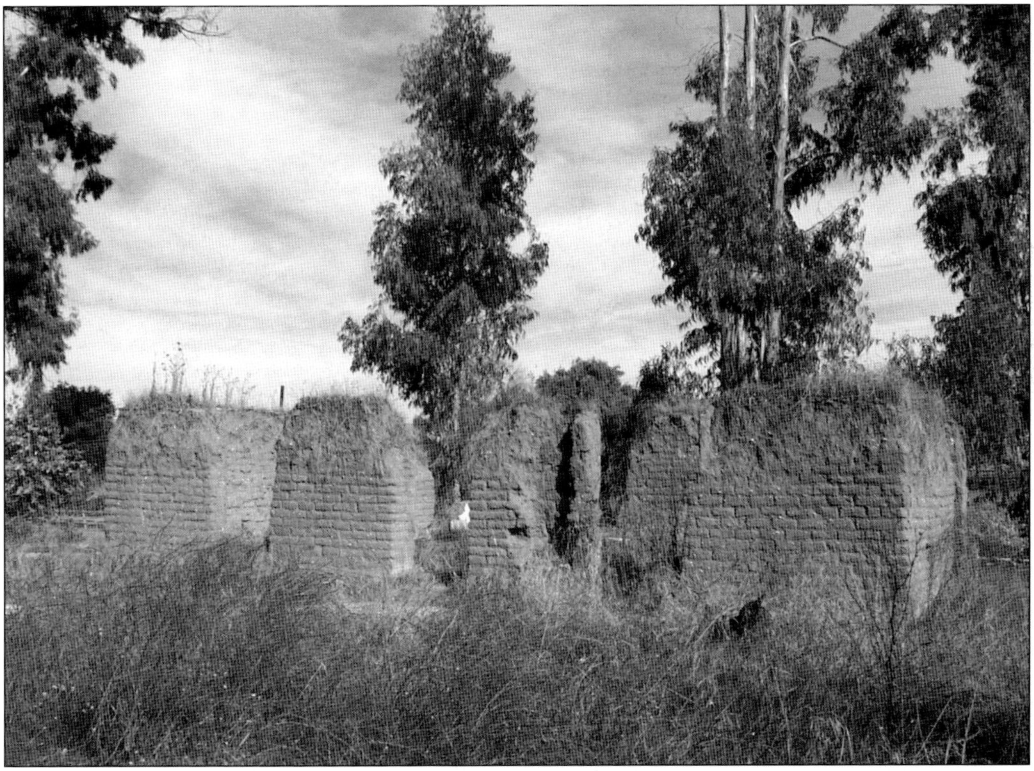

This ruined structure illustrates the construction of an adobe building. Adobe blocks were layered straddling the two beneath. Bricks were sliced to accommodate doors and windows. The interior wall was plastered with adobe and layered with whitewash. Outside walls were chinked with adobe mud. Wood planks across the top of walls supported rafters. The roof was constructed of tule bundles sealed with tar from local tar pits. (Photograph by author.)

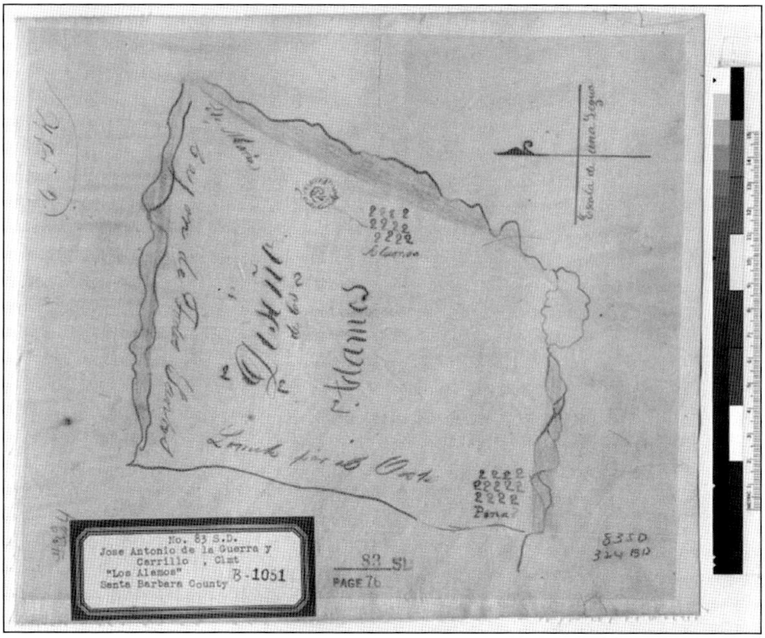

A *diseño* is a hand-drawn map used to describe in detail a land grant or property boundaries. Jose de la Guerra submitted this map to define his Los Alamos Rancho grant boundaries. Naturally occurring features, even those as impermanent as trees and bushes, were used as markers. The Los Alamos Rancho was likely named for the proliferation of cottonwood trees in the area.

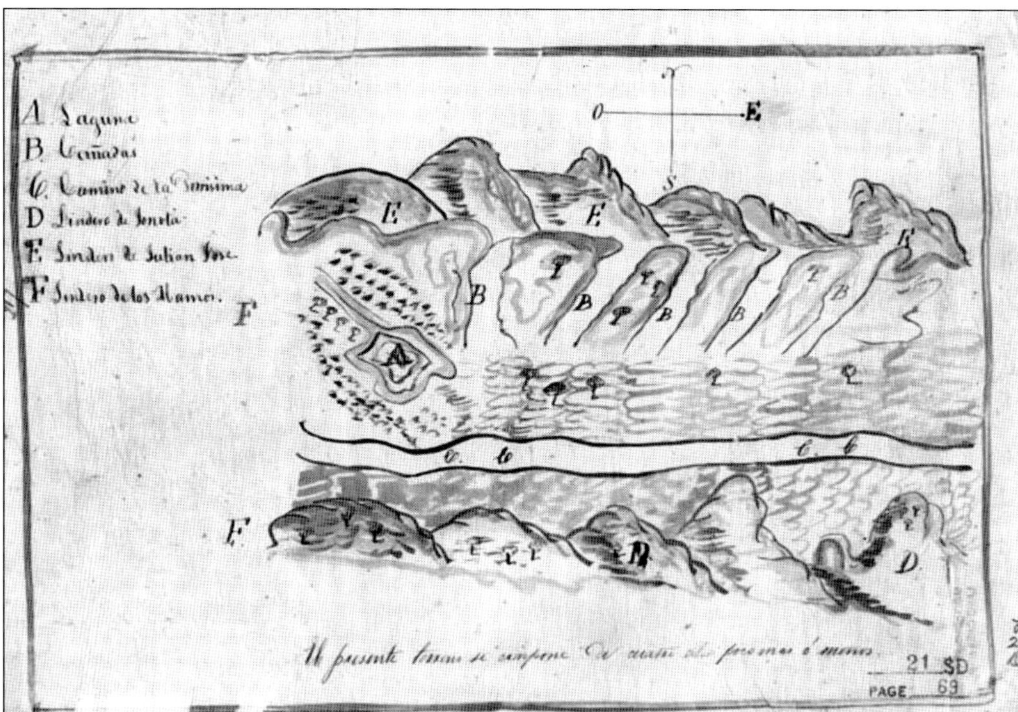

The Rancho La Laguna diseño is detailed and artfully drawn. The lake exists today, although it is much smaller. The Purisima Road runs through the property. Los Alamos Rancho is to the west, Rancho Jonata to the southeast, and Rancho San Julian lies to the south. Cañadas were drawn between hills. Dr. J.B. Shaw purchased part of this ranch for himself and part of Los Alamos Rancho for Thomas Bell.

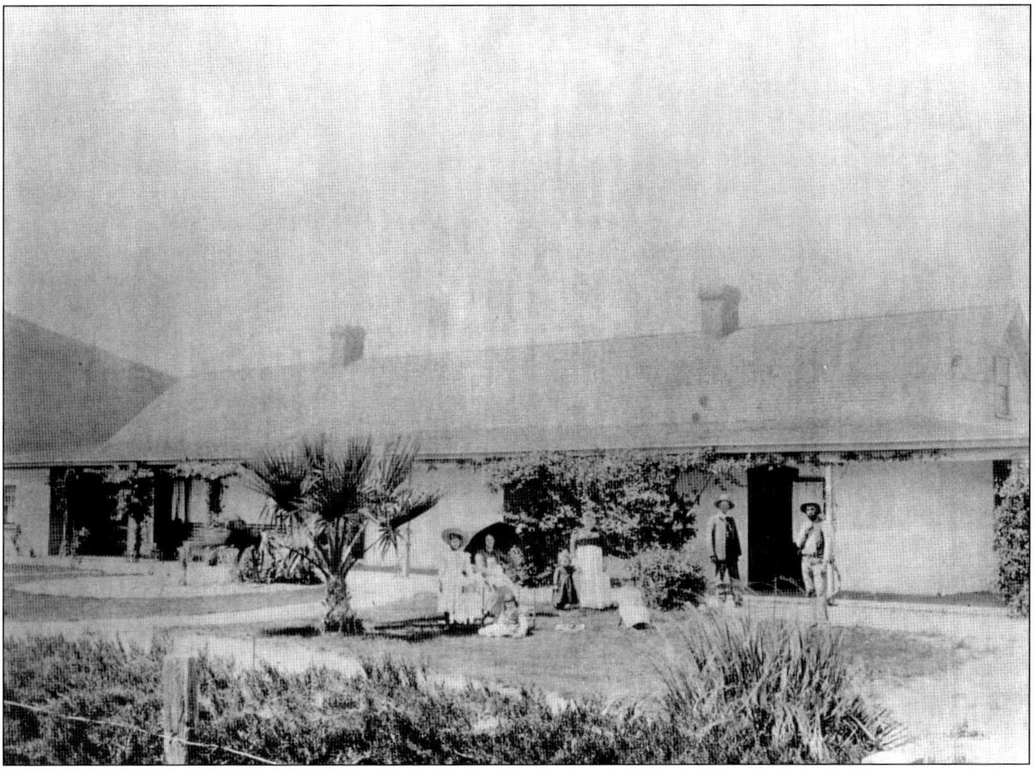

This is the original adobe house built by Chumash Indians for Jose Antonio de la Guerra y Noriega. His grandson Dario Oreña and family are pictured. They are, from left to right, daughters Ynez Elena and Beatrice, Señora Herminia Oreña and baby, daughters Anita and Marguerite with nurse Graciosa, daughter Herminia, Don Dario Oreña, and Alfred Oreña. A small room (far left) was reputedly available for the bandit Salomon Pico. (Courtesy of C&S Scheller.)

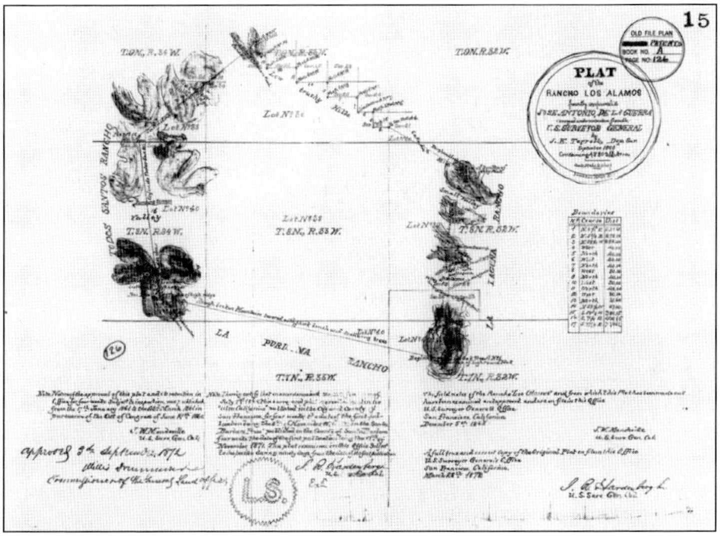

Following the American seizure of California, land-grant diseños were redrawn and resubmitted. This Los Alamos Rancho plat map was submitted by Jose de la Guerra to the surveyor general and published in the city and county of San Francisco for a period of four weeks, published in the city and county of Santa Barbara for four more weeks, and held in the US surveyor general's office for 90 days until approved.

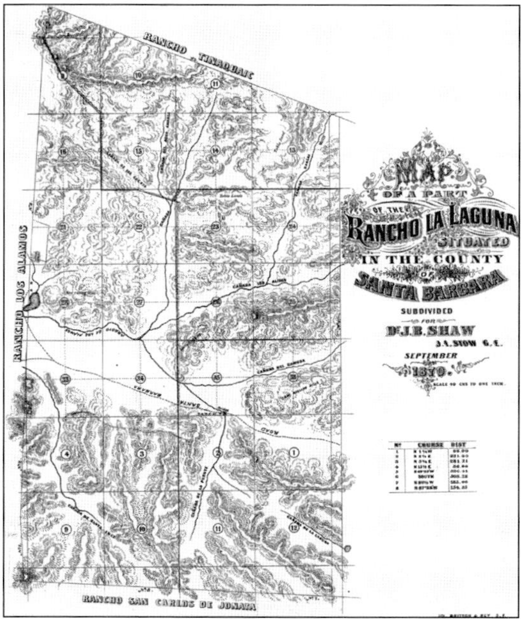

J.T. Stow subdivided the Rancho La Laguna map (pictured) for Dr. J.B. Shaw in 1870, drawn by the lithographers Britton & Rey of San Francisco in incredible detail. The Cañada de Los Alamos (center right) follows San Antonio Creek. The dots drawn above the lake at far left are the residence buildings of J.B. Shaw.

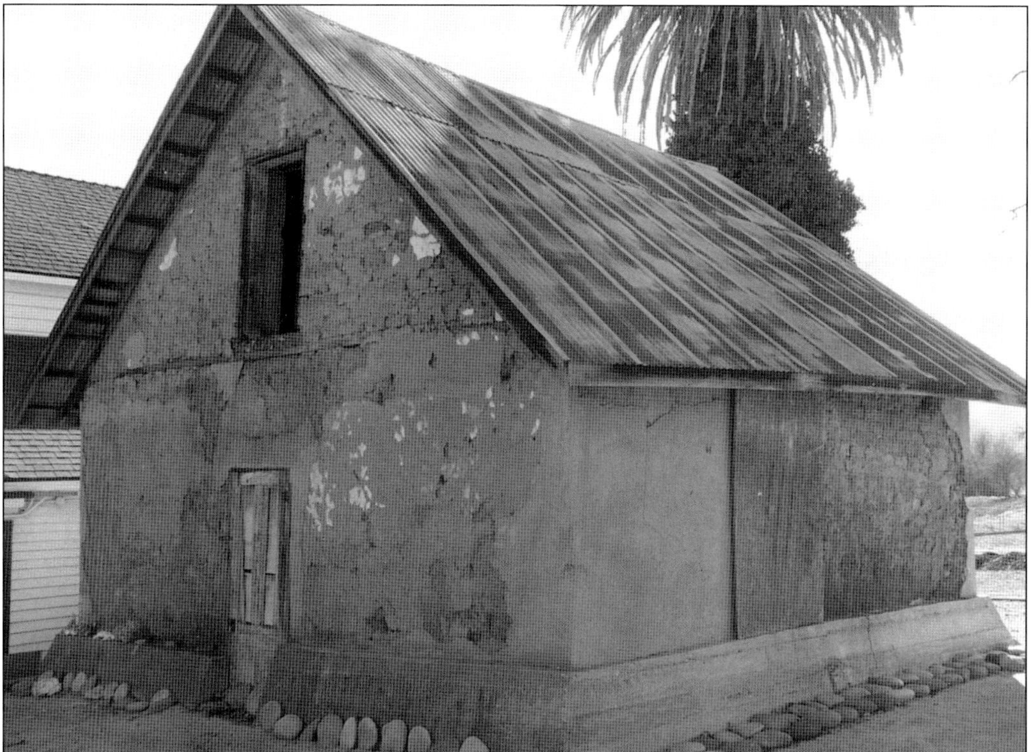

After purchasing 14,000 acres of the Rancho La Laguna, Dr. James Shaw lived in this adobe, built by grantee Octaviano Gutierrez. He built a two-story Victorian home in 1890 for himself and his family and kept the adobe for guests. The adobe found use as a guesthouse, storage facility, and rental unit over the years. It still stands just yards behind the Victorian structure. (Photograph by author.)

This ruin of an adobe is located on the Las Flores Rancho in the Los Alamos Valley. Although tentatively thought to have been built by Antonio Estrada, the current ranch owner, Jeanette Sainz, is unsure. Buildings constructed of adobe have demonstrated great durability, but, once the roof is gone, the adobe material erodes much more quickly. (Courtesy of Jeanette Sainz.)

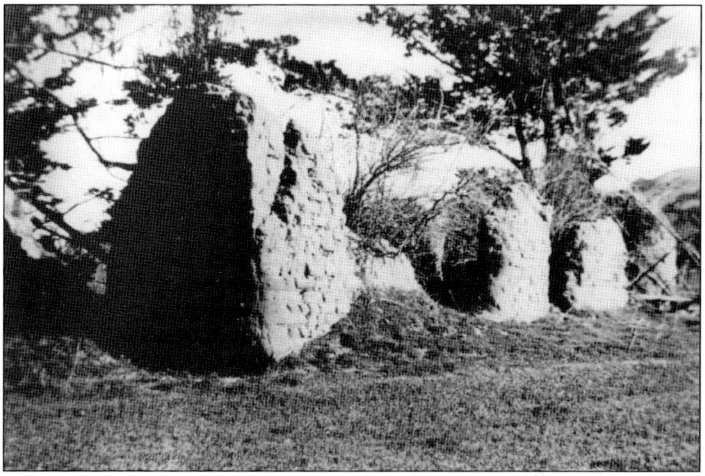

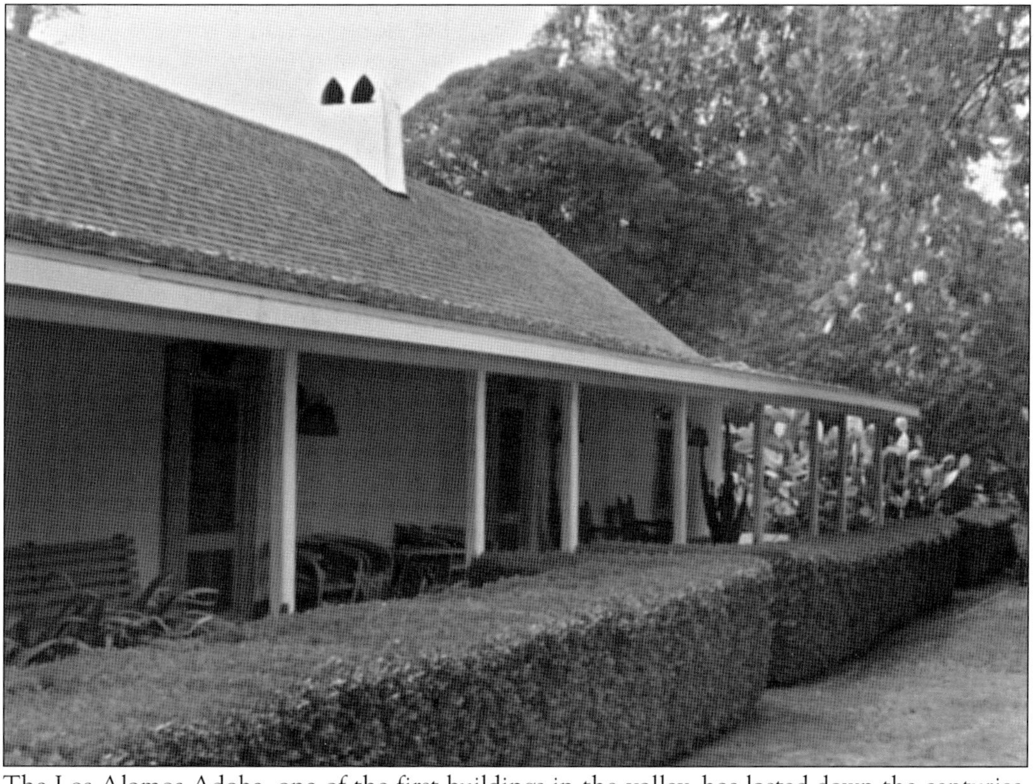

The Los Alamos Adobe, one of the first buildings in the valley, has lasted down the centuries. Adobes were built of bricks made from soil containing a small amount of gravel, mixed through with straw, then poured into molds to bake in the sun. Currently owned and maintained by Sherry and Carson Scheller, this adobe is essentially unchanged from historic times. (Photograph by author.)

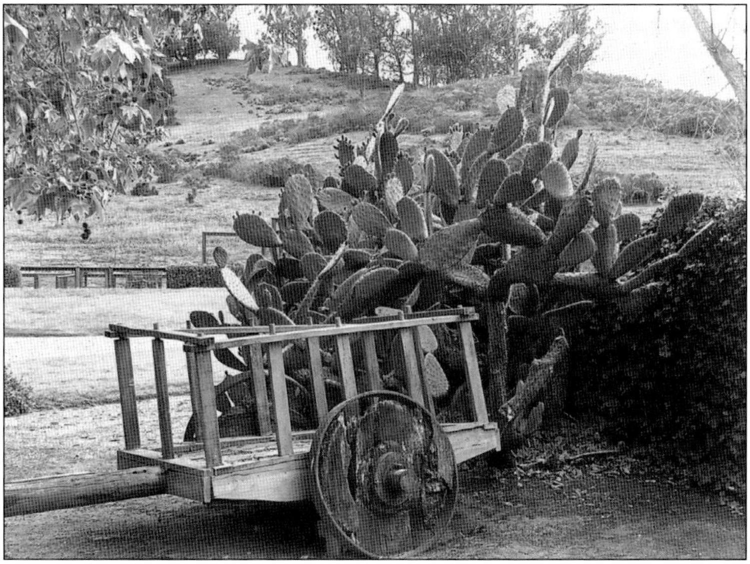

The two-wheeled cart, called the carreta, was the best way to haul cargo during the early Spanish period. A team of oxen usually pulled it. This carreta is on the grounds of the Los Alamos Adobe. The wheels are original, but the body was rebuilt. For many years, this carreta, drawn by a pair of oxen, participated in the Los Alamos Old Days Parade. (Photograph by author.)

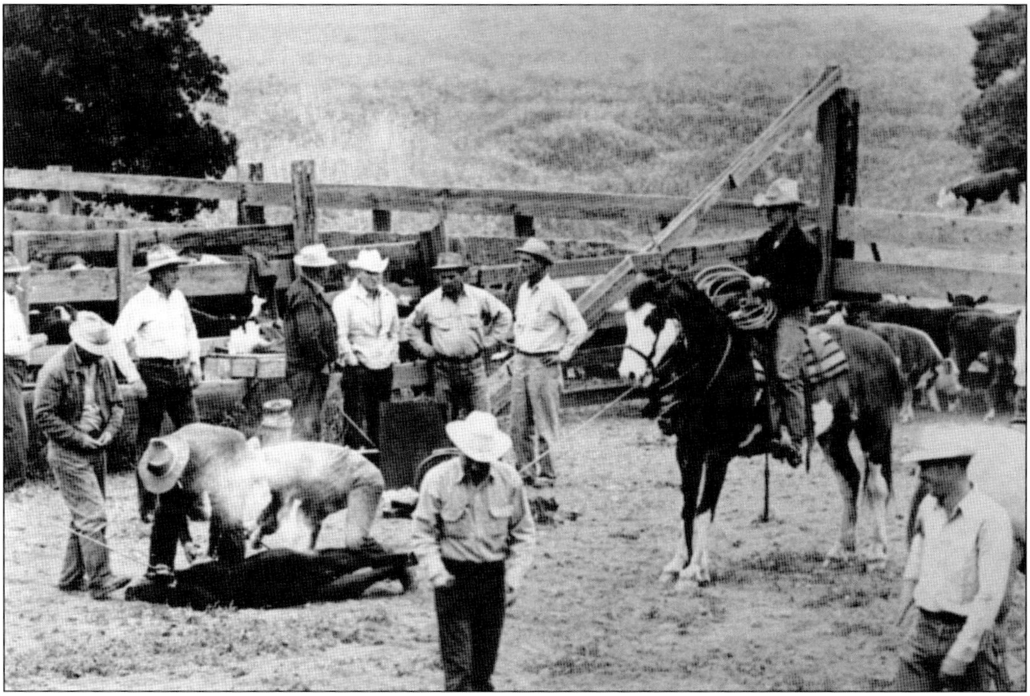

At the time of the great Spanish and Mexican ranchos, cattle roamed freely. The only way to determine ownership was by branding and ear tagging. Once a year or more, neighboring ranchos united to separate, brand, and tally the cattle of each rancho. The rodeo, which continues today, is an occasion for celebration. In this photograph of the Las Flores Ranch, Frank Tognazzi secures a calf for branding. (Courtesy of Jeanette Sainz.)

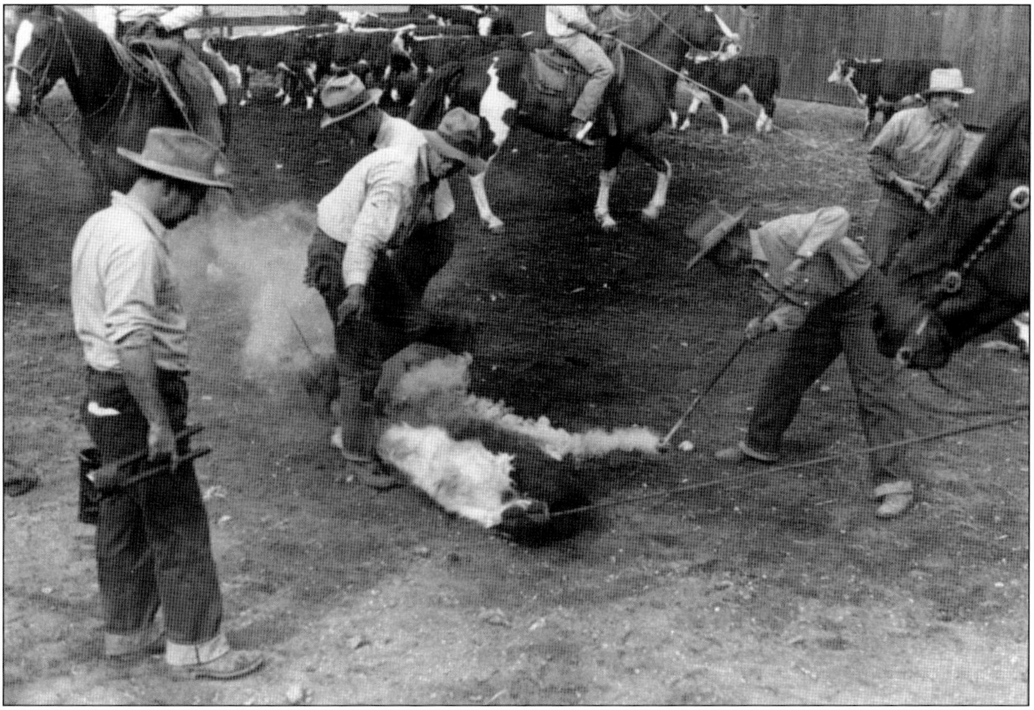

This photograph captures the fast action as a calf is roped and thrown in preparation for branding. The branding iron smokes while the calf is held motionless by two taught ropes and a knee on the neck. A cowboy reaches for a tool from a man standing nearby with the oyster bucket. (Courtesy of Jeanette Sainz.)

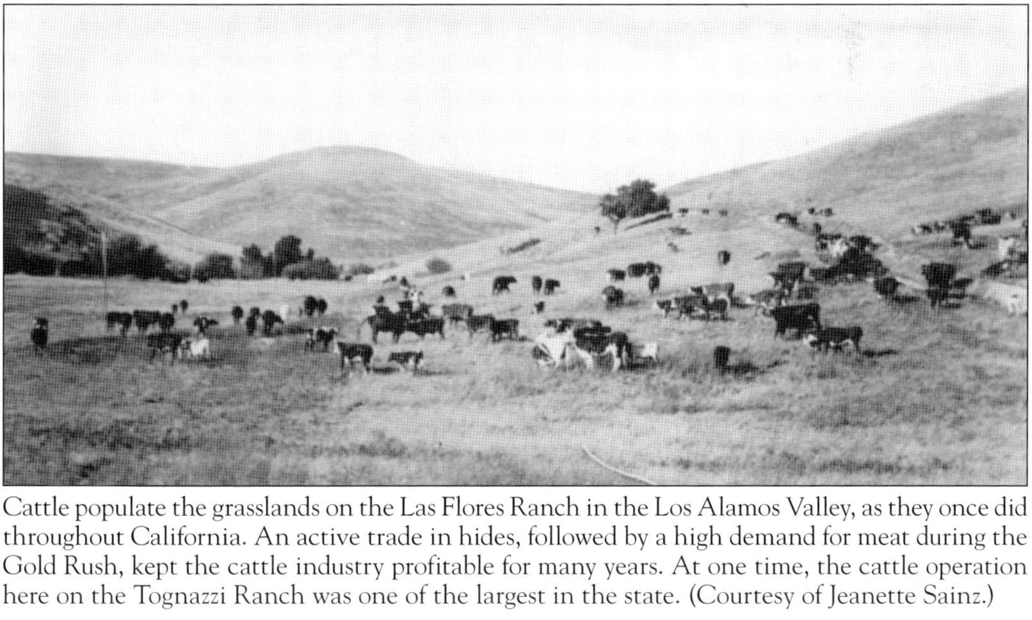

Cattle populate the grasslands on the Las Flores Ranch in the Los Alamos Valley, as they once did throughout California. An active trade in hides, followed by a high demand for meat during the Gold Rush, kept the cattle industry profitable for many years. At one time, the cattle operation here on the Tognazzi Ranch was one of the largest in the state. (Courtesy of Jeanette Sainz.)

Ten Commandments for Stage Passengers

The following list of rules was posted on all stagecoach station walls and on the ceiling of the coaches themselves.

Adherence to the Following Rules Will Insure A Pleasant Trip

1. Abstinance from liquor is preferred. If you must drink, share the bottle. To do otherwise makes you appear selfish. And don't overlook the driver.
2. If ladies are present, gentlemen are urged to forego smoking cigars and pipes, as the odor of same is repugnant to the weaker sex. Chewing tobacco is permitted if you spit with the wind, not against it.
3. Gentlemen passengers must refrain from the use of rough language in the presence of ladies and children. This rule does not apply to the driver, whose team may not be able to understand genteel language.
4. Robes are provided for your comfort during cold or wet weather. Hogging robes will not be tolerated. The offender will be obliged to ride outside with the driver.
5. Snoring is disgusting. If you sleep, sleep quietly.
6. Don't use your fellow passenger's shoulder for a pillow. He or she may not understand and friction could result.
7. Firearms may be kept on your person, for use in emergencies. Do not discharge them for pleasure, or shoot at wild animals along the roadside. The noise riles the horses.
8. In the event of a runaway, remain calm. Jumping from the coach may kill you, leave you injured, or at the mercy of the elements, highwaymen and coyotes.
9. Topics of discussion to be avoided have to do with religion, politics, and above all, stagecoach robberies or accidents.
10. Gentlemen guilty of unchivalrous behavior toward lady passengers will be put off the stage. It is a long walk back to Santa Barbara. A word to the wise is sufficient.

Can you imagine a ride from Santa Barbara over the San Marcos Pass in a stagecoach? Remember, it was not on the nice paved highway of today, but was over very rugged terrain.

This list of rules was found posted on all stagecoach station walls and the ceilings of the coaches themselves. Travel in Santa Barbara County in the mid- to late 19th century was an adventure. The run from Santa Barbara to Los Alamos was uncomfortable and often dangerous. An outrider was employed with a shovel to scrape mud from the coach's wheels. To prevent injury or accidents during robberies, drivers traveled unarmed. (Courtesy of LAMC.)

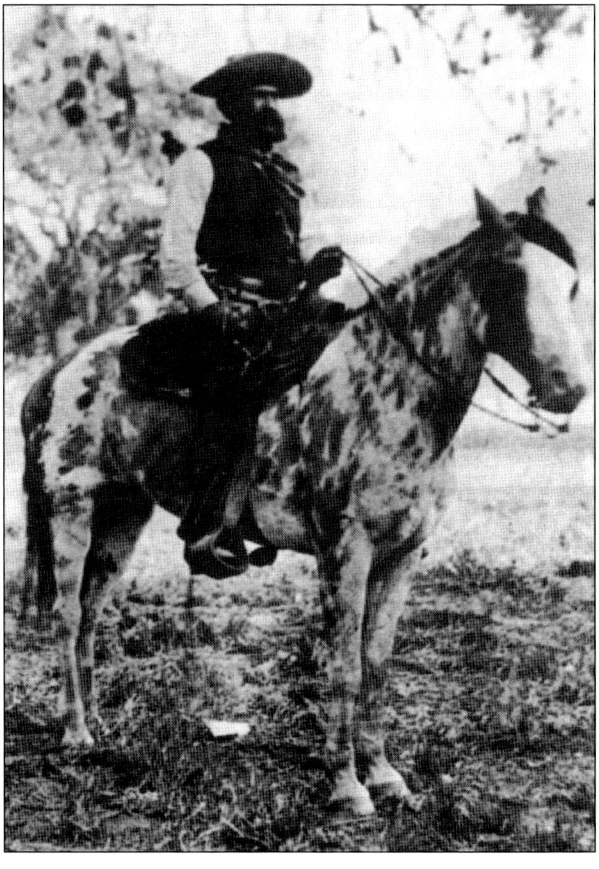

This photograph was taken in 1887 at Rancho El Roblar in the Los Alamos Valley. The man was named Chino Bronco. He and his horse are in traditional vaquero gear, including a slick-fork saddle, chaps, rawhide reins, and a spade bit with rein chains. The vaquero and his horse were integral to the history of the valley. (Courtesy of LAMC.)

Three

A Town Is Born
Early Los Alamos

Not often in life do plans work out precisely as hoped, but they did for financier Thomas Bell and Dr. James B. Shaw when they platted the town of Los Alamos. The two men came to live in Los Alamos Valley in the 1870s, after Dr. Shaw, at the bidding of Thomas Bell, purchased two adjoining 14,000-acre lots from the Los Alamos and La Laguna Ranchos. The first property was intended for Bell to provide a home for his nephew John, and the second was for Dr. Shaw himself. In 1876, each owner set aside an equal portion of land for a square-mile townsite. It is no coincidence that the stage line moved from its Foxen Canyon route to a route through Los Alamos Valley that same year. The town plat the men drew up called for a north-south street that divided the two ranches, named Centennial Street in honor of the nation's recent birthday. The town area was then divided into 24 equal blocks, each halved by an east/west alley. Each block was further divided into 26 lots. The men included such details as locations for a church and a school and names for each street. The town plat even appears to suggest a railroad right-of-way, including a depot (where the current one stands) and an outhouse. Again, it is unlikely to be a coincidence that, in the same year, the Pacific Coast Steamship Company replaced the tram that existed from Port Harford with a narrow-gauge railroad and extended the line to San Luis Obispo. No doubt, these two prescient men had already dreamed of the railroad coming to Los Alamos.

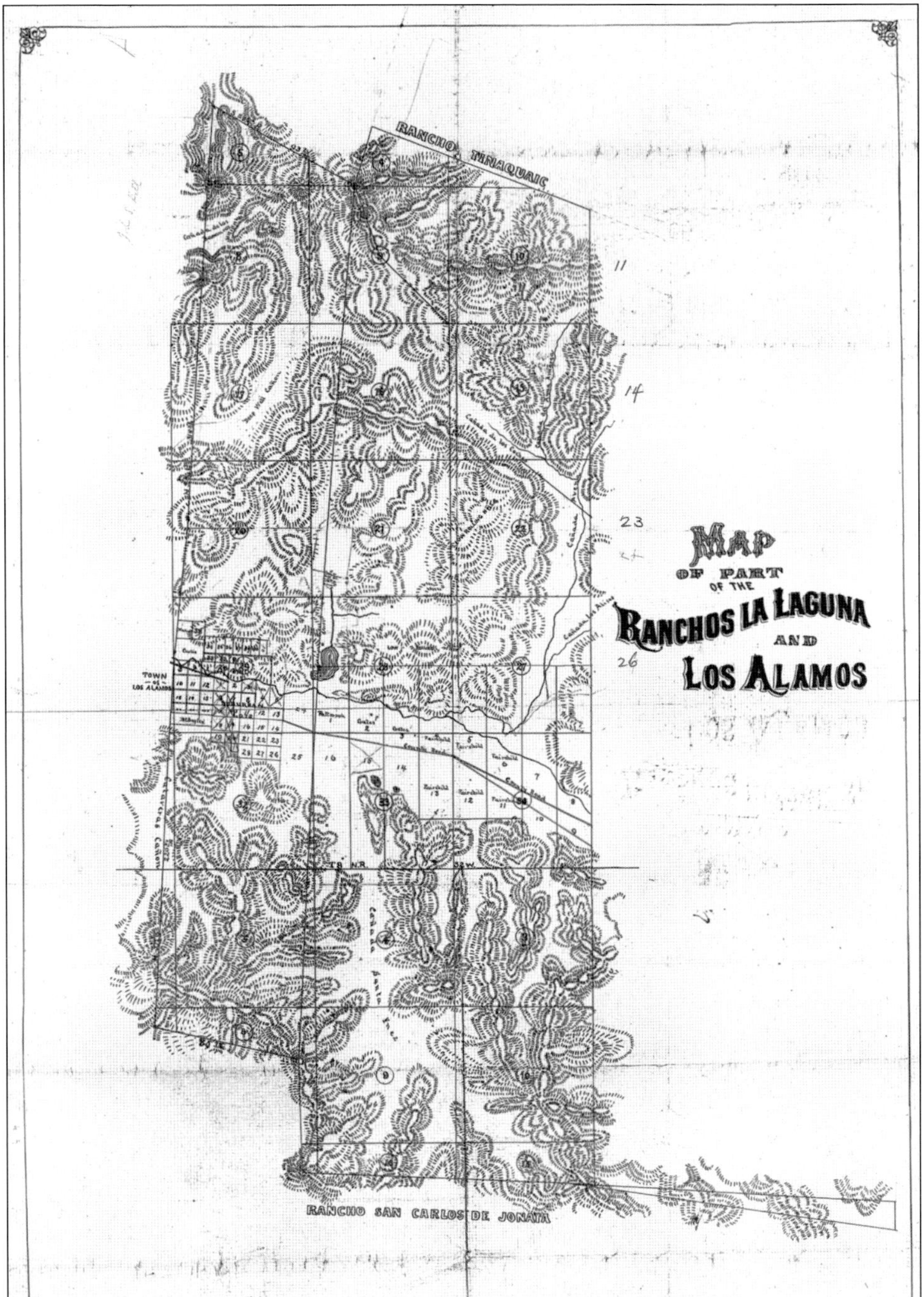

This extremely detailed map shows those portions of Rancho La Laguna parceled by Dr. Shaw, including number 29 and the plat for Los Alamos. The parcels not shown are presumably those that have no portion designated for sale. Note that Drum Canyon, south of Los Alamos, is identified by its original designation, Calaveras Cañon, named for human bones found there.

This is the deed transferring Los Alamos properties from Dr. James Barron Shaw to his son James Barron Shaw Jr. Dr. Shaw bought land in the valley largely on speculation of future growth an as a fine location for his descendants to live. Dr. Shaw had another residence in Santa Barbara, where he spent much of his time when he was not traveling.

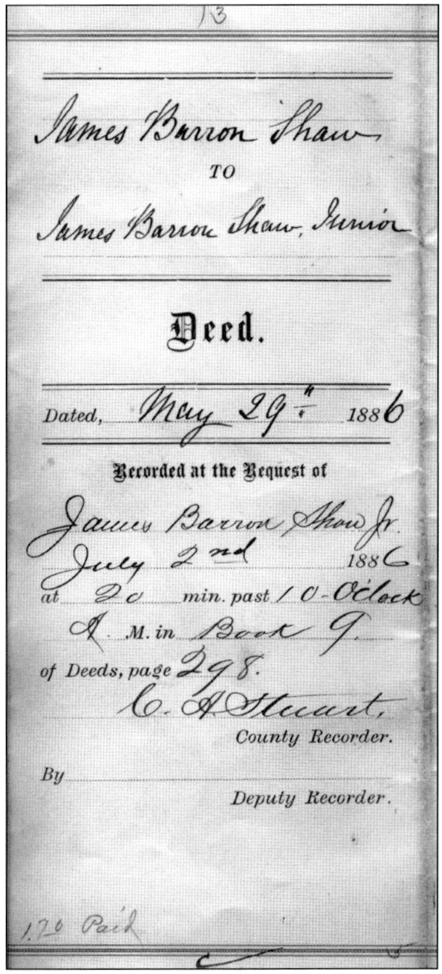

James Barron Shaw

TO

James Barron Shaw, Junior

Deed.

Dated, May 29th 1886

Recorded at the Request of

James Barron Shaw Jr.

July 2nd 1886

at 20 min. past 10 O'clock

A. M. in Book 9.

of Deeds, page 298.

C. A. Stewart,

County Recorder.

By

Deputy Recorder.

1.70 Paid

This plat map of Los Alamos is dated September 15, 1876. The town was divided into 26 blocks, with streets and alleys. The intention for Main Street to become the business thoroughfare may be seen. Interestingly, the Central Coast Railway, which did not arrive in Los Alamos until 1882, seems to appear as a right-of-way and depot, suggesting that Dr. Shaw may have been acting on inside information.

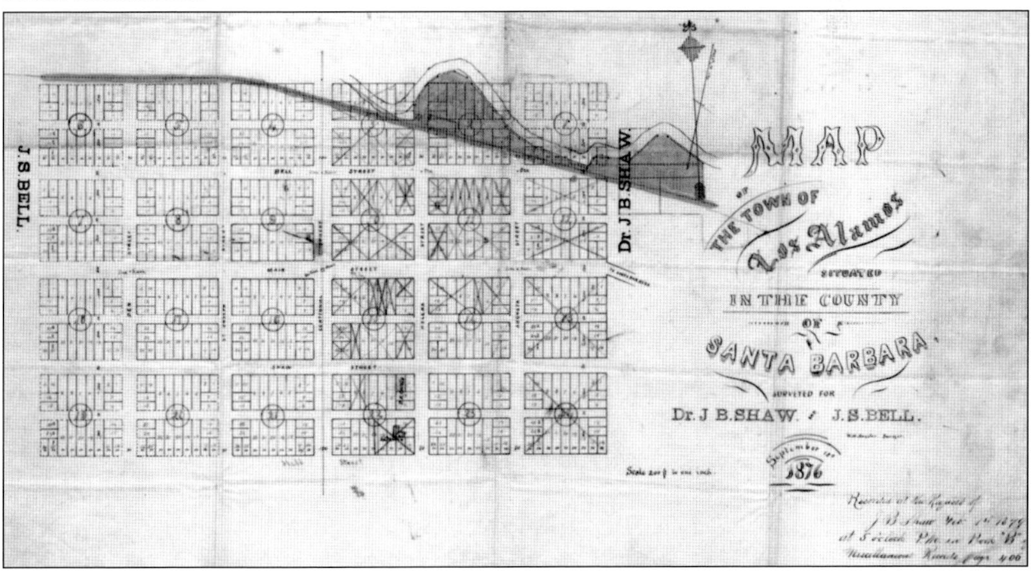

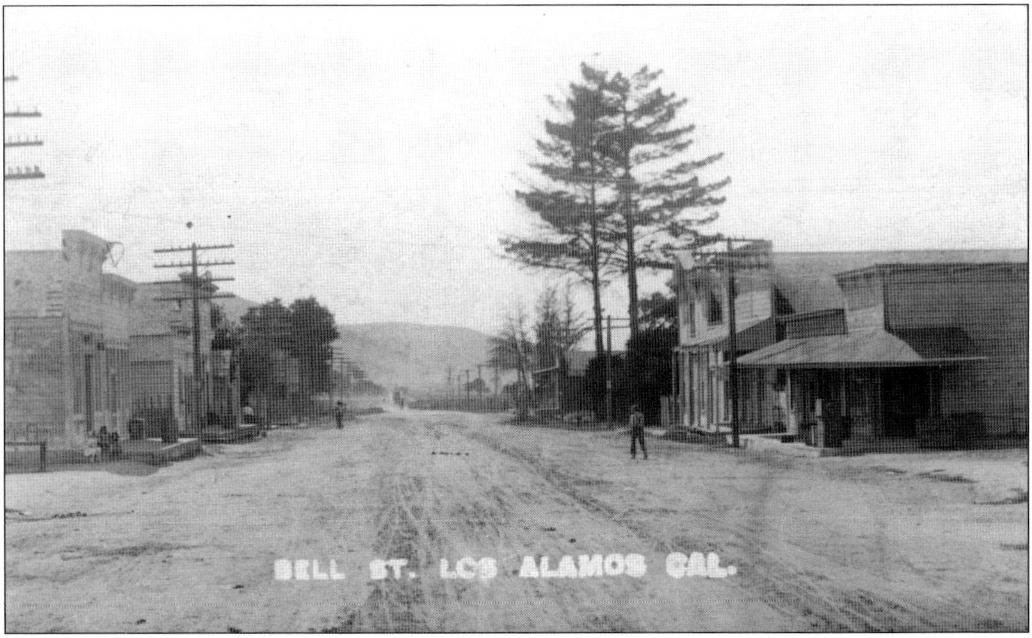

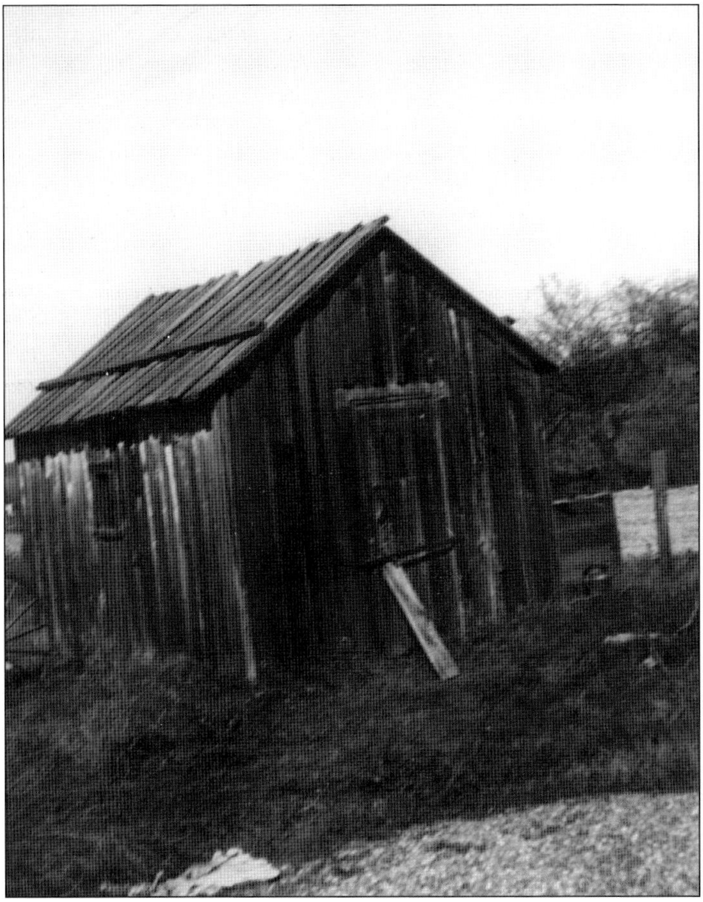

This west-facing photograph of Bell Street was taken some time around 1915. The building at far left is Pearson's Cheap Cash Store. A barbershop stands two stores down, where the first Union Hotel once stood. At far right is Sam Boradori's merchandise store. The Meat Market porch is visible at center right. A horse-drawn covered wagon approaches town from the west.

Originally built on Waite Street in 1880, this old Los Alamos jail was later demolished. A new one was built on Centennial and Leslie Streets in 1887. The story is told of a prisoner who sawed out a portion of the jail wall, selected a good horse and saddle, and rode away after leaving a note of appreciation for the accommodation.

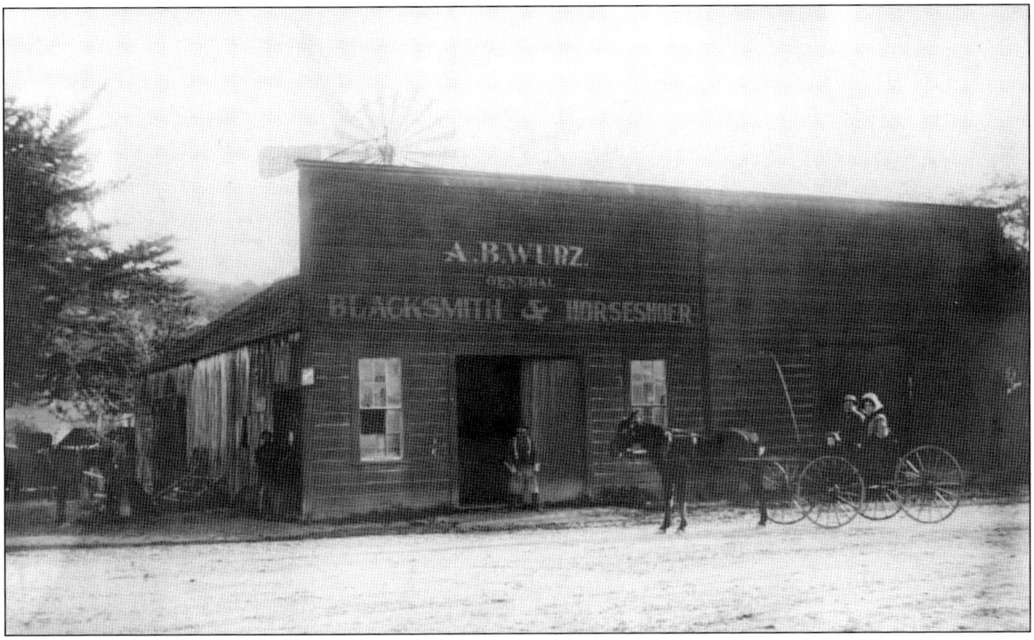

C.H. Pearson built the first blacksmith shop in 1879 (above). He operated it jointly with Frank Whitcher. At that time, there were two blacksmith shops in Los Alamos, the second operated by Homer Waite on the street that now bears his name. Pearson went on to establish himself in the general merchandise business and sold his shop to William Gewe in 1882. Gewe expanded the business and built a home on the same block of land (below). He later sold the business to A.B. Wurz, who operated it until 1923, when he finally sold it to E.A. Robbins for a filling station. Wurz operated his business at two locations: the first where Collins Market now stands, and the second at 325 Bell Street.

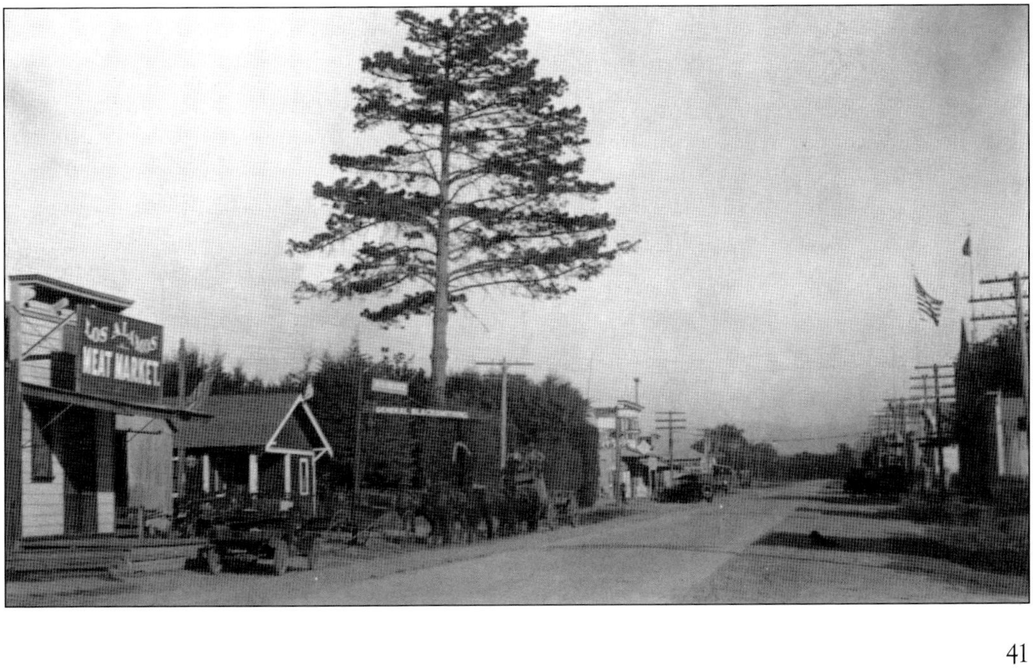

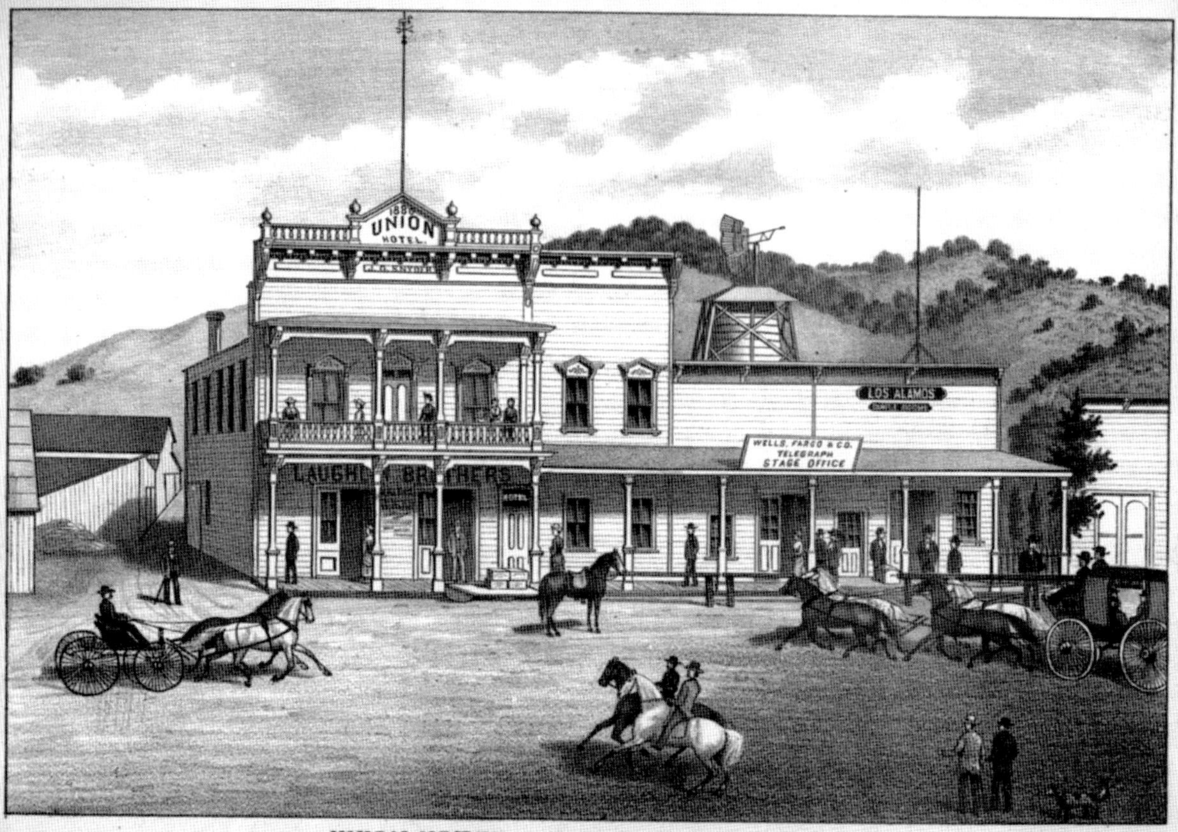

UNION HOTEL, J. D. SNYDER OWNER & PROPR.
LOS ALAMOS, SANTA BARBARA CO. CAL.

John B. Snyder built the Union Hotel in 1880, with accommodations on the second level and rental space below. Henry and Ozell Laughlin operated a mercantile store there. Here, the original hotel entrance is seen to the right of the Laughlin Brothers store. Snyder added an adjoining structure to the Union Hotel in 1882, with extra rooms on the second floor. In 1887, the brothers bought Alex Leslie's Pioneer Store and moved. The original Union Hotel housed the Wells Fargo & Company Express Office, the telegraph office, and the stage office. By 1887, the hotel had a total of 22 rooms on the second floor. The Sample Rooms were rooms in which traveling salesmen could display their wares. The hotel burned to the ground in 1893.

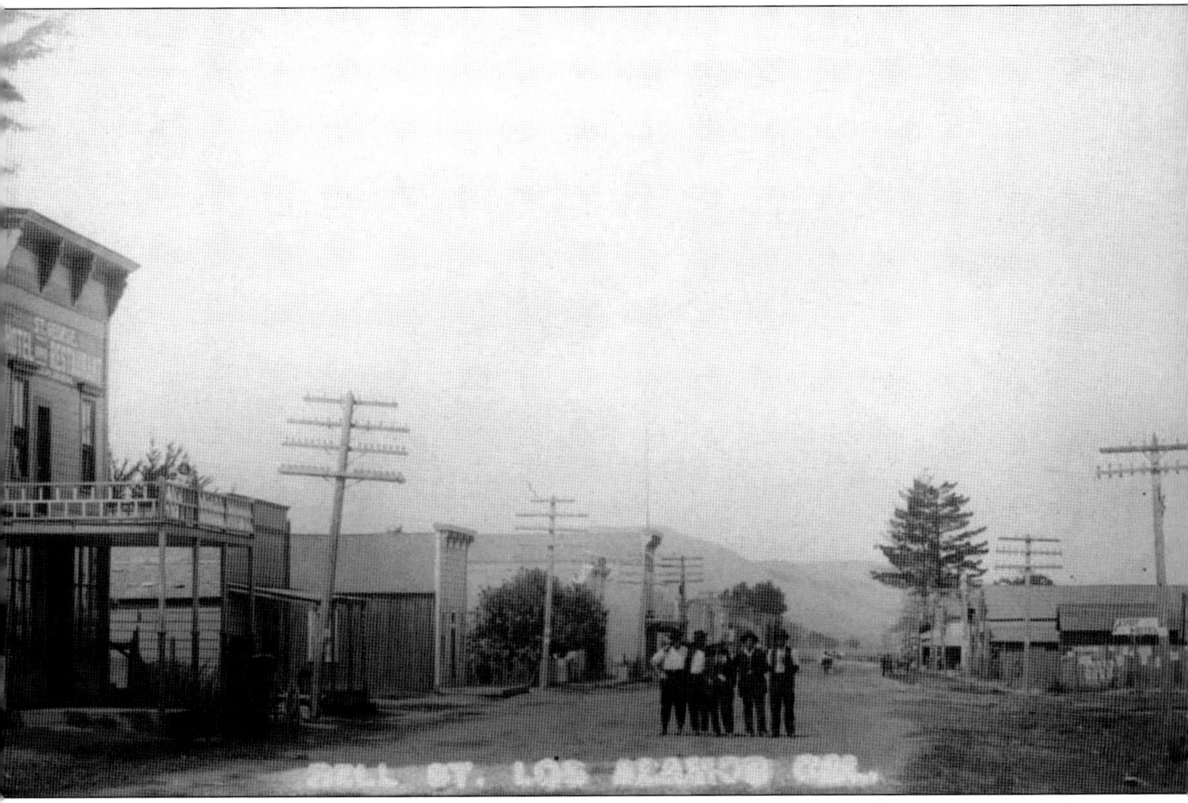

The Queen Lily Soap advertisement dates this photograph to the mid- to late 1890s. Here, five unidentified men stand shoulder to shoulder in the middle of Bell Street for the camera. The St. George Hotel (left) stood in the vacant lot west of the present Well Bread Bakery. The tall pines on the right mark the location of the Leslie house.

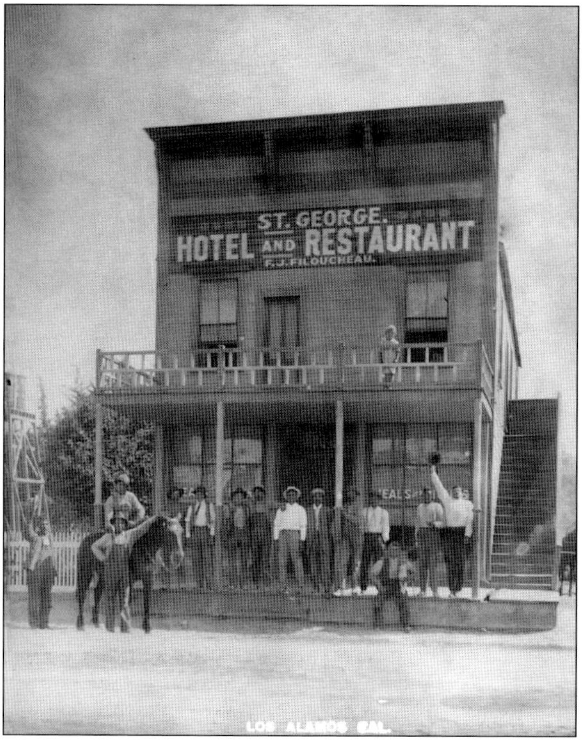

A happy crowd gathers at the St. George Hotel. Note the little girl on the balcony. The hotel and restaurant burned down in 1919. A man named Mr. Goodman would drive a surrey with fringe on the top to meet each train at the station, calling out "Come to St. George hotel, a place where anybody can eat." Manager and chef F.J. Filoucheau was known up and down the coast as an excellent cook.

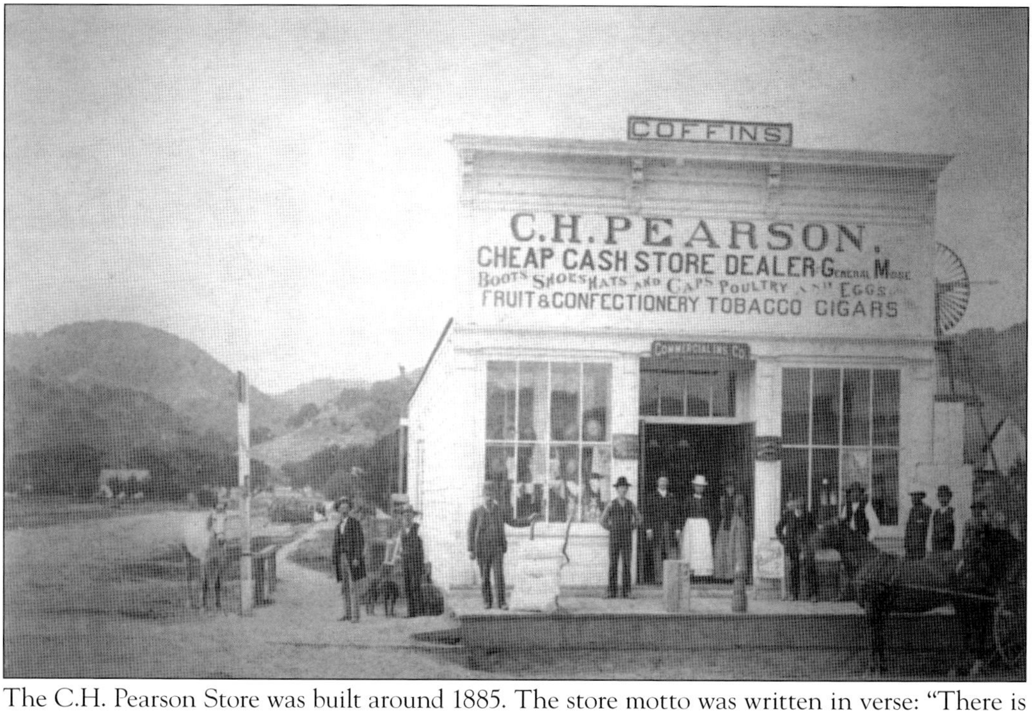

The C.H. Pearson Store was built around 1885. The store motto was written in verse: "There is Pearson's Cheap Cash Store / They meet you at the door / They try to please and never tease / And when you are inside / They'll meet you with a smile / With ribbons and laces to deck ladies faces / At Pearson's Cheap Cash Store."

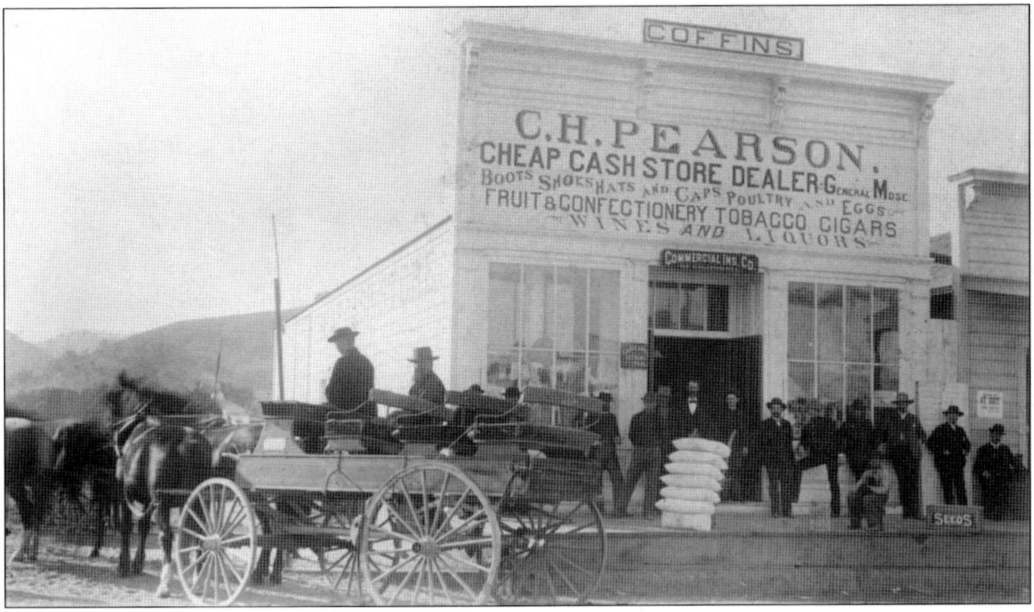

C.H. Pearson was a man who pulled himself up by the bootstraps. When it came time to learn the merchandising business, he worked as a clerk for the Laughlin Brothers before opening his own business. When he did, his store reflected his personality. This photograph illustrates the wide variety of goods Pearson carried. When he saw there was no undertaker in town, he took up that business, as well. Here, C.H. Pearson (center, white shirt) stands among his friends.

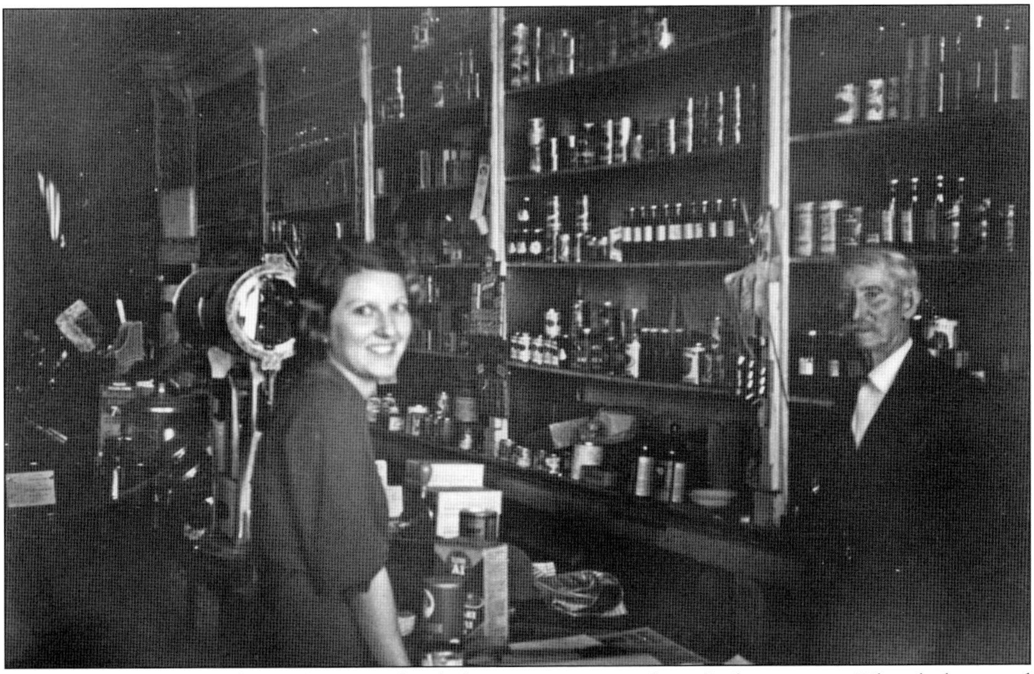

C.H. Pearson pauses for a photograph while serving an unidentified customer. The shelves and counter space around them are stocked to overflowing with a great variety of goods. After Pearson's death, Knott's Berry Farm purchased the entire interior of his store for an exhibit illustrating a typical general store of the era.

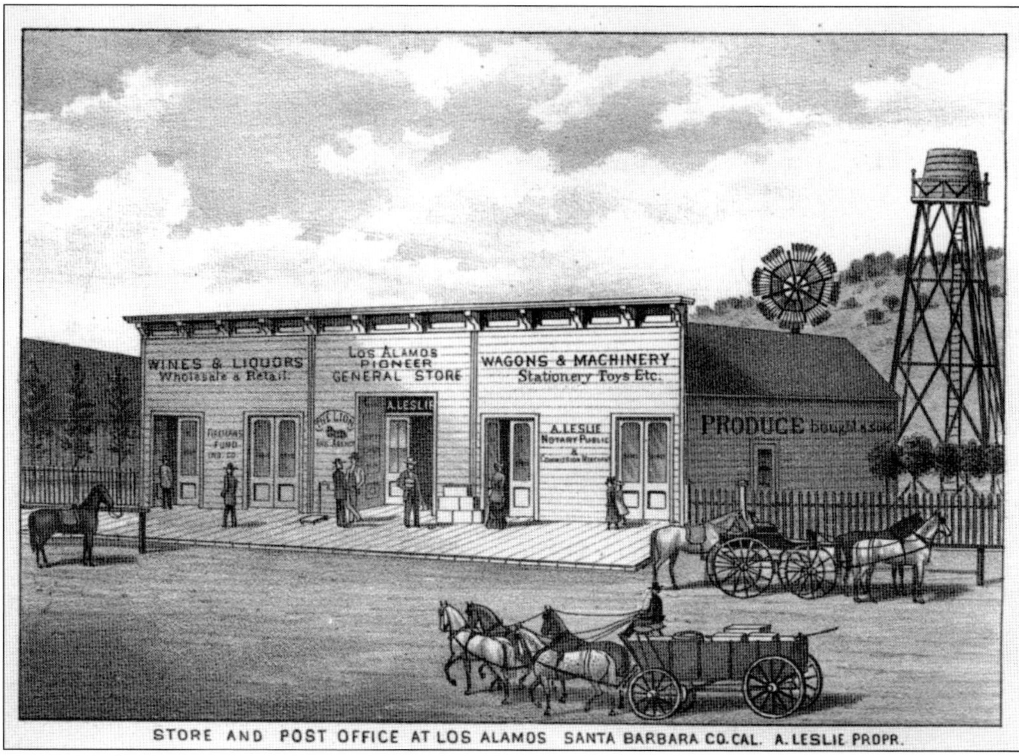

In 1877, Alex Leslie constructed his Pioneer General Store, seen here in a drawing. The building housed three stores: a general merchandise store, a toy and candy store (which housed the post office), and a liquor store. He added a second floor that included a meeting hall in 1882. Leslie sold the building to the Laughlin brothers in 1887. The building, along with the Union Hotel, burned to the ground on February 16, 1893.

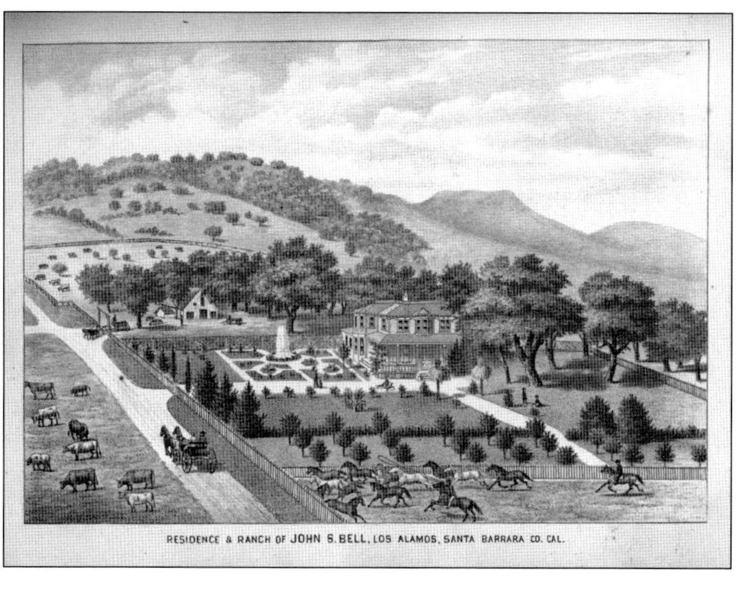

This is an 1895 drawing of the home Thomas Bell built for his nephew John Stewart Bell on a ranch west of town. It was torn down in the mid-20th century. John Bell married, and he and his wife raised five children on the ranch. He planted grains and built a flour mill in Los Alamos. His son Charles explored beet-sugar refining, and his daughter Carrie married the town doctor, George Luton.

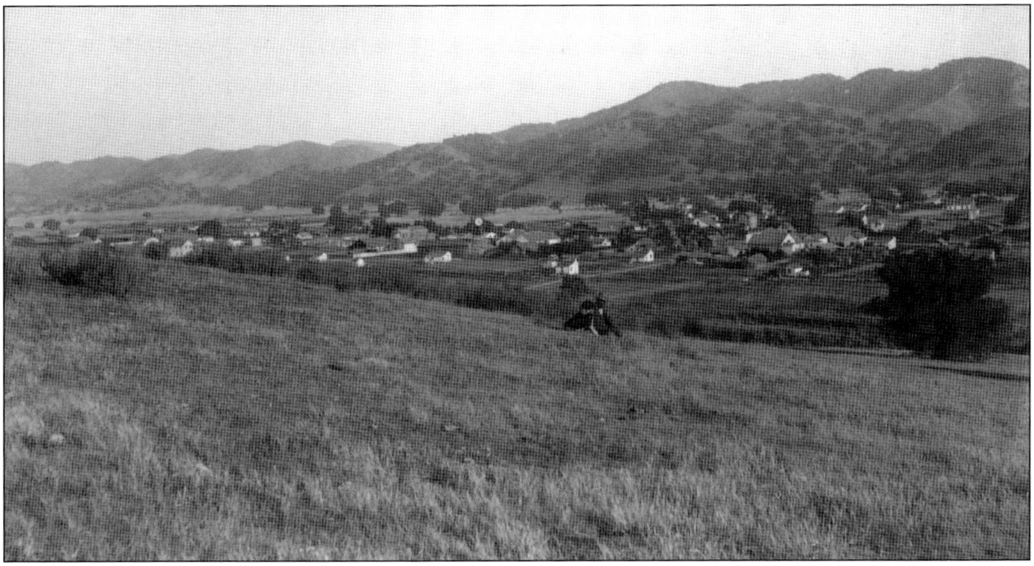

This south-facing photograph of Los Alamos was taken at the turn of the century. The flagpole of the first school building can be seen at the far edge of town, above the man's head. The Fairchild Hotel (later Depot Hotel) is the large white house at far left. The original Union Hotel is in the center of town, directly over the dog's head.

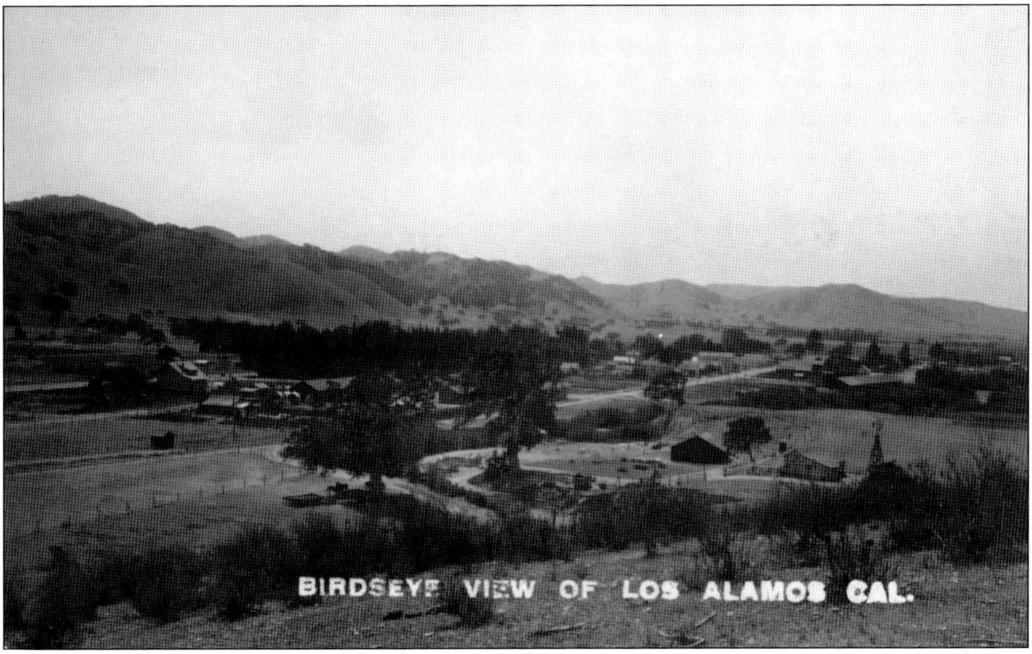

Los Alamos is seen from the southeast some time between 1910 and 1919. The second school building stands alone at left in the distance. The train depot is the angled building on the right; the white Depot Hotel is seen just beyond it. The two-story St. George Hotel is the tall building on the south side of Bell Street (center right).

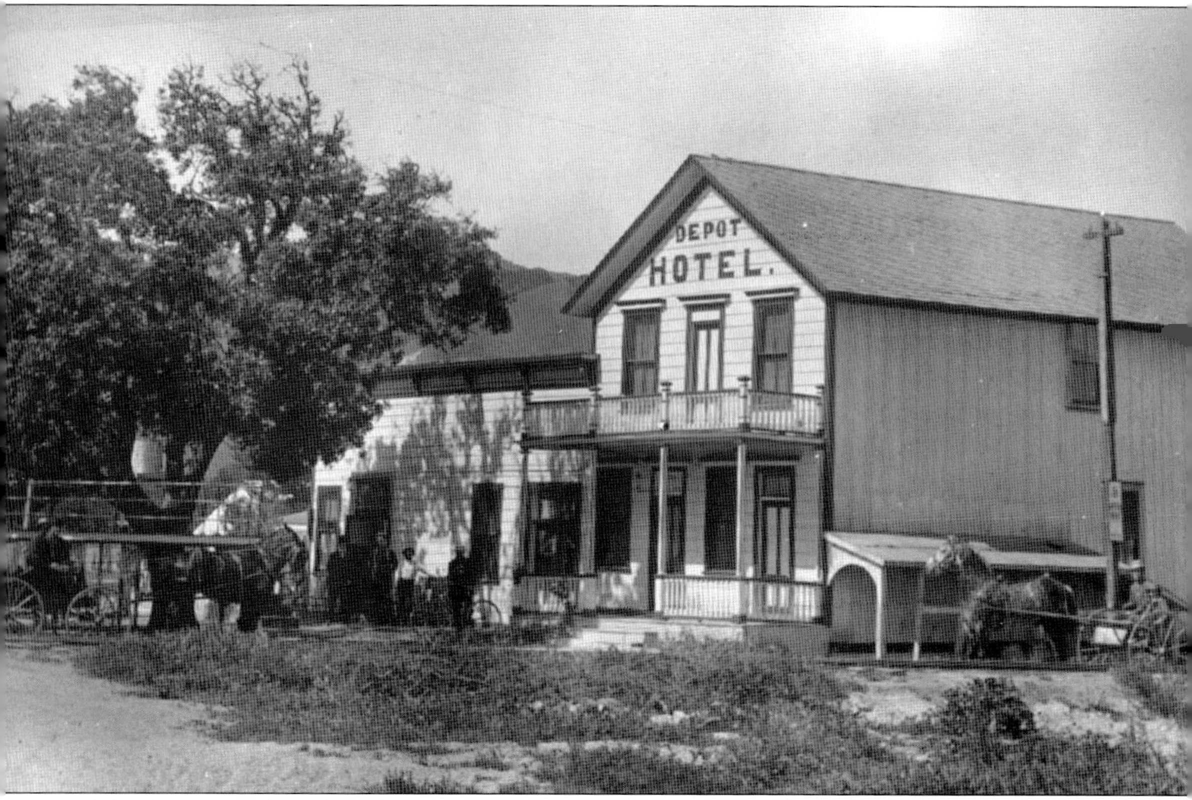

The Depot Hotel was built for Fred Beck as a brewery. Since then, it has been the Oak Tree Hotel, Fairchild Hotel, a brothel, a dentist's office, and the Depot Hotel, among other establishments. The sign over the door beneath the balcony reads "Ladies Parlour," suggestive of other activities. A keen eye will see train tracks across the foreground.

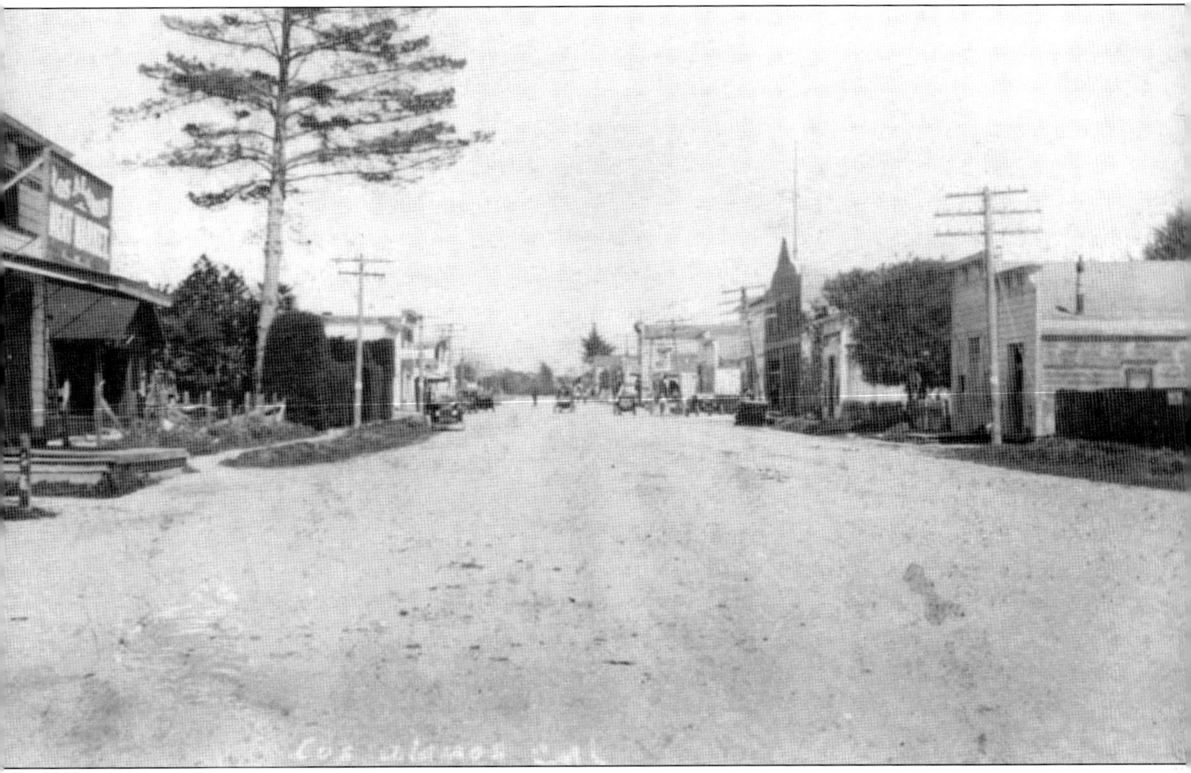

Bell Street is shown in this east-facing photograph between 1915 and 1918. The Los Alamos Meat Market is at far left, and beyond it is the Alex Leslie home, hidden behind the hedges. At far right is the Kahn building, torn down later by Al Scolari to expand the California Garage. In earlier days, the stage stopped at an old adobe building just west of the Leslie property, and Kahn served meals to travelers.

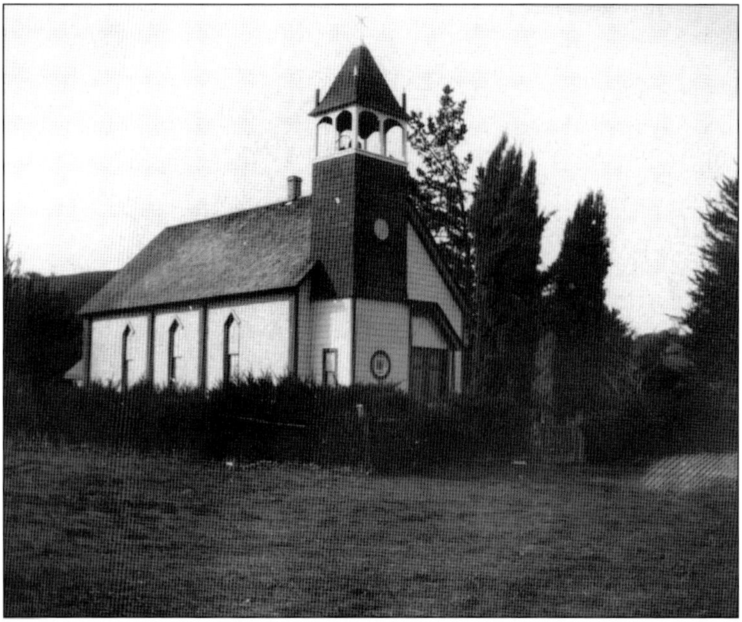

The Presbyterian church on Main Street was built by a Methodist congregation and then sold to the Presbyterians in 1900. The original 15 Presbyterian congregation members first met in 1882 in the schoolhouse. The church building was severely damaged in the 1902 earthquake. It was then rebuilt, and a belfry was added. Alice Linsemayer, the pastor's wife, painted the simulated lead-glass windows. The annex was added in 1949.

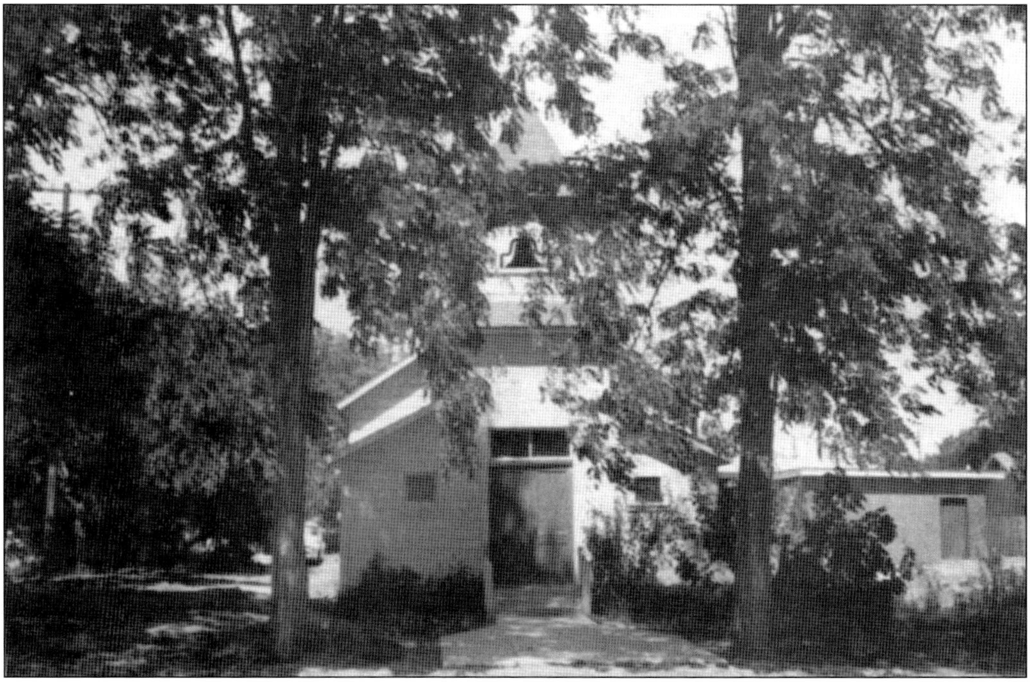

This building was constructed as a home for Mrs. Harvey in 1890. Thomas and Jerry Foxen converted it into the Catholic church in 1905 with the help of volunteers. The current Catholic church building was erected immediately behind the first, which was then removed. Prior to the building of this church, most Los Alamos Catholics attended services at the Santa Ynez Mission. (Courtesy of LAMC.)

Four

Town and Valley
Growing Together

Once the town of Los Alamos was born, valley and town grew in concert—what benefited the valley, benefited the town, and vice versa. The cattle industry, dairy industry, and ever-expanding agriculture left their economic stamp on the community. Then came the discovery of oil and the growth of the oil industry. The first well drilled in the area, named Esperanza, was sheared off its casing in the 1902 earthquake; the pool was never relocated. The best-known strike was well No. 3, Old Maude, on the Careaga Ranch west of Los Alamos. It came a gusher, and hundreds of visitors came to see it. Oil was subsequently discovered and developed on the Bell estate, El Roblar Ranch, Gato Ridge, Wickenden and Rickard properties, Calaveras Canyon, and the Las Flores Ranch, bringing jobs to people of the valley and wealth to the landowners. Oil changed the pattern of people's lives and increased the flow of traffic and capital to the town of Los Alamos. The 1902 earthquake was a little-known yet significant event; it struck with an intensity equal to the San Francisco quake four years later. The shocks were felt for four days and forced residents to flee to safety. Many buildings were severely damaged, and they had to be rebuilt or abandoned. In the valley, meanwhile, the two large ranchos gradually diminished as parcels were rented and sold. Gaspar Oreña purchased 4,000 acres of the Los Alamos Rancho. Dr. J.B. Shaw sold 3,000 acres of the Rancho La Laguna to Frederick Wickenden and 4,000 acres to Francis T. Underhill, which became the property now known as El Roblar Rancho. Over the years, the farseeing town fathers enticed the stagecoach, the railroad, and State Highway 101 to the valley, all of which played a part in the economic growth of both town and valley.

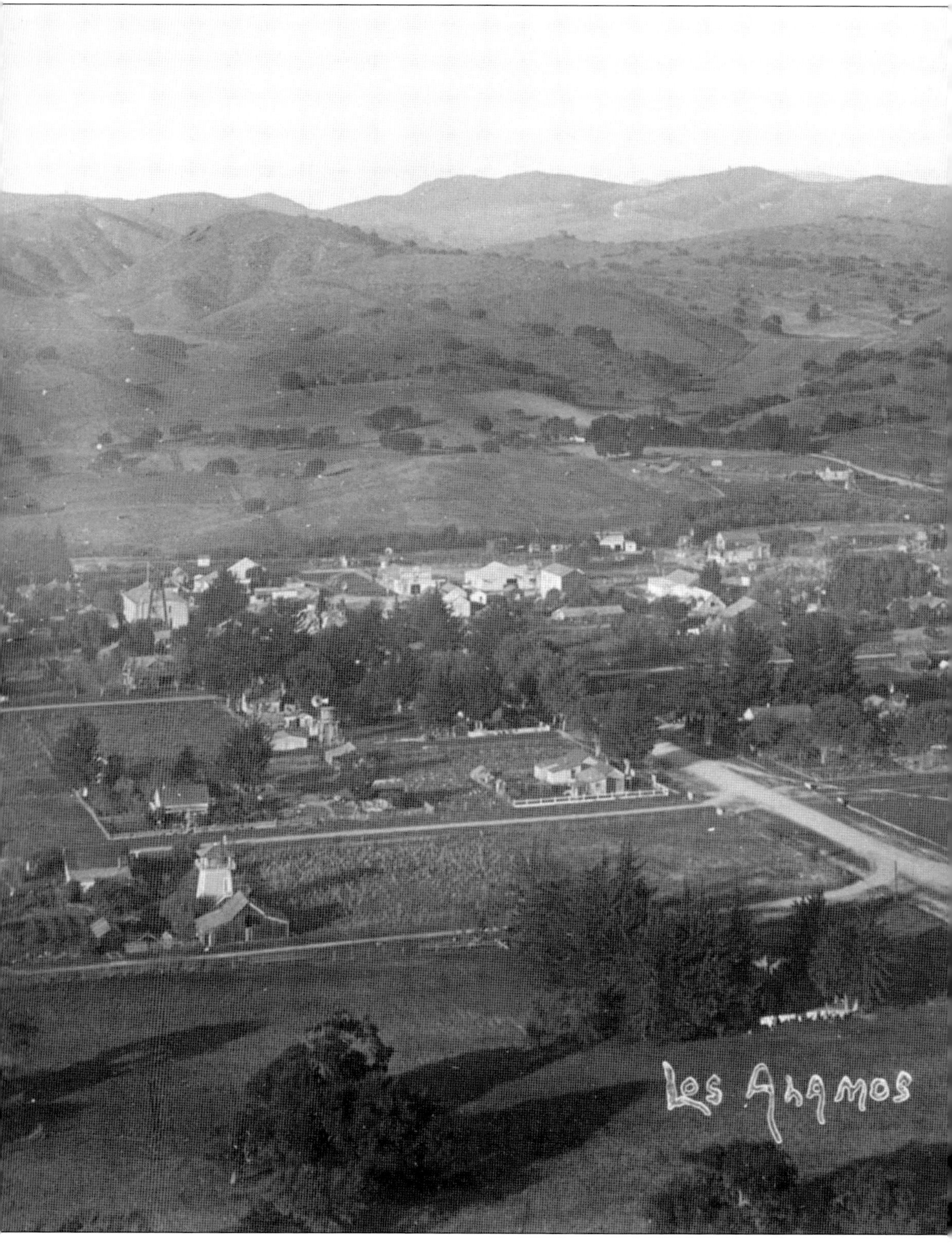
Los Alamos

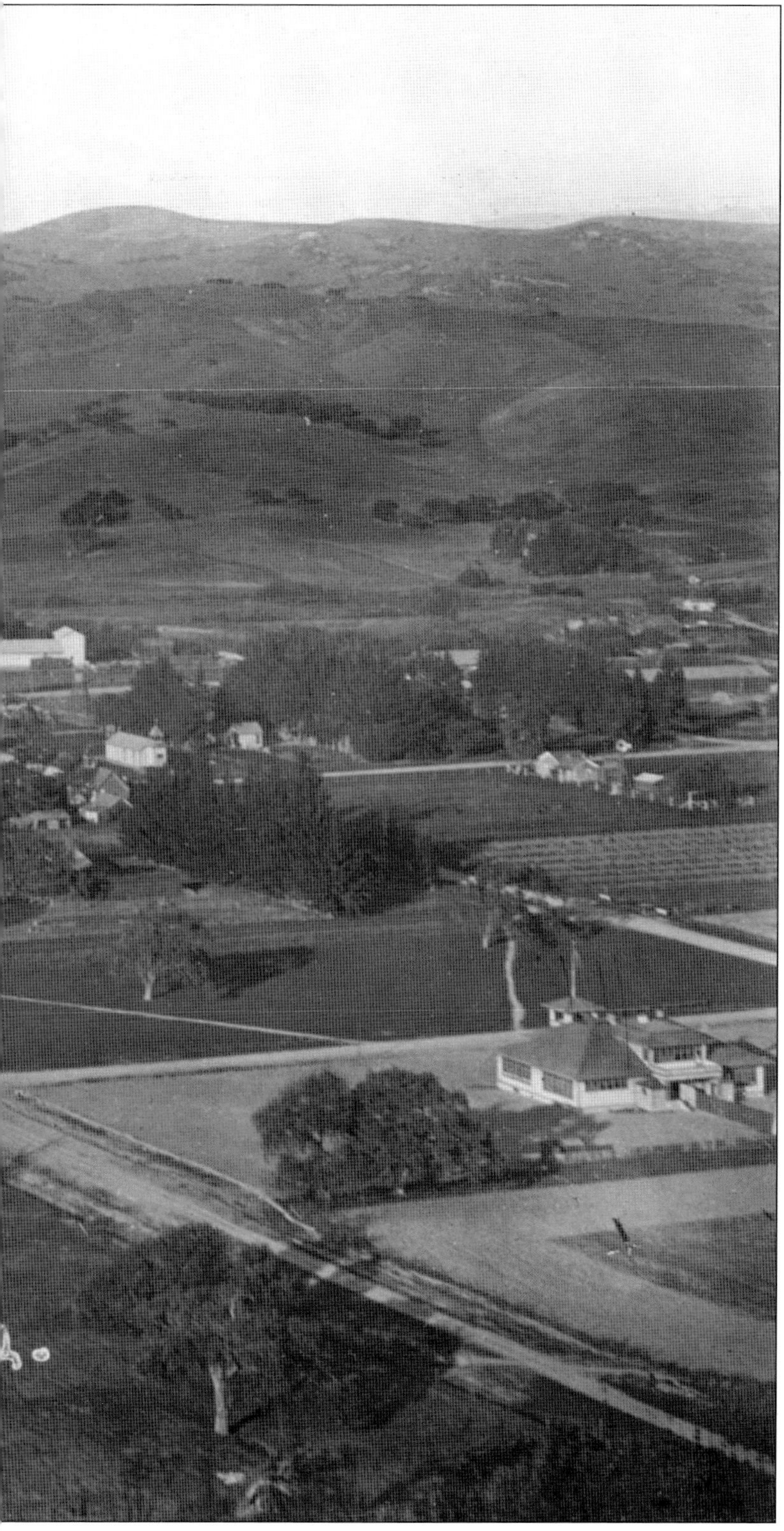

This bird's-eye view of Los Alamos was captured from a hilltop south of town between 1910 and 1919. The grammar school is visible at lower right, surrounded by bare earth. A large white building directly above it beyond the trees is the first of the two Catholic churches. Below it to the left is the Presbyterian church. The Central Coast Railway depot is the large white building right of center, with two large water tanks visible to its left. Sharp eyes might make out a freight car in front of it. Just to the left of the water towers and barely visible above the trees is the Depot Hotel. To the left, toward the town center along Bell Street, the two large white buildings with gaping doors are the livery stables and mills. The other large building at left, with a flagpole and a tall water tower behind it, is likely the Los Alamos Hotel. Beyond the town are the rolling Solomon Hills. (Courtesy of LAMC.)

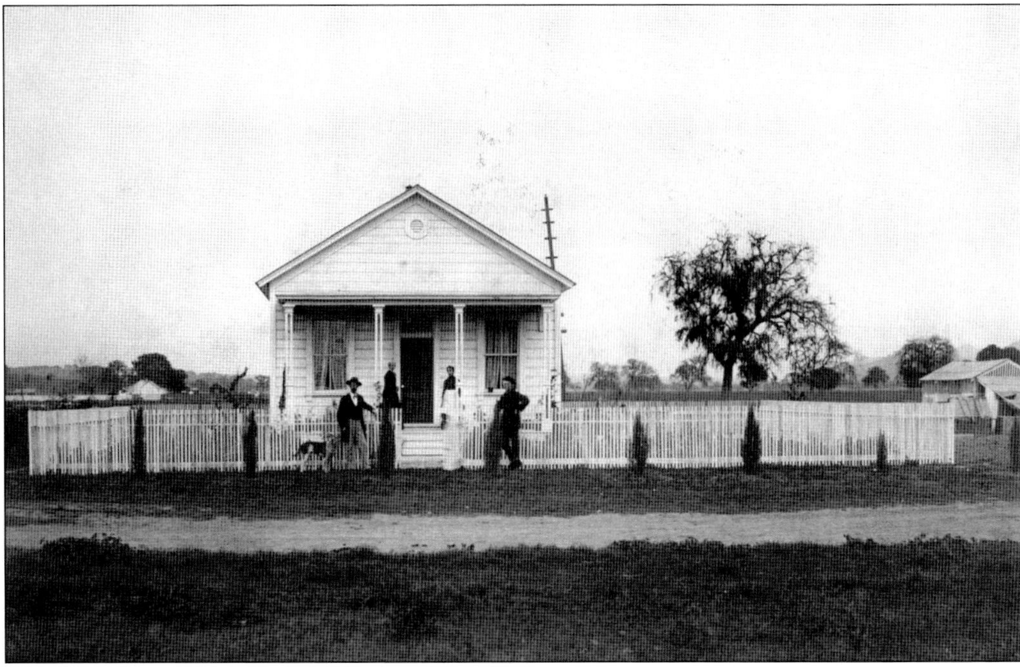

On this and the facing page is a sequence of images of the C.H. Pearson home, from its earliest days in Los Alamos to the present. These photographs show not just the changes to Pearson's house over the years but the growth of the town of Los Alamos as well. Charles Pearson came to Los Alamos in 1879 and joined an established business as a blacksmith. He built his home (above) in 1882. In 1886, after time spent as a clerk at the Laughlin Brothers general store, he began his own mercantile business. Pearson traveled home to Canada in 1891 to marry Nettie Spafford. His success in the mercantile business is made evident by an addition to the house (below), his fine horses, and new carriage. Centennial Street is in the foreground.

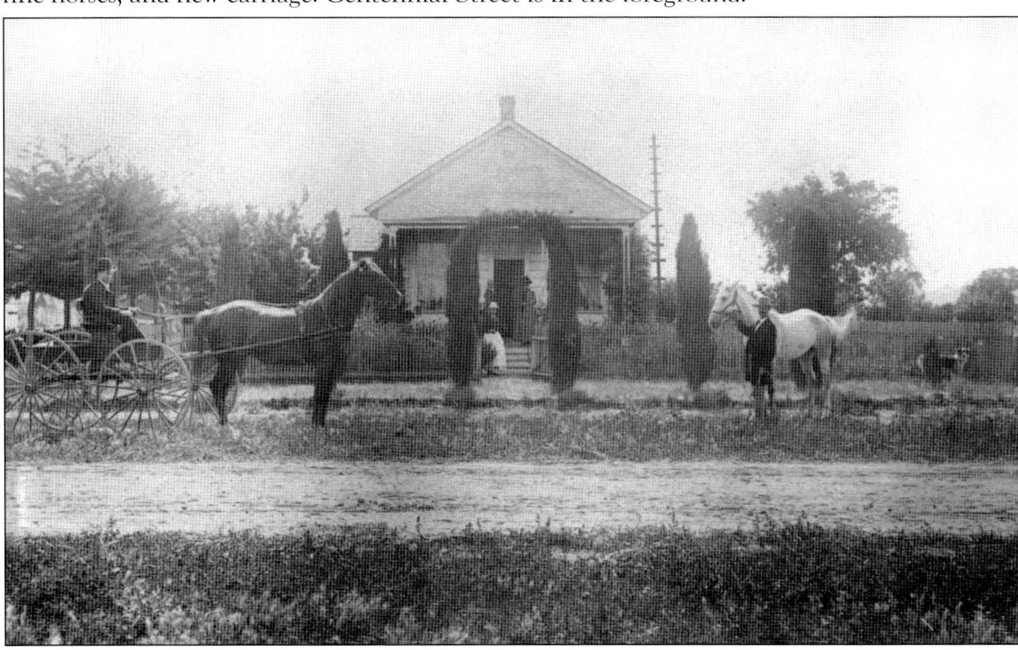

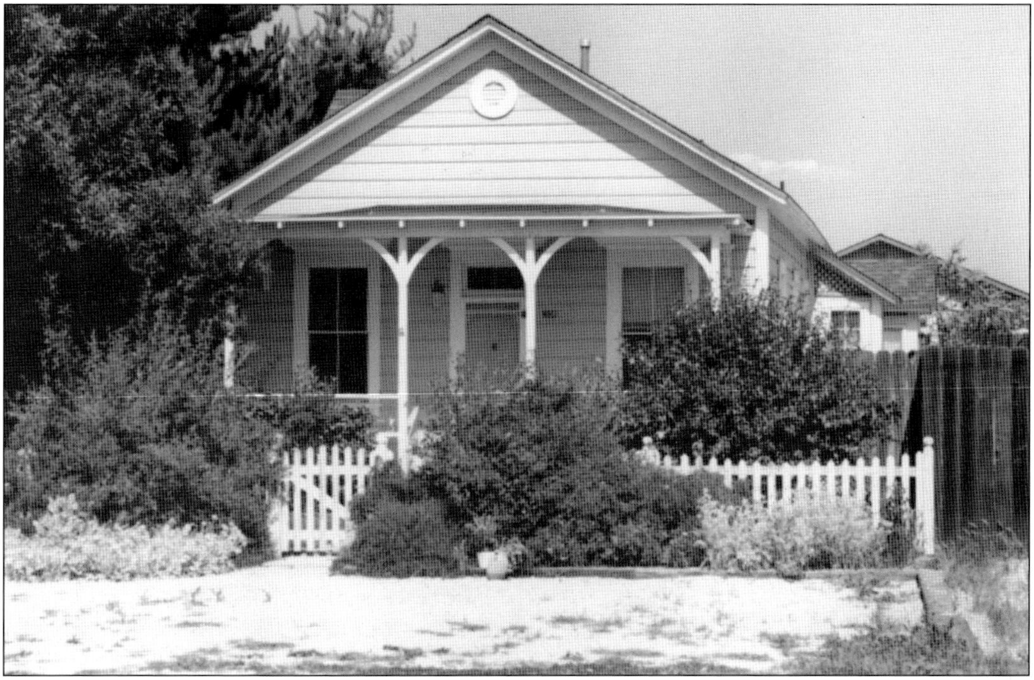

The growth of the town of Los Alamos can be seen by the proximity of other houses in the above photograph, taken in 1982. The shade trees that threaten to envelop the house were planted long ago by Pearson himself. Another addition has been made to the south side of the house, yet its character remains largely unchanged. People who knew him described Charles Pearson as honest, tactful, and always ready to please. The below photograph was taken by the author for this publication. The house appears much as it did originally, except for a more populated neighborhood. Like many historic buildings in Los Alamos, it has been well maintained.

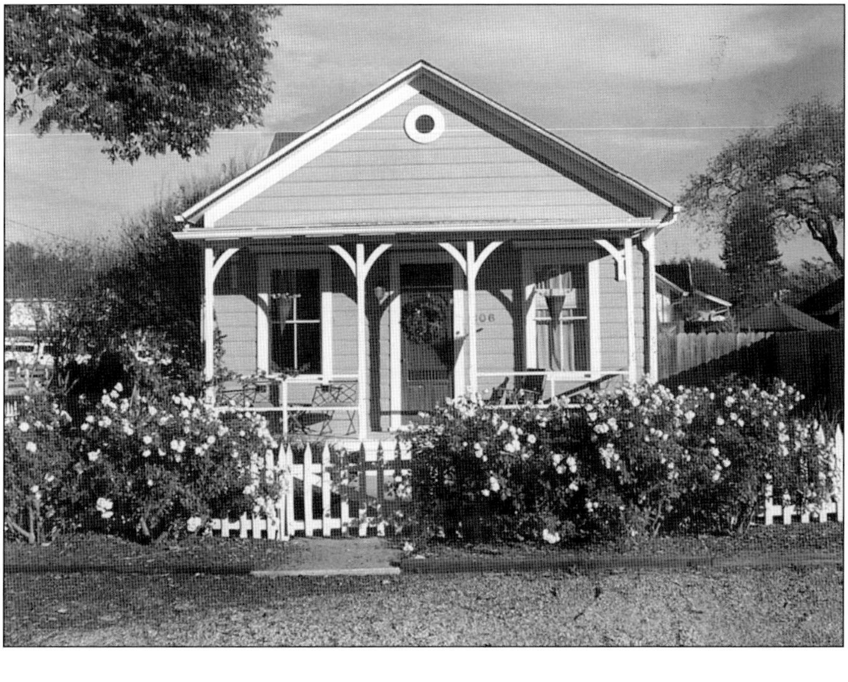

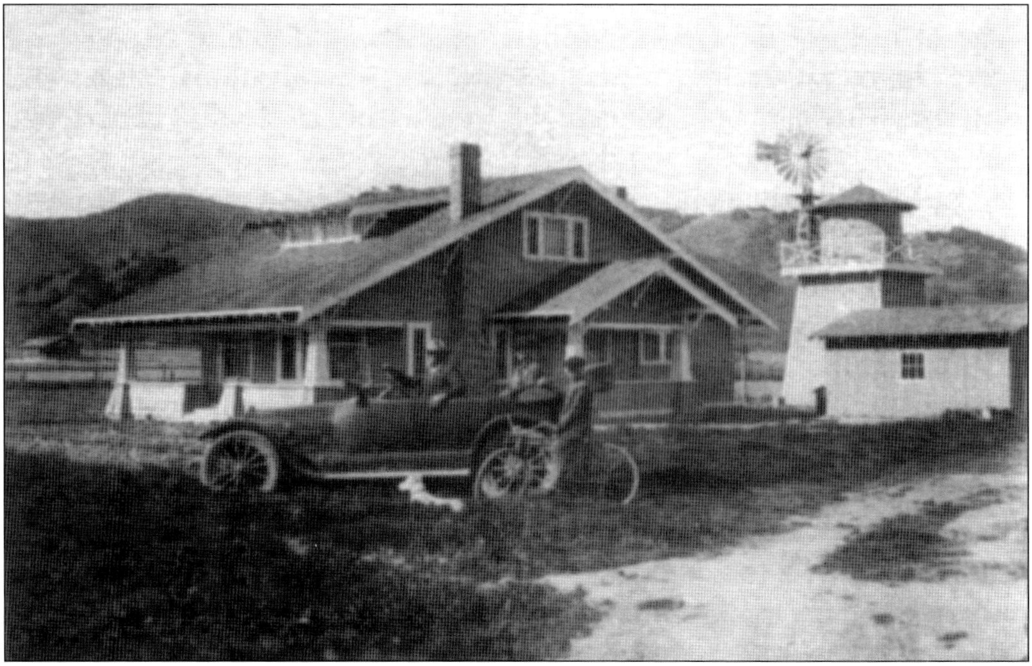

The Robbins family poses proudly for a photograph in front of their home. The bicycle and automobile were standard modes of transportation at this time, as they are today. The use of a windmill and water tank was the best system for supplying water to the household. Water underlying the Los Alamos valley floor was easy to access by such a system, and most homes had them. (Courtesy of LAMC.)

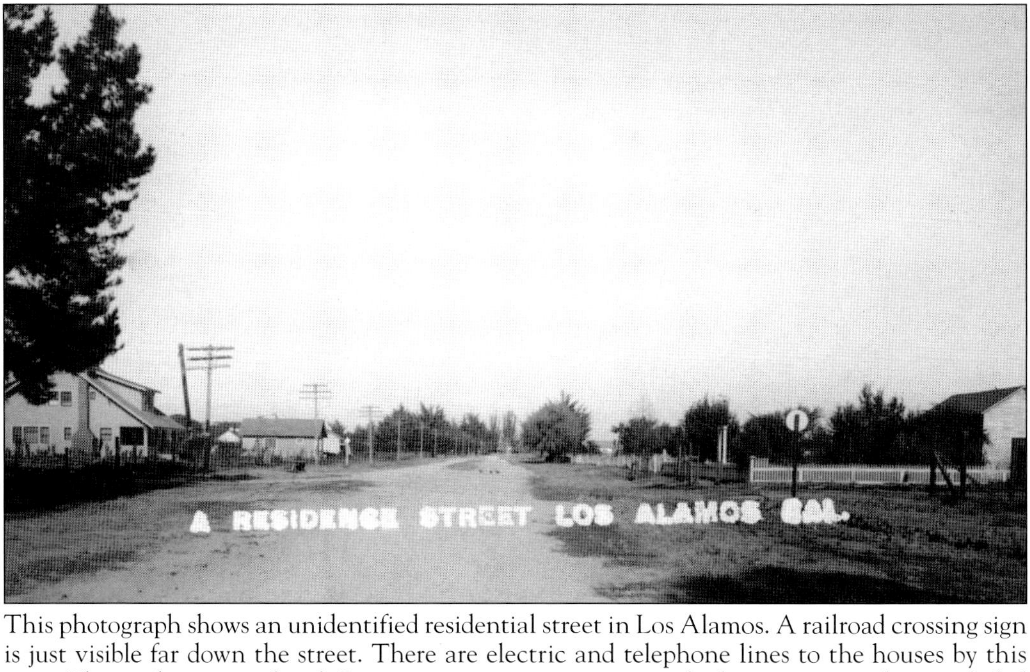

This photograph shows an unidentified residential street in Los Alamos. A railroad crossing sign is just visible far down the street. There are electric and telephone lines to the houses by this time. The road is not surfaced. Since no mountains appear on the horizon, it can be concluded that this photograph, taken in the early 1900s, looks east.

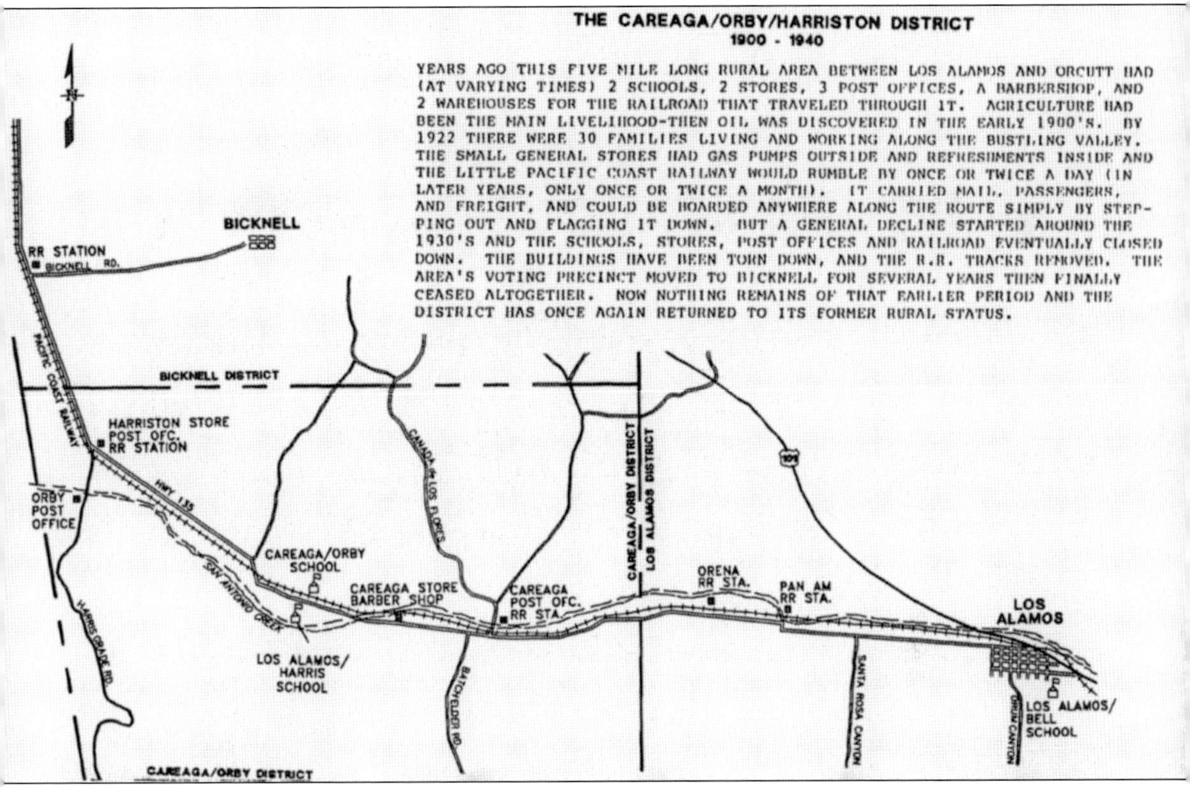

This map of Los Alamos Valley shows the location of the schools pictured on the next pages. None of the roads shown branching off Highway 135 are still in public use, with the exception of the Harris Grade Road. A flurry of post offices have come and gone, as well. Name changes to the school districts, as some expanded and others appeared, can mean confusion for historians.

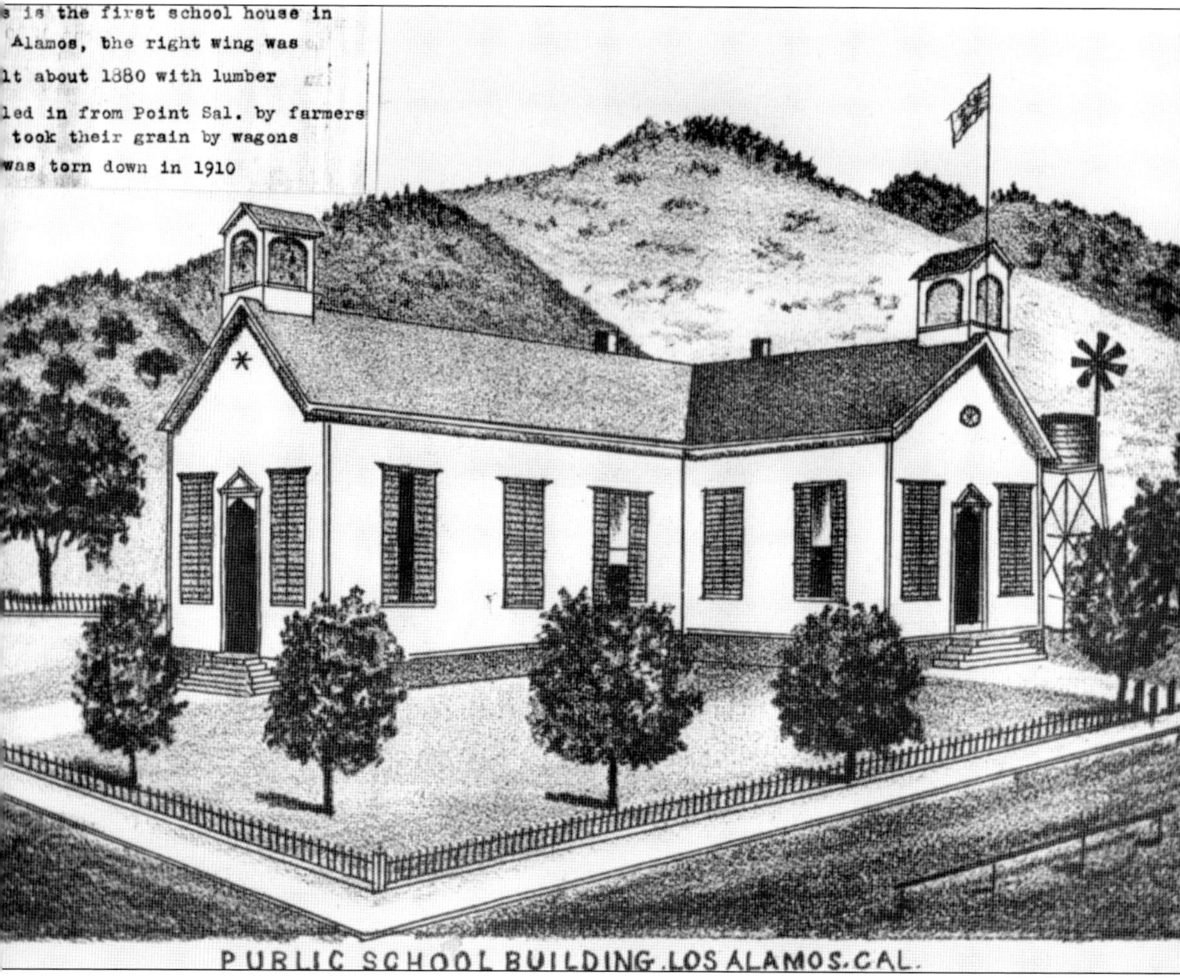

This drawing depicts the first school structure built in Los Alamos, the Bell School. The Bell School District was established in 1877, and this building was erected shortly thereafter. It was built of wood and brick. The lumber was shipped to Point Sal and thence to Los Alamos by wagon. Originally built as a rectangle, a later addition gave the school an ell shape. It was dismantled in 1910. (Courtesy of Olga Reed School.)

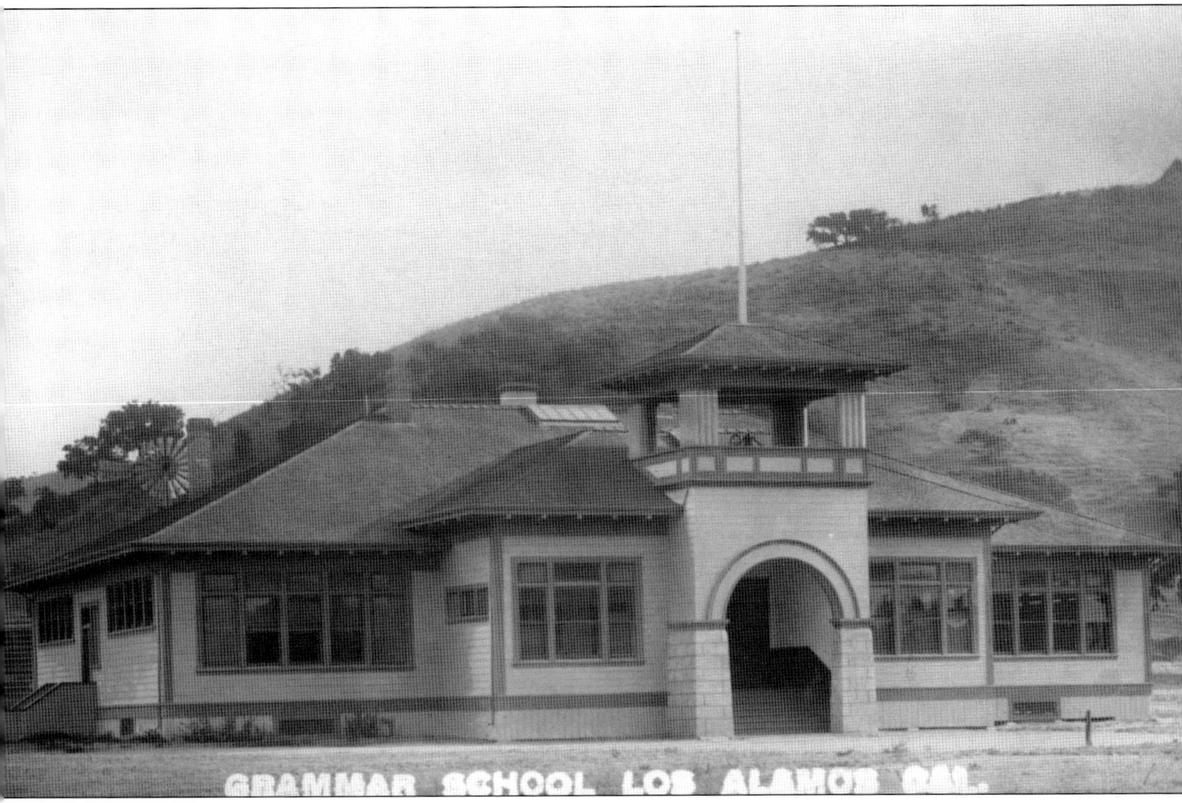

This beautiful new schoolhouse was completed in 1910 after the first structure was razed. While it was being constructed, school was held in the parsonage of the Presbyterian church. A windmill behind the school (from Fairbanks, Morse & Company) supplied it with water. The building was destroyed by fire in 1919. (Courtesy of Olga Reed School.)

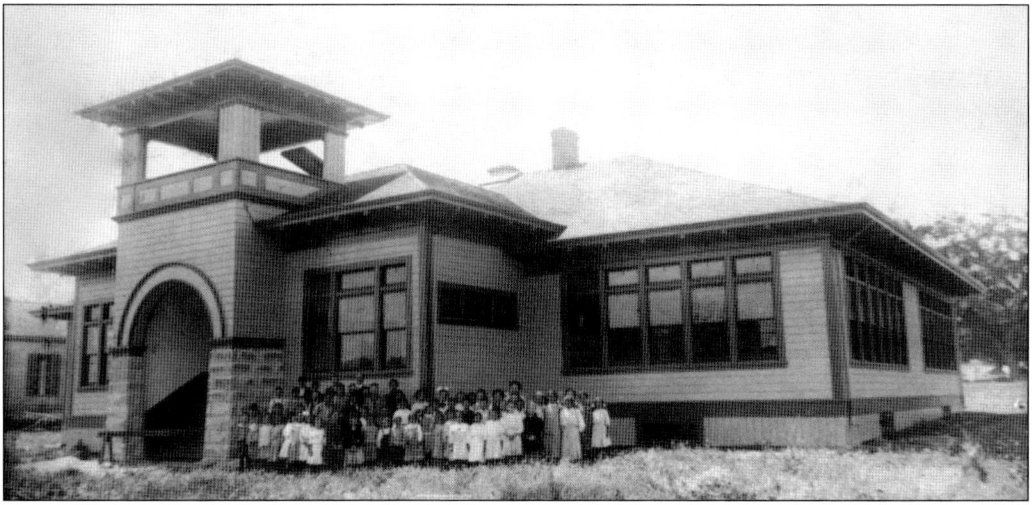

In 1909, sixty students and their teachers stand proudly in front of their new school. A sawhorse across the entrance steps suggests the newly built school is not yet quite complete. A large bell with a rope pull was installed in the tower to call the children to school. The building would burn to the ground in less than a decade.

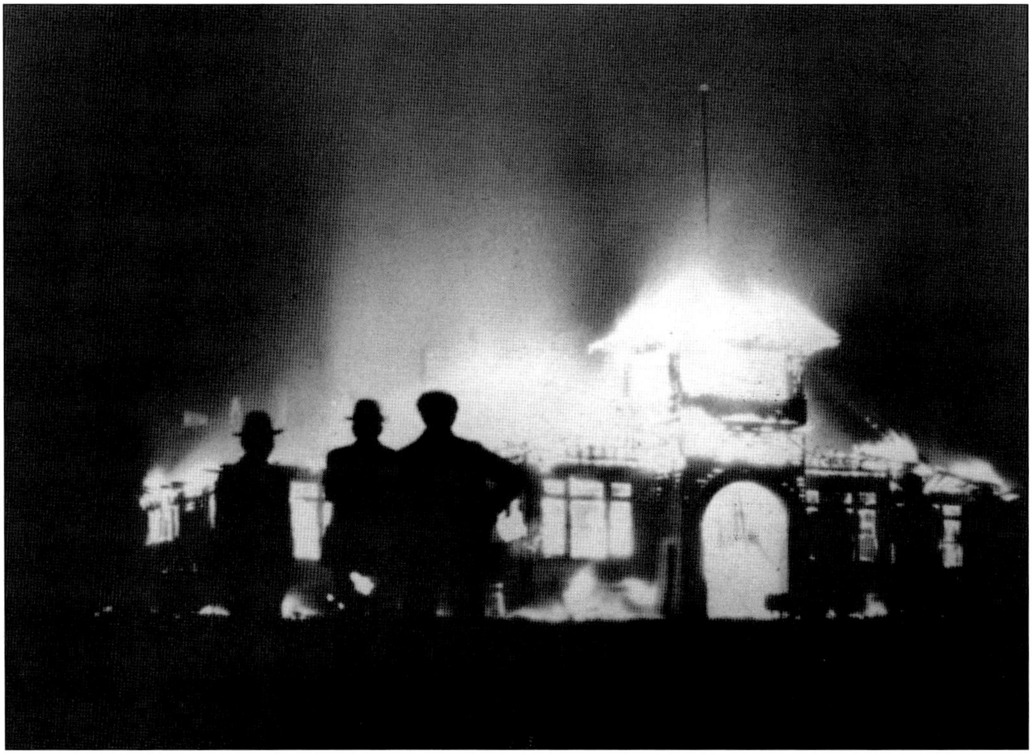

The second school building is hopelessly engulfed in flames as citizens of Los Alamos watch. A new stucco building was erected to fireproof standards and completed in 1920. A large gymnasium/auditorium building was added in 1952. In 1962, the stucco schoolhouse was razed, and a new office and classroom building was constructed to meet California earthquake standards.

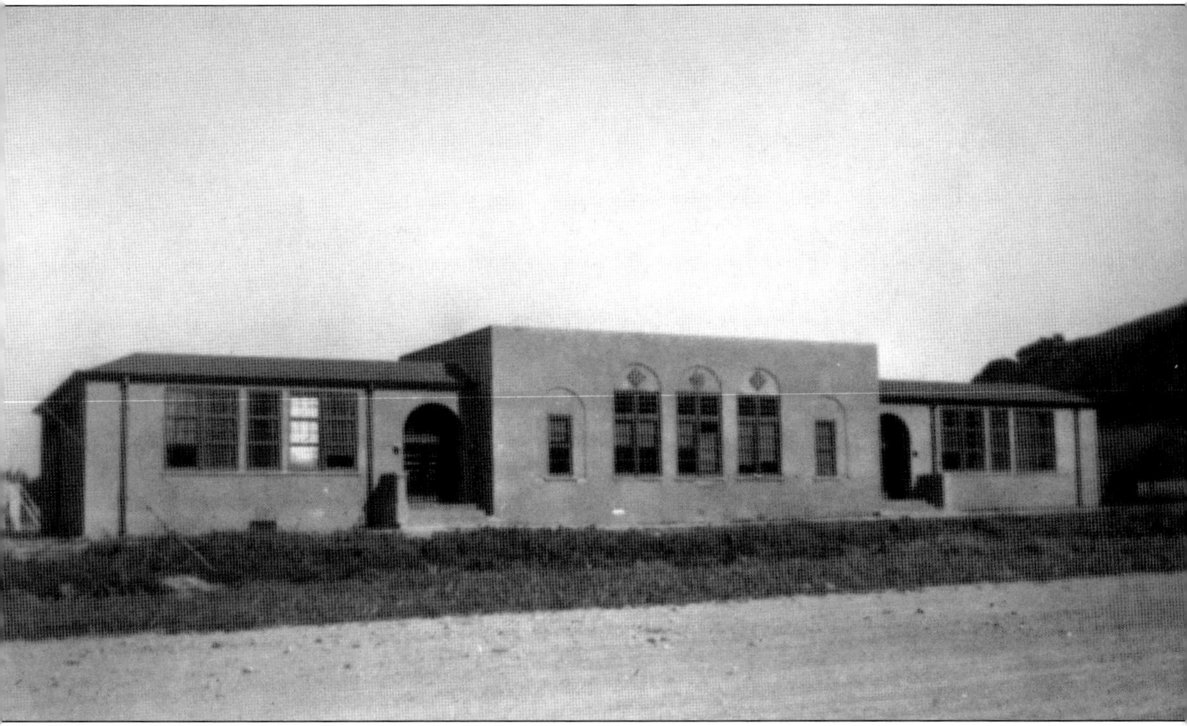

While the stucco school building was being razed and the new classroom unit was under construction, school was taught in the gymnasium. In 2000, another building was added to the existing buildings with four classrooms, a computer lab, and a library. A special fenced-in play area could be shared among the kindergarten classrooms. Later, a modular unit would be added and a 1/6-mile track constructed for athletics. (Courtesy of Olga Reed School.)

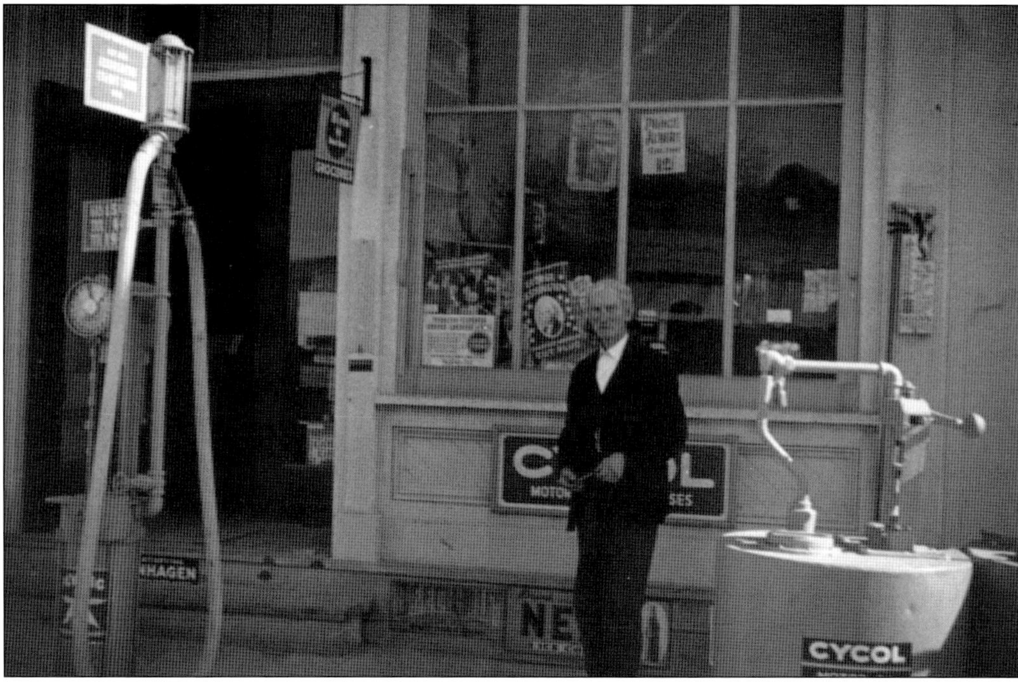

Ever the opportunist, Charles Pearson (pictured) was quick to bring gasoline and oil products to his store. On the boardwalk in front of his Cheap Cash Store is a Flying A gasoline pump, with gas selling at 15¢ per gallon (before tax). A hand-pumped barrel of Cycol motor oil is to the right.

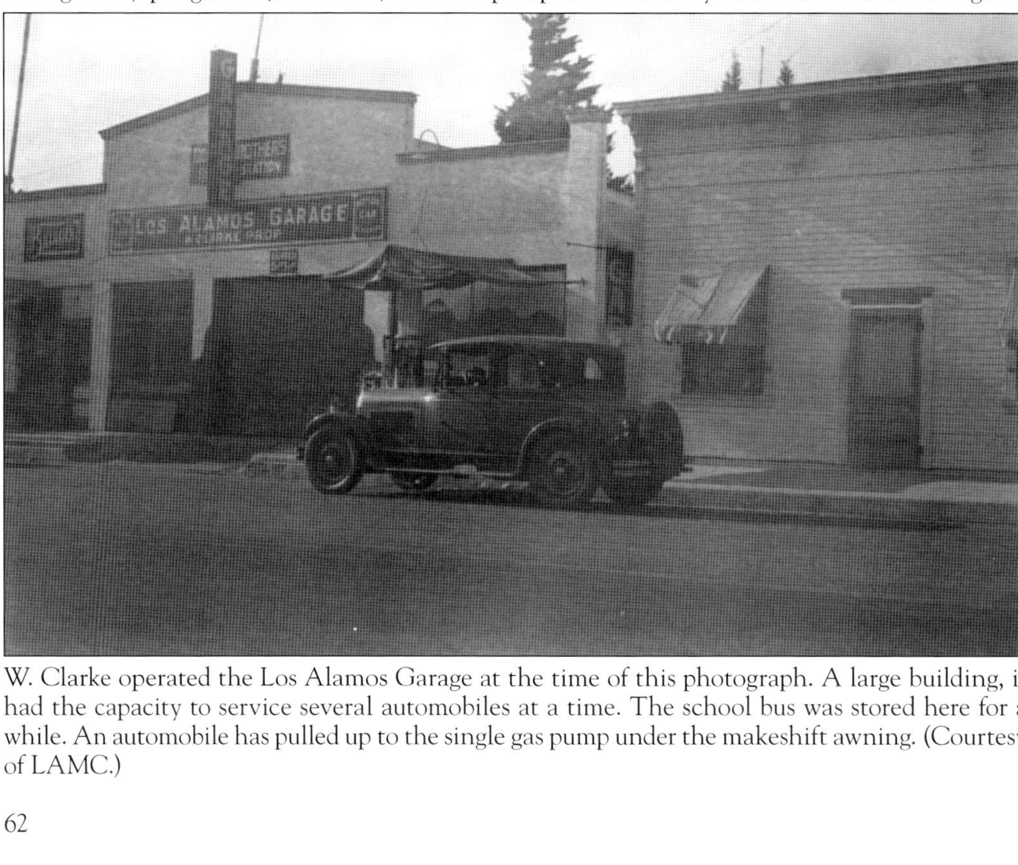

W. Clarke operated the Los Alamos Garage at the time of this photograph. A large building, it had the capacity to service several automobiles at a time. The school bus was stored here for a while. An automobile has pulled up to the single gas pump under the makeshift awning. (Courtesy of LAMC.)

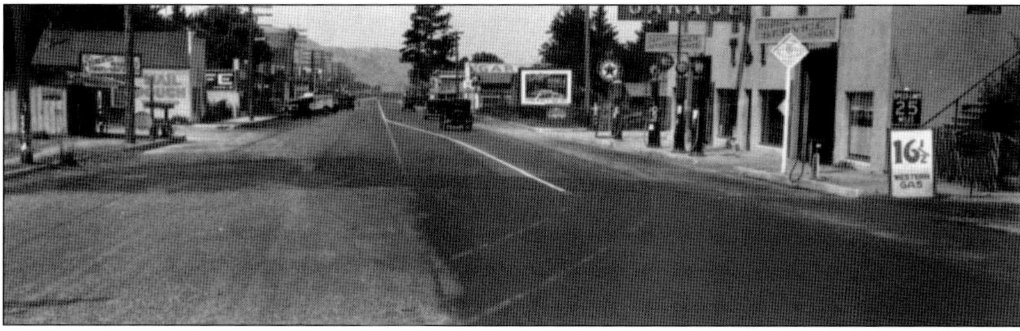

Los Alamos experienced an automobile boom in the 1920s. Americans hit the road, traveling farther and faster, and California was no exception. California's Highway 101 passed directly through Los Alamos, and the town was optimally located for a rest stop and filling station. Service stations and garages bloomed in the town. The T&T Garage (far right) offered gasoline and automobile services.

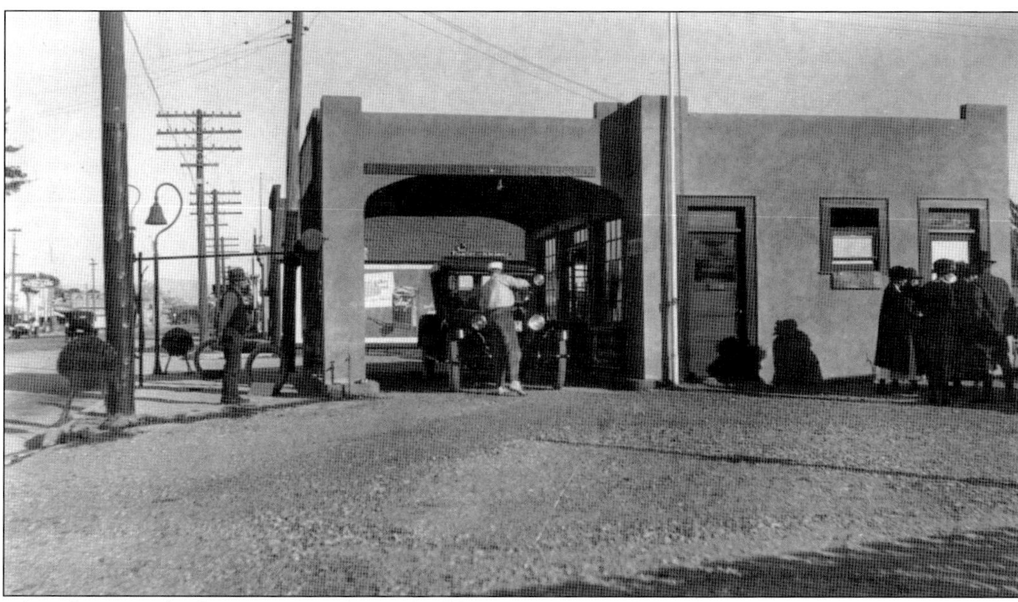

This photograph illustrates another valuable service offered by filling stations in Los Alamos: the restroom. Several ladies and a gentleman wait their turn at the El Camino Real service station's unisex bathroom. The attendant checks the oil in the automobile as the owner looks on. The sign just above the automobile, under the canopy, advertises Foster & Kleiser, an outdoor advertising media group founded in 1901.

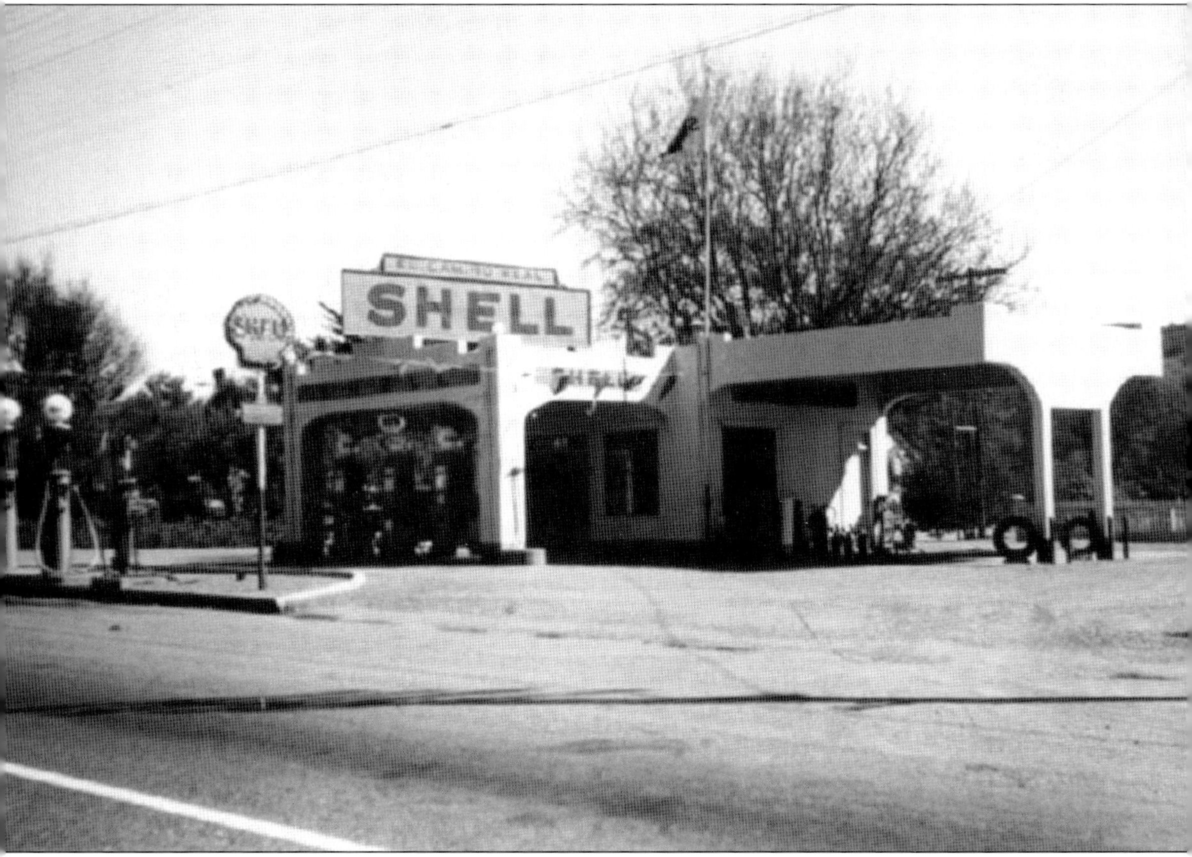

The El Camino Real station takes on new life as the El Camino Shell. As seen here, a modern-looking Shell station has blossomed from the more basic look of its predecessor. It was necessary to keep up appearances in the service station business in Los Alamos to stay competitive. Such stations lined the streets when Highway 101 ran through the town.

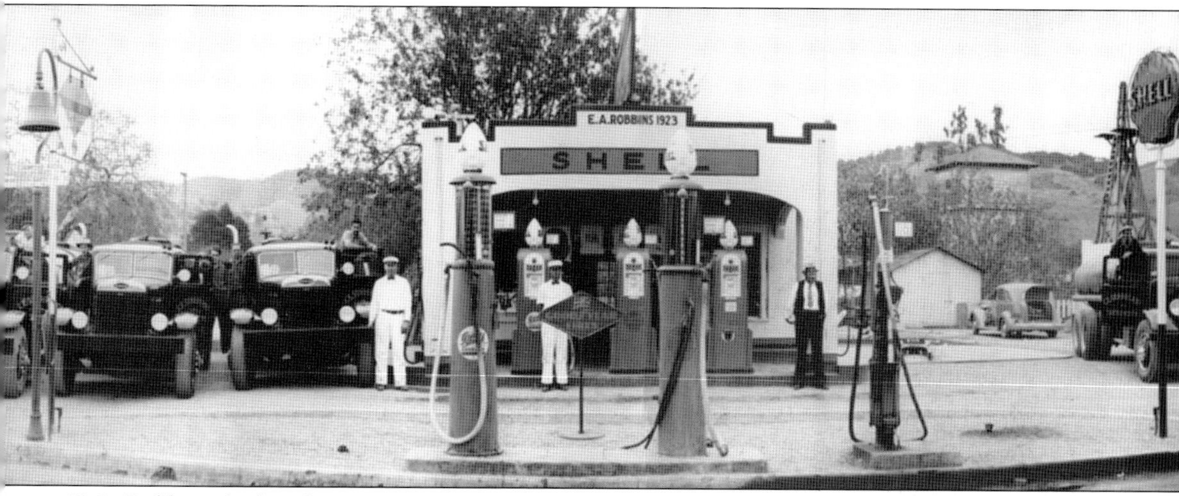

E.A. Robbins (right of center, in suit and tie) proudly shows off his Shell Gasoline station, repair facility, and fleet of gasoline trucks at his location on Bell Street in Los Alamos. The Robbins family has operated gasoline stations at this site continuously since 1923. One of the gasoline pumps, although no longer functional, can still be seen in front of Collins Market today.

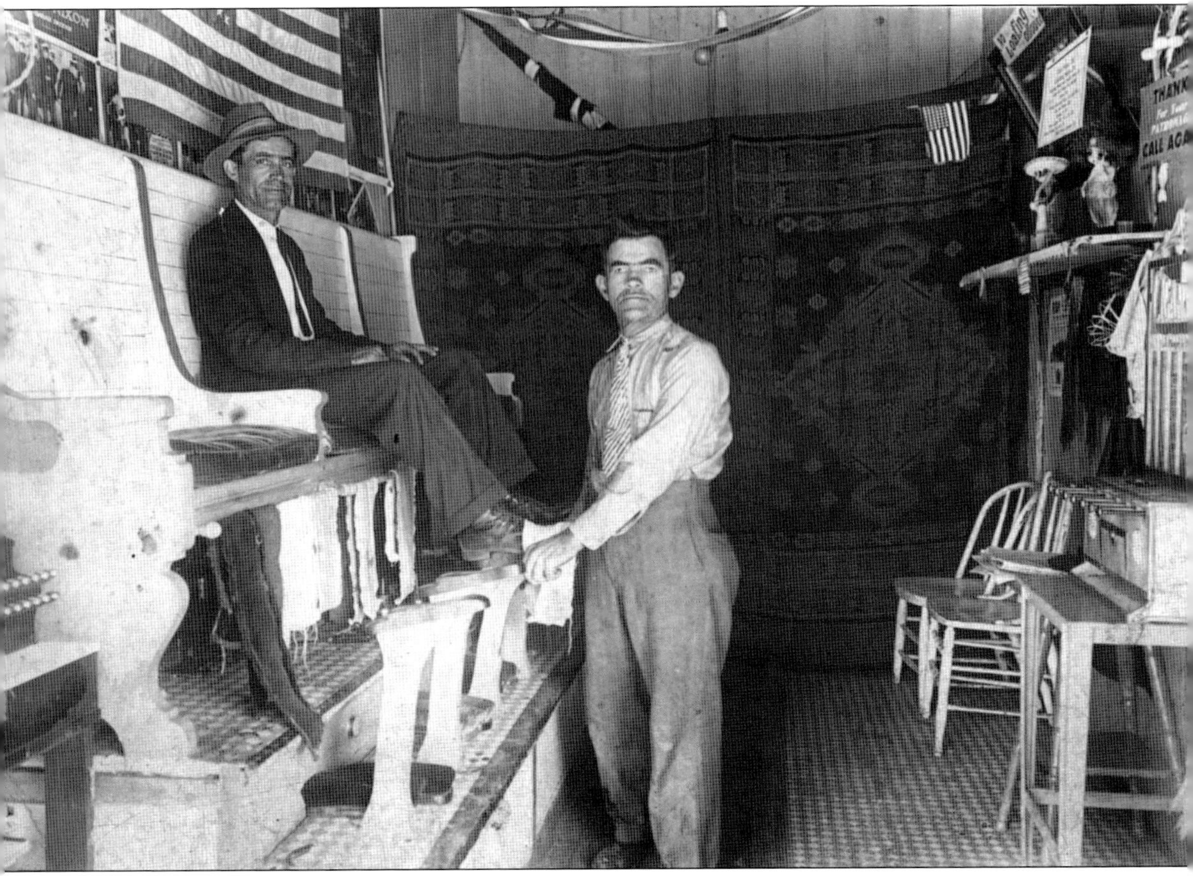

A resident receives a shoeshine in a rather eclectic shop in Los Alamos. A traveling shoemaker, it was said of the craftsman that he enjoyed his canned heat, and the earlier one had one's shoes repaired, the better. This multi-skilled man reputedly played the concertina very well.

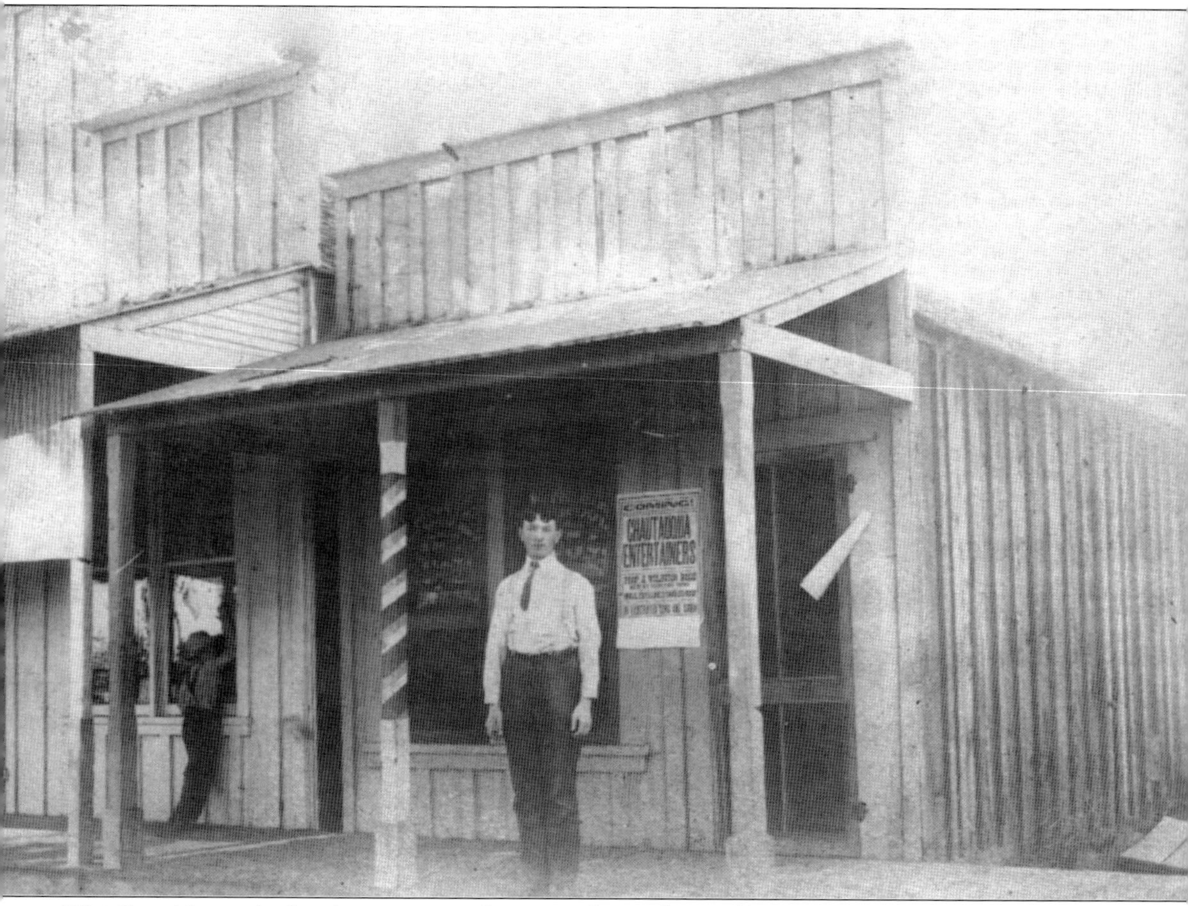

This Los Alamos barbershop, once a saloon, was located on Bell Street, east of where Bell Street Farms stands today. Just east of the barbershop, and appropriate to its craft, a dance hall and pool hall stood. On its west side were a gambling hall and a saloon. The barber, Leonard Simmons, is seen here around 1900.

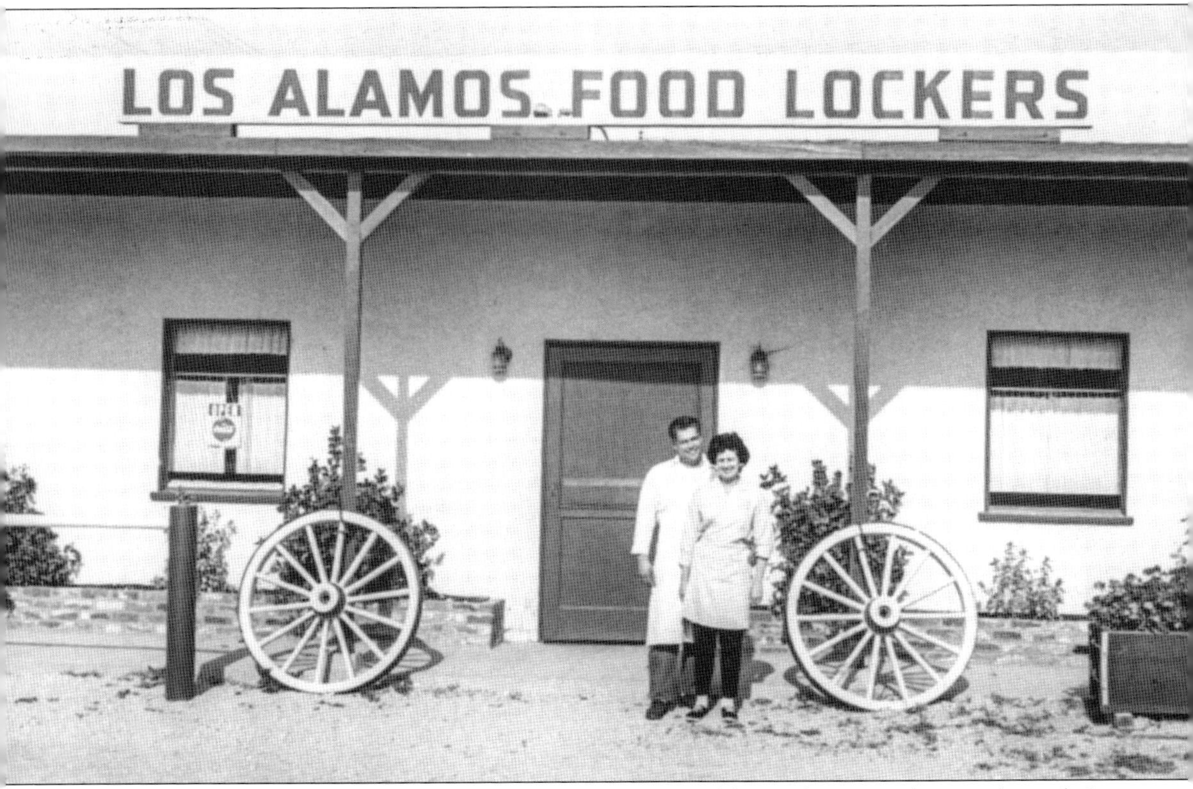

The popular story is told of Joaquin Henry Gonzales and his wife, Jessie, driving through Los Alamos in their new Ford Model A when it quit. Taking this as an omen, and liking what he saw, Joaquin determined to make Los Alamos his home. In 1957, the couple opened a meat locker/butcher business. By 1992, they had altered the building to its current appearance, now the Los Alamos Market. (Courtesy of Charlie Gonzales.)

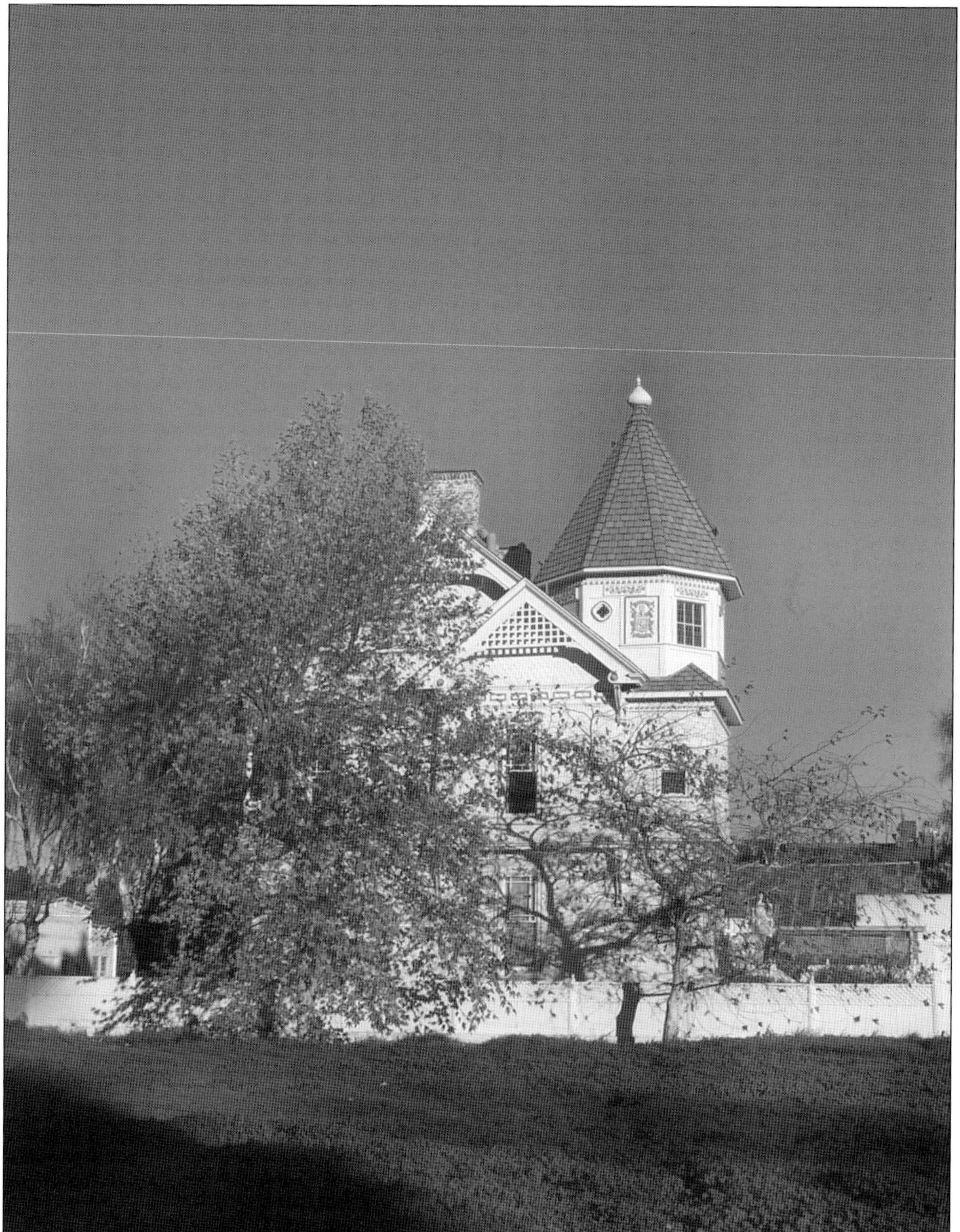

This beautiful Victorian house is not native to Los Alamos. In fact, it came from Nipoma, where it once was the home of a Russian immigrant couple. Dick Langdon moved the building to Los Alamos to be a bookend with his Union Hotel, which he was restoring as a period piece. In this bed-and-breakfast, each room is designed thematically, and every bathroom is disguised within the wall. (Photograph by author.)

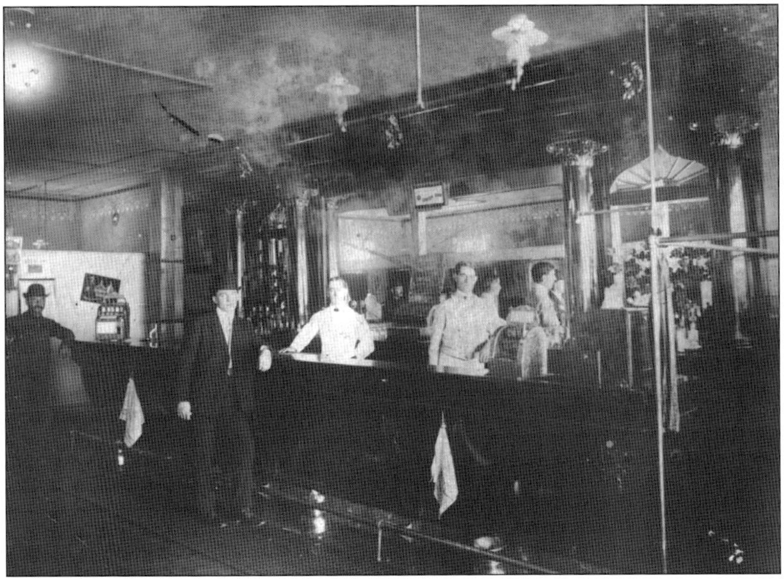

This great old mahogany bar resides in the Union Hotel. Over the years, it has been used in many ways, including as an ice cream bar, a wine bar, and a liquor bar. Since the hotel was built in 1915, the bar has remained a functional part of it. A sign over the cash register warns, "No Drinks Exchanged for Hot Air."

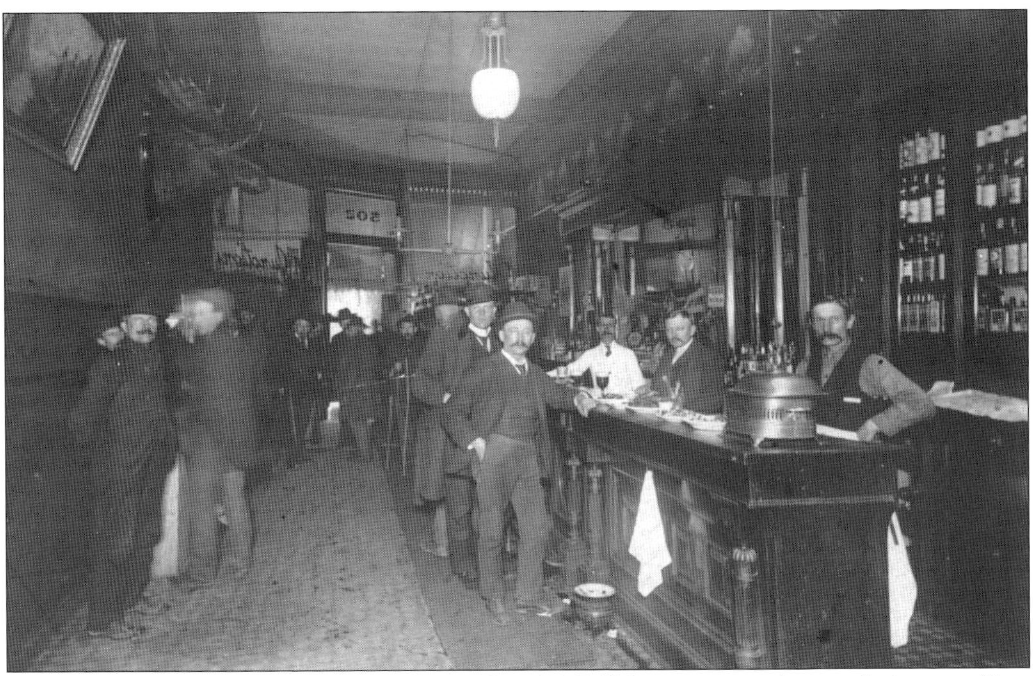

This saloon, named the Junction, was located at 502 Bell Street, across from today's post office. It may have been named for its position at the junction of Bell and Helena Streets. There was lodging associated with the saloon; in fact, in 1887, classes were held here while the schoolhouse was being enlarged. (Courtesy of Jeanette Sainz.)

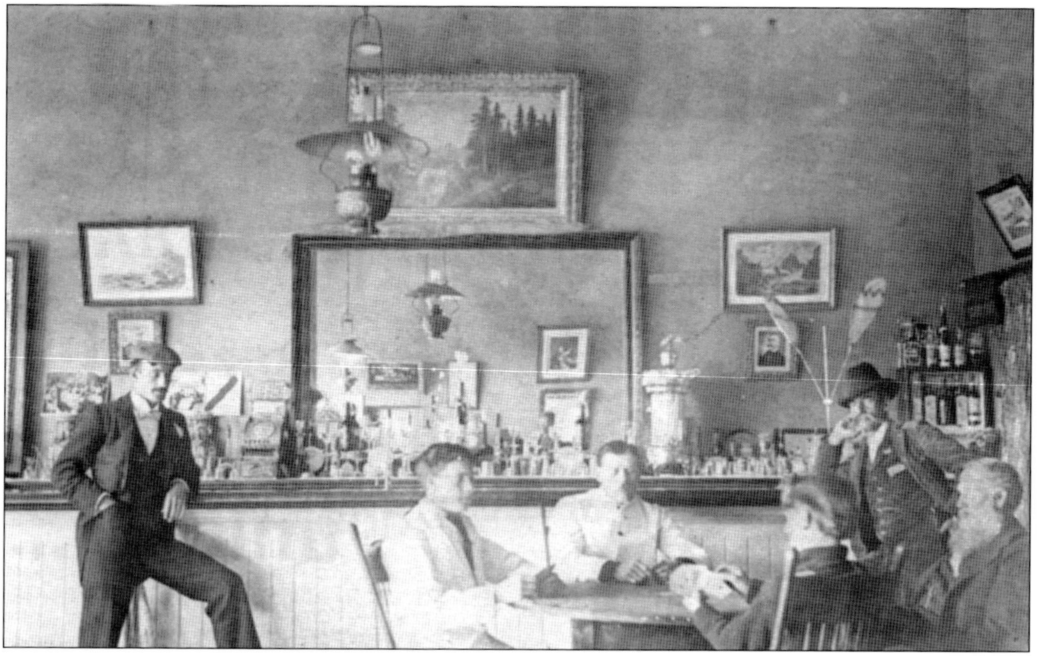

In 1889, there was a saloon east of today's Bell Street Farm on Bell Street. Next to it was a gambling hall. It was said that "you could set a clock each day as Henry Holt walked by to the gambling hall." Taken in 1899, this photograph shows gentlemen enjoying a card game in a card room and bar, possibly that same gambling hall on Bell Street. (Courtesy of LAMC.)

Los Alamos' second jail building was erected in 1887. This building, located on the corner of Centennial and Leslie Streets, was constructed more substantially than the wood-slat jail on Waite Street. This jail eventually had water, electricity, and comforts suitable to the more modern era. Although the time of roving bandits was past, the town constable, Pete Coiner, and, later, Ed Robbins, continued to find use for a jail building.

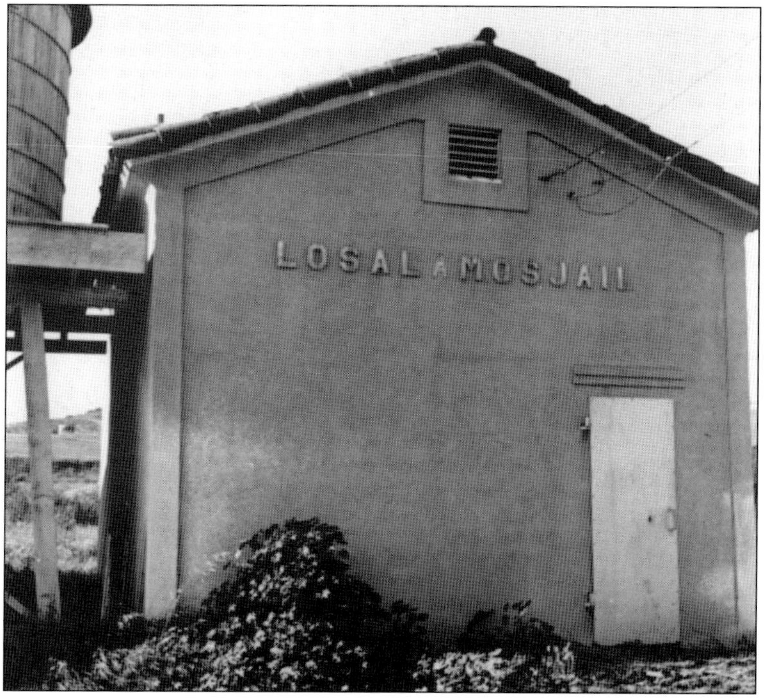

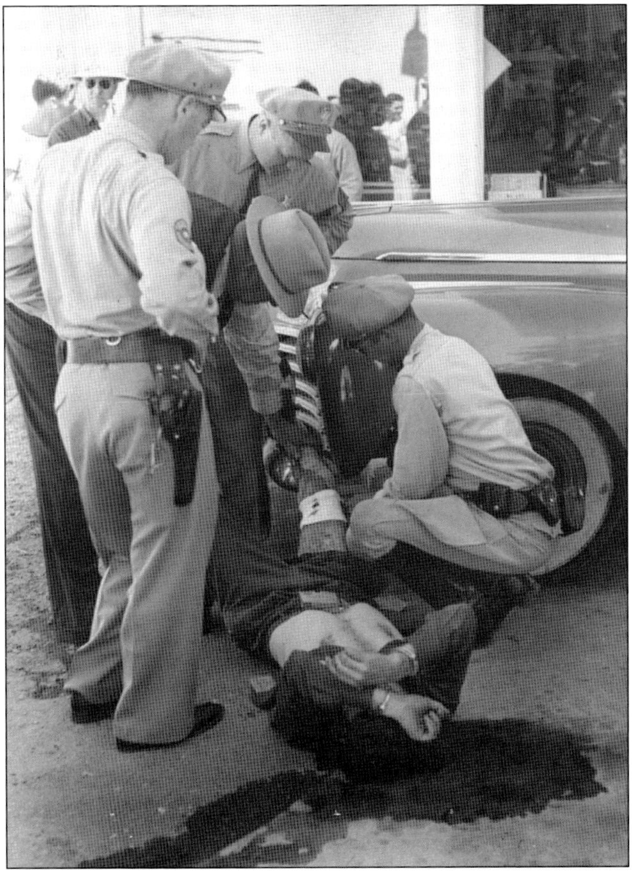

An unidentified patrolman applies a bandage to the leg of a would-be robber and wanted man. The man in the white hat (second from left) bending to assist by holding the victim's leg is constable Ed Robbins. A curious crowd gathers around. The shooting occurred in front of the 76 station on Bell Street.

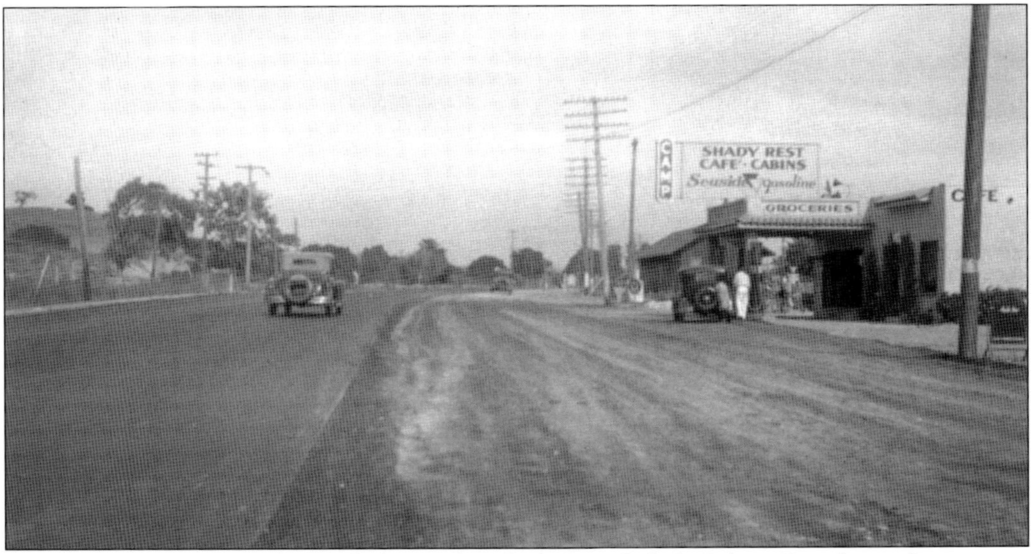

In the 1920s, an automobile is pulled up at the Shady Rest Café & Cabins Seaside gasoline station for service along busy Highway 101. The building today, now Bob's Well Bread, looks much the same. Both the narrow-gauge track and the San Antonio Creek are close by, to the left of the highway. The hill on the far left is now adorned with the Sky View Motel. (Courtesy of LAMC.)

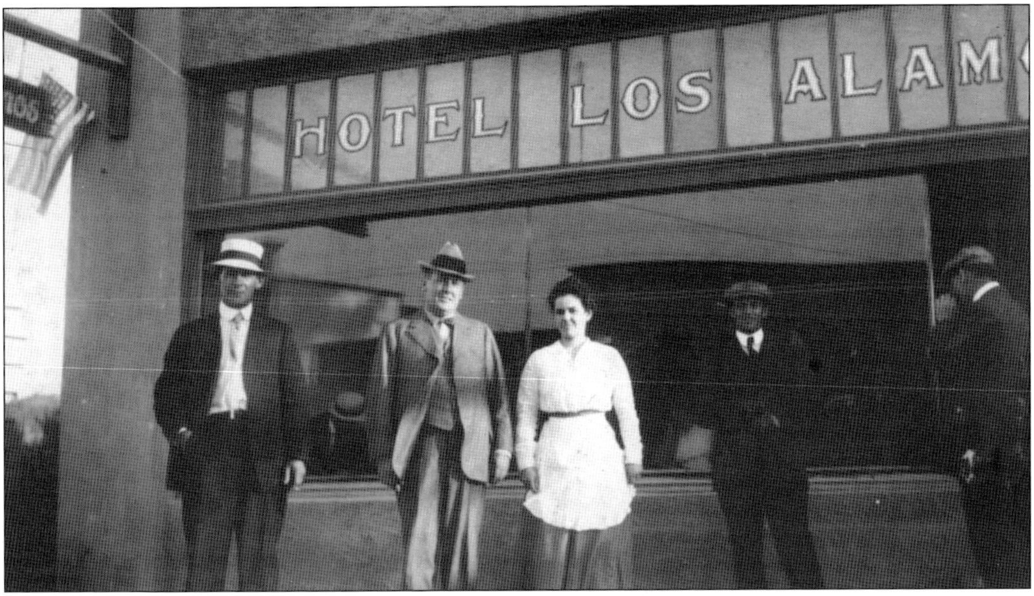

After a two-decade hiatus, this large hotel was built on the footprint of the old Union Hotel. Named simply Alamos Hotel, later owners changed it to Hotel Los Alamos (above). The Hotel Los Alamos was built of stucco and looked quite different from the Union Hotel. An unidentified group, possibly hotel staff, poses before the hotel. Apparently, the man at far right did not get the memo.

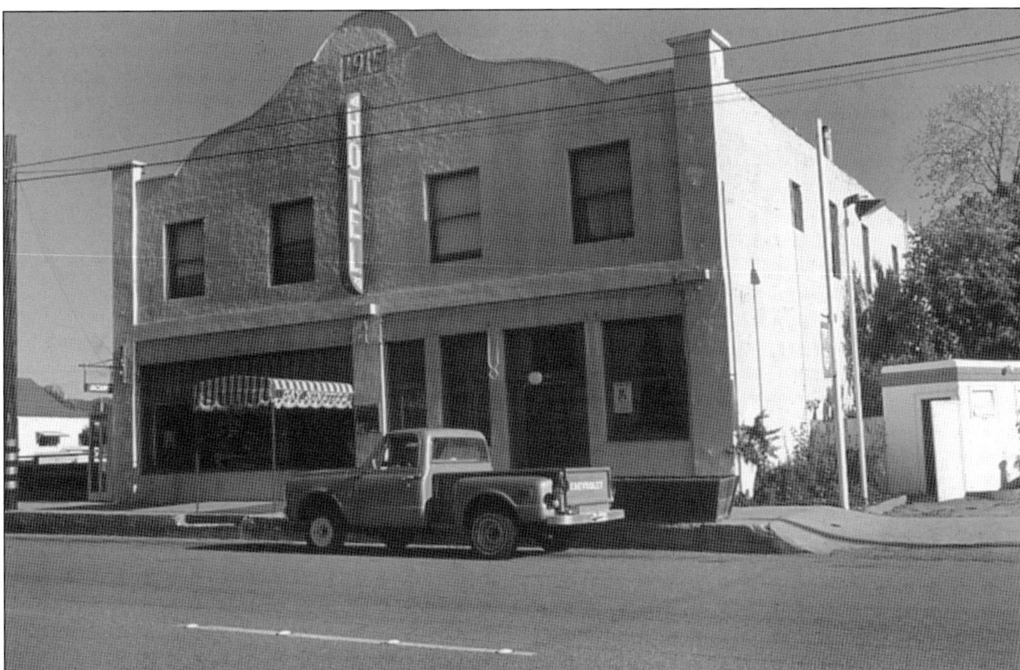

The Hotel Los Alamos experienced a number of management changes over the years. Under Jake and Mary Stine, it became the Gay Nineties Hotel (pictured). In later years, Dick Langdon would rename it the Union Hotel and reconstruct a facade to resemble the original hotel of that name.

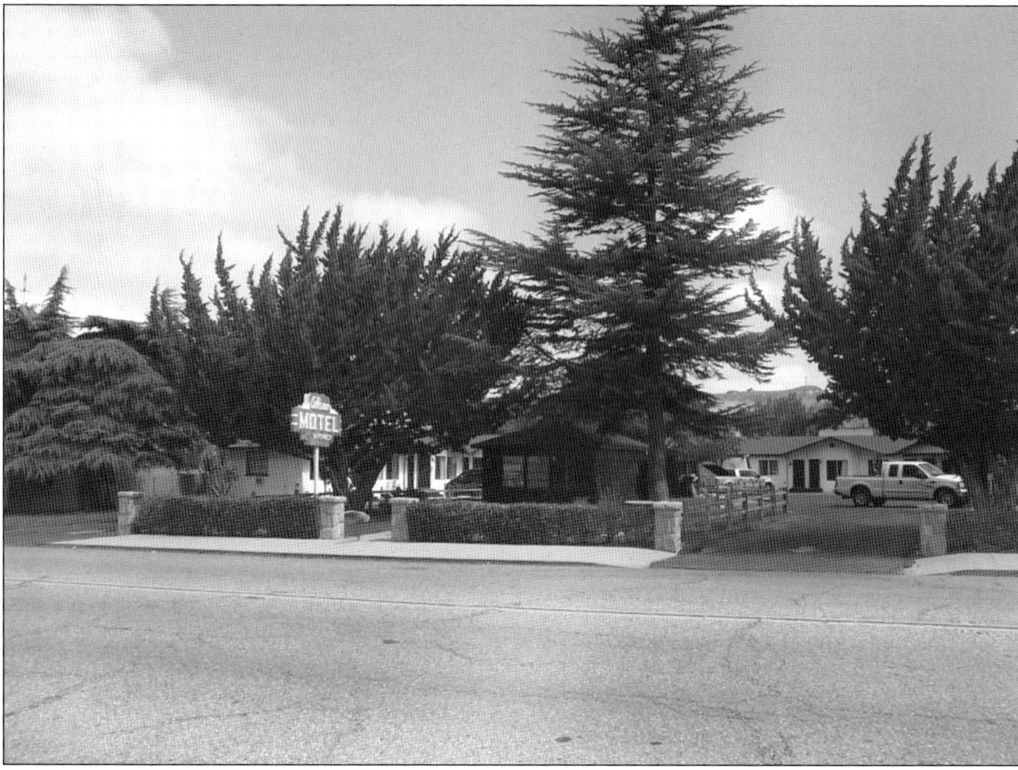

The Alamo Motel is a classic representation of its time, the mid-1960s. Each small but well-furnished cabin along the circular drive had an accompanying garage for the traveler's automobile. Later, the garage was walled in and added to the small cabin to increase the size of the unit. The motel, located in the heart of Los Alamos, continues to be popular and has added a wine-tasting room. (Photograph by author.)

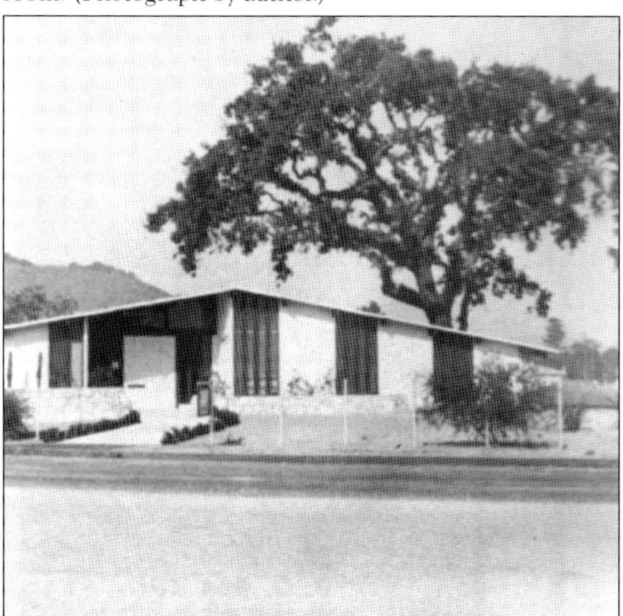

Charles Pearson's daughter, Agnes Pearson, was likely the first librarian in Los Alamos. While the school librarian, she started a town library in her father's store in 1940 with her personal collection and donations from the town's people. In 1961, it closed, and the books were passed to the Santa Maria Library. The Los Alamos Library (pictured) was built in 1966 and served Los Alamos until 1988. (Courtesy LAMC.)

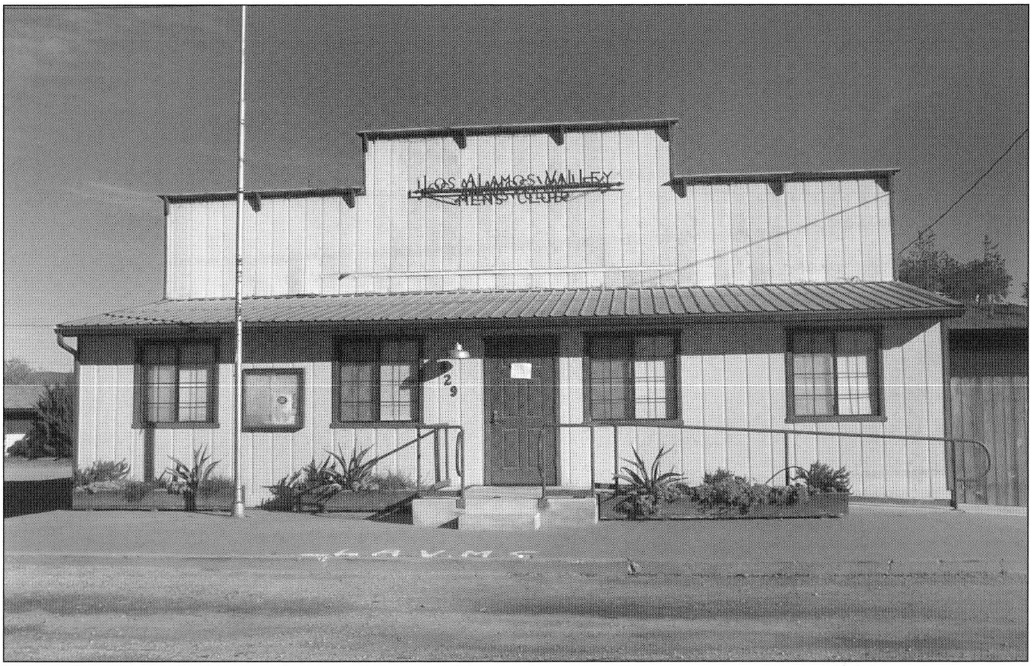

In 1946, the men of Los Alamos decided to organize a men's club, perhaps a response to the Justamere Club formed by women in 1924 to provide for the needs of the community. The Los Alamos Valley Men's Club building, a mess hall from the Santa Maria Air Base, was disassembled and then reassembled on Leslie Street in Los Alamos by members in their spare time. (Courtesy of LAMC.)

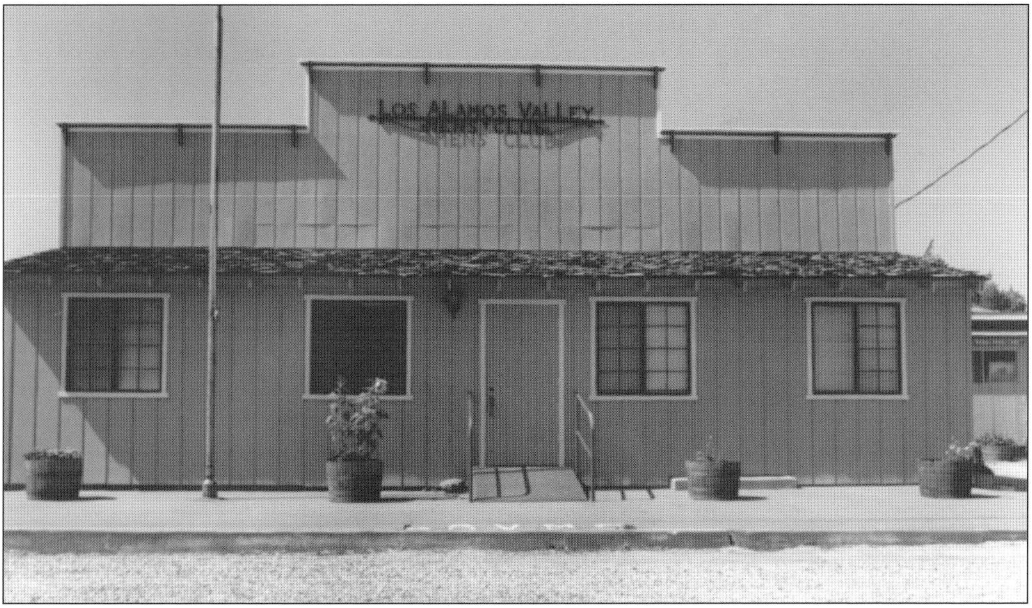

The Los Alamos Valley Men's Club building is 40 feet by 90 feet and contains a large hall, dining room, taproom, kitchen, and barbecue patio. Improvements have continued over the years, including handicapped access and a weather entrance. Despite its name, the club now includes women, who are well represented in the officer ranks. (Courtesy of Olga Reed School.)

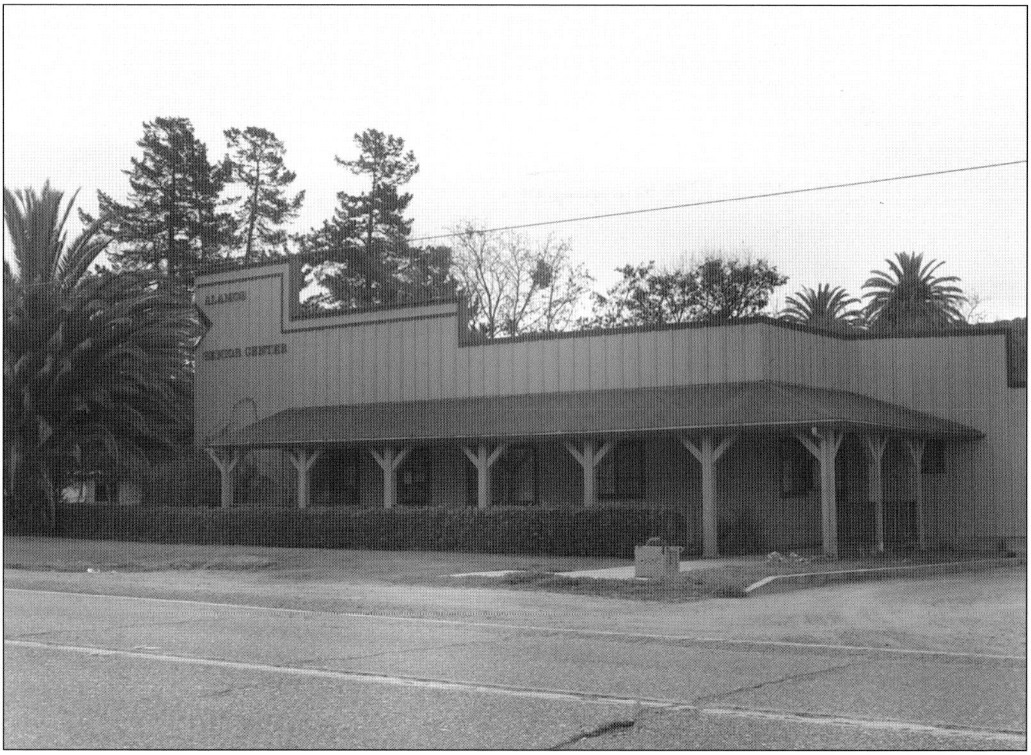

The Los Alamos Valley Senior Citizens, an all-volunteer organization, began fundraising for a senior center facility in 1980. Additional funding came from grants and the Savings Association Mortgage Company. The ground breaking took place on May 12, 1989, and the building was completed by April 1990. The center offers a number of health, entertainment, and educational programs for the valley seniors. (Photograph by the author.)

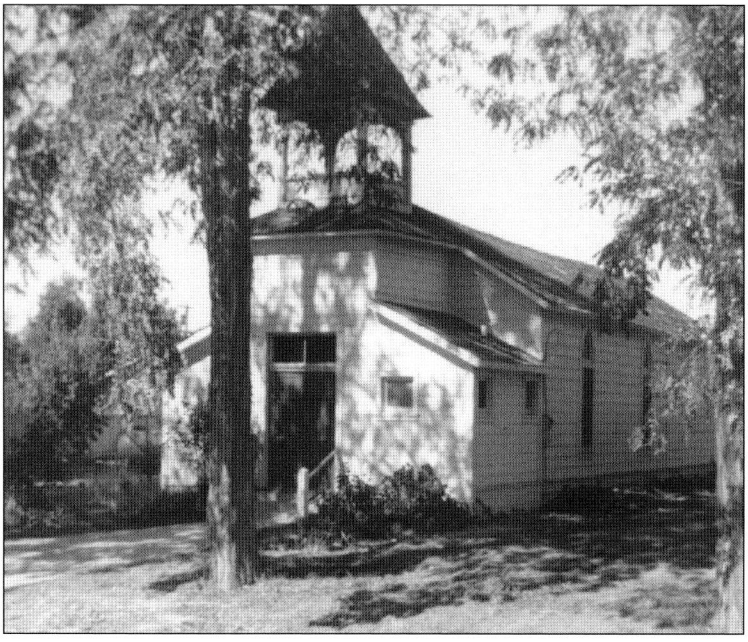

Following the secularization of the missions in 1834, the priests at the Santa Ynez Mission ministered to the Catholic community in Los Alamos Valley. Not until 1905, when Fr. Mathias Ternes became pastor for the three towns of Santa Maria, Guadalupe, and Los Alamos, was a Catholic church constructed in Los Alamos. St. Anthony Catholic Church was renovated from a private home.

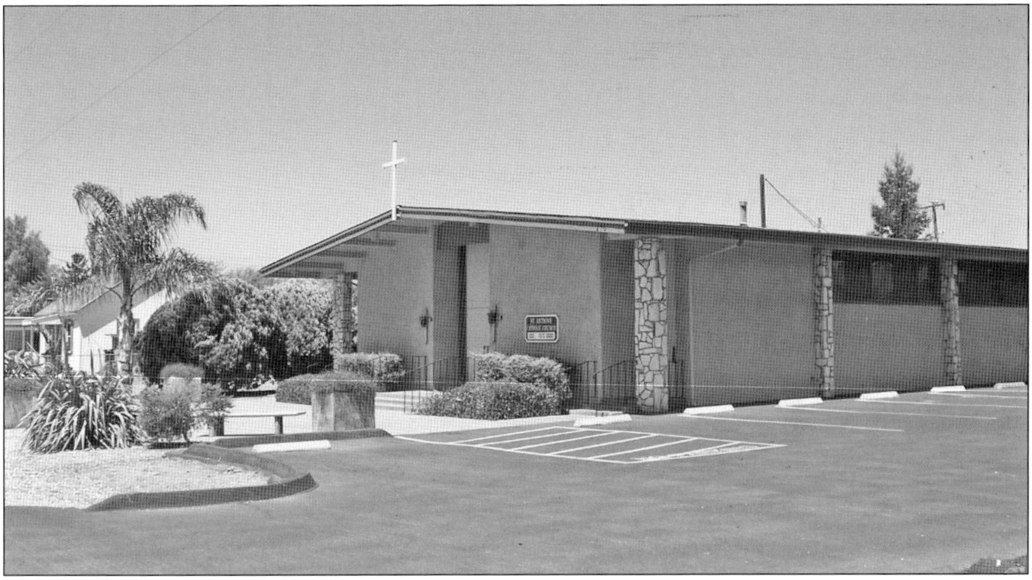

The second Los Alamos Catholic church was built in 1966 on the north end of the same lot as the first church. The new church was dedicated in 1967, and the first marriage ceremony united Virginia Bumman and Michael Farris. The old church building was moved to the King Ranch west of Los Alamos. A large parking lot now occupies that space, serving an increased congregation.

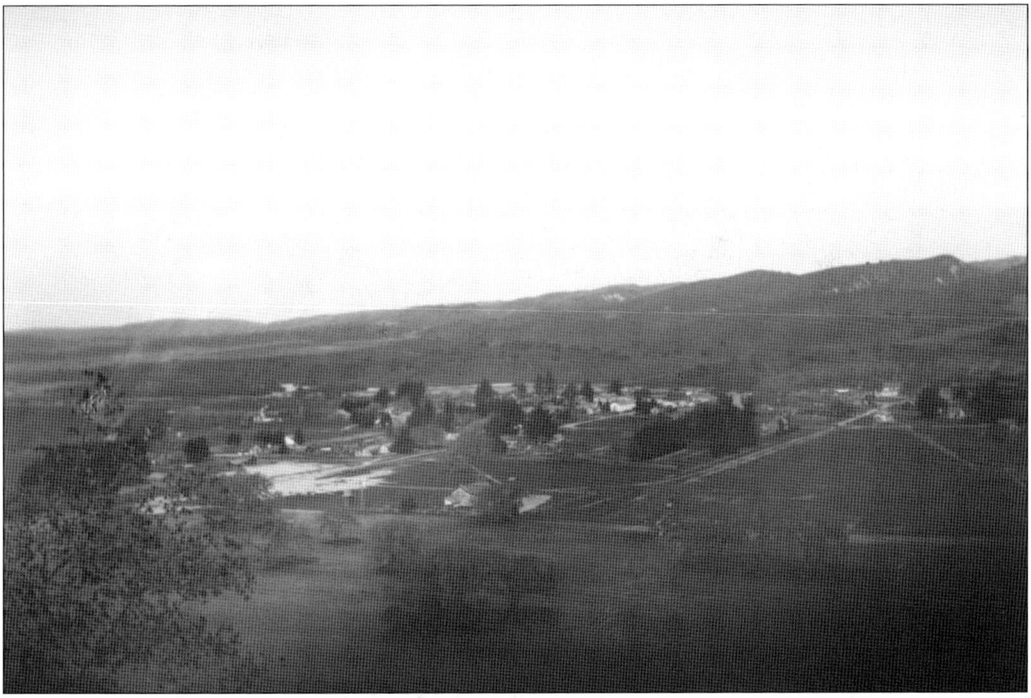

This photograph, taken some time between 1905 and 1919, shows the original Catholic church (center right) in its location on the south section of the lot, diagonally opposite the Presbyterian church. The school at lower center is the second building; it burned down in 1919. A large area of south Centennial Street (lower left) appears to be flooded. Severe flooding occurred in Los Alamos in 1911.

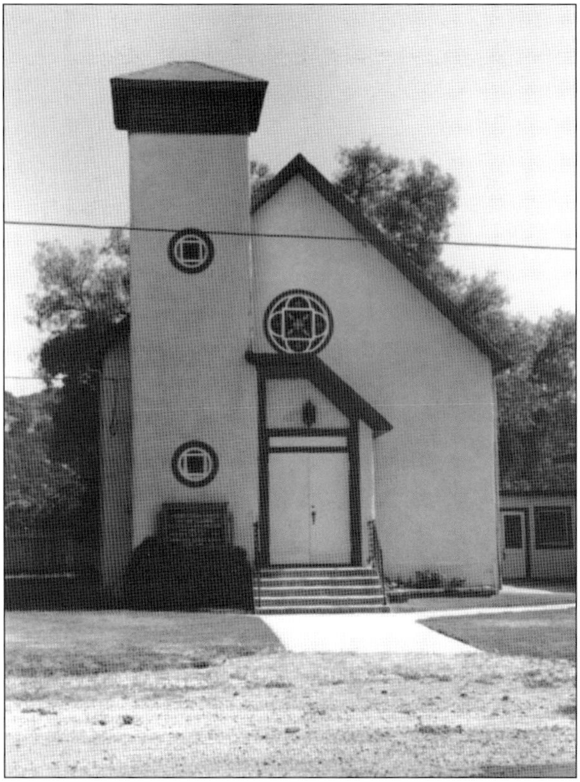

This structure was the first church of any denomination to be built in Los Alamos. It was dedicated in 1887 under the auspices of the Methodist Church and cost $2,000 to erect. The Presbyterians, who had been meeting in a private home, purchased the building for themselves in 1900. (Courtesy of Olga Reed School.)

In this 2004 photograph of the Cottonwood Community Church, the old Presbyterian church sign has been removed, and a new one proclaims "Cottonwood Community Fellowship." The name change came with the desire to be a welcoming congregation to everyone in Los Alamos, not just Presbyterians. The church, severely damaged in the earthquake of 1902, was repaired through a grant from other churches and from donations by members. (Photograph by author.)

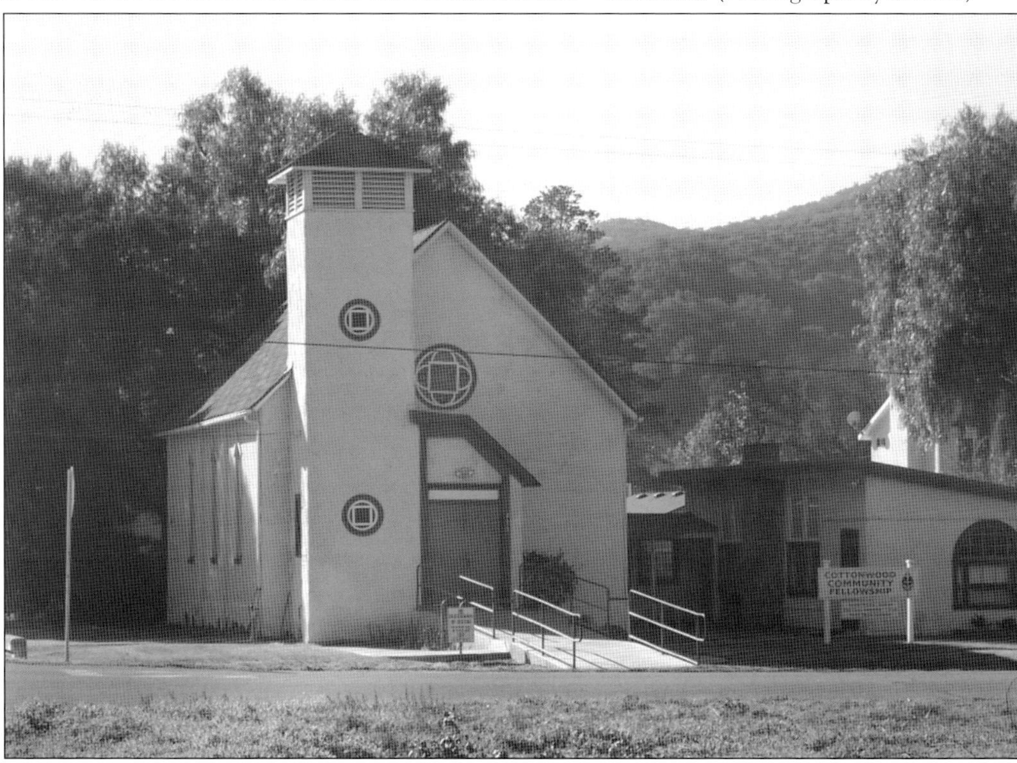

This is the Victorian home built by Dr. J.B. Shaw on his ranch northeast of Los Alamos. This recent photograph shows that the building has been well kept over the years. Dr. Shaw lived in the original Gutierrez adobe, located just behind the house, for several years until his new home was built in 1890. (Photograph by author.)

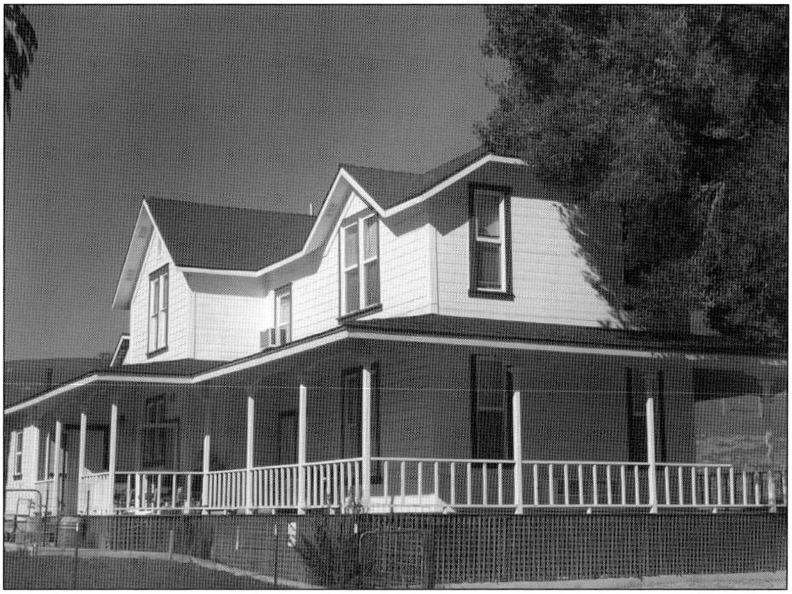

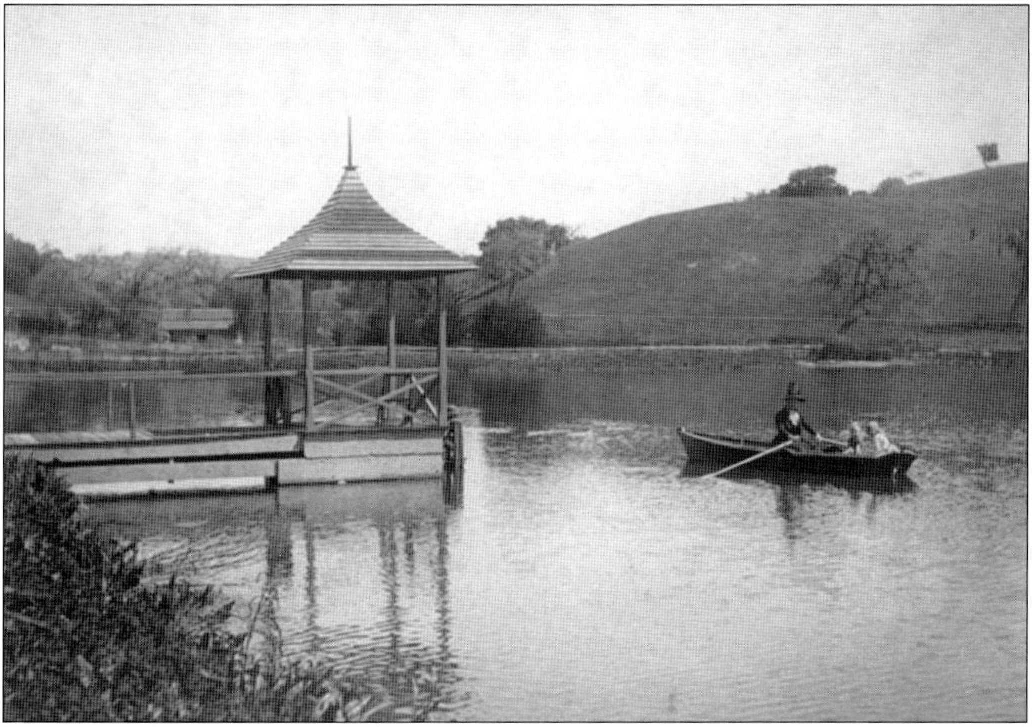

At first glance, this photograph might appear to depict a scene in Edwardian England. In fact, it shows an outing on the lake at J.B. Shaw's La Laguna Ranch. At the time, the lake extended most of the way from the residences down to San Antonio Creek. Visible in the photograph are a barn and the adobe (just behind the gazebo's second post from the left).

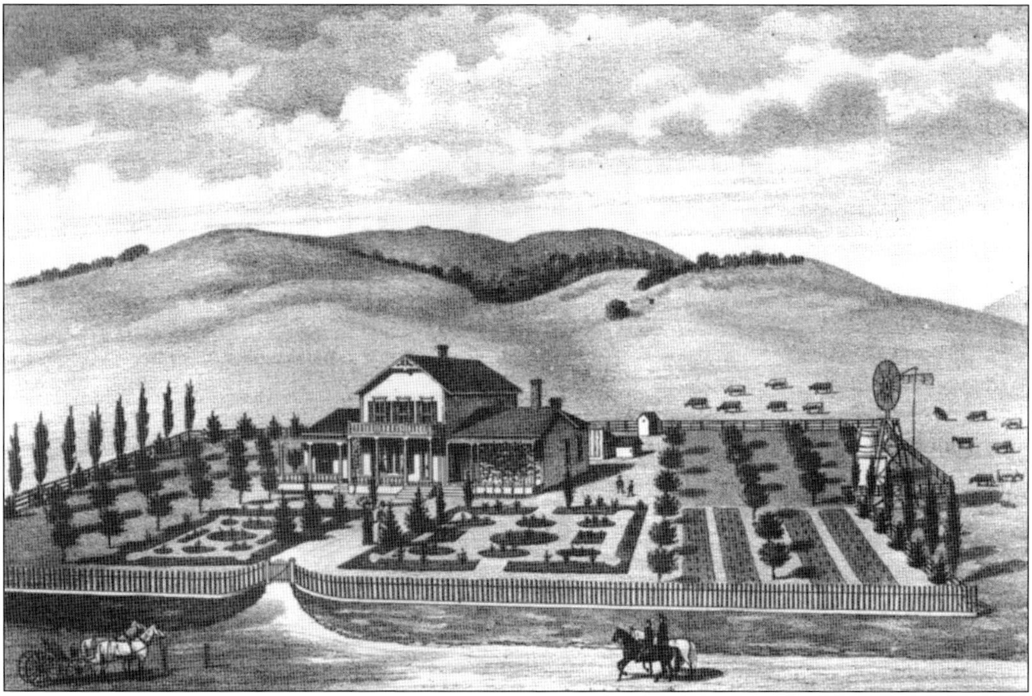

This illustration depicts the large home built by the Careaga brothers on their ranch. While grazing cattle was the first business of the brothers, the discovery of oil on their land near the turn of the century assured their future. The Careaga Ranch is situated at the western end of Los Alamos Valley.

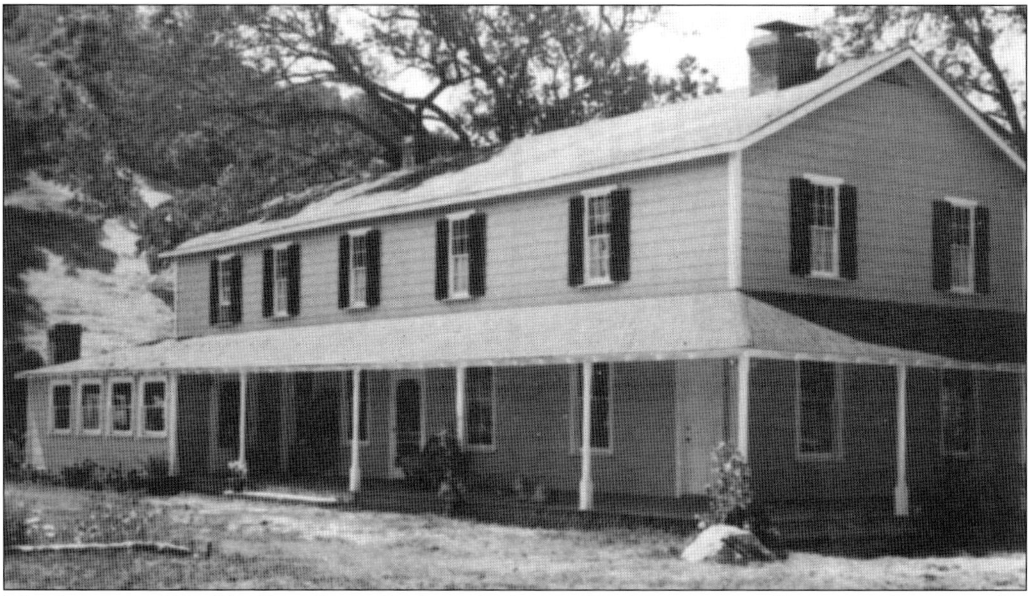

This home on El Roblar Ranch was built in the late 1880s. It was originally a part of the Rancho La Laguna. It was remodeled in the 1980s by Mr. and Mrs. W.P. Blair and purchased in 1885 by F.T. Underhill, an Eastern capitalist, for his winter retreat. Under the supervision of George T. Coles, Underhill raised 300 head of cattle and quality-blooded horses. (Courtesy of LAMC.)

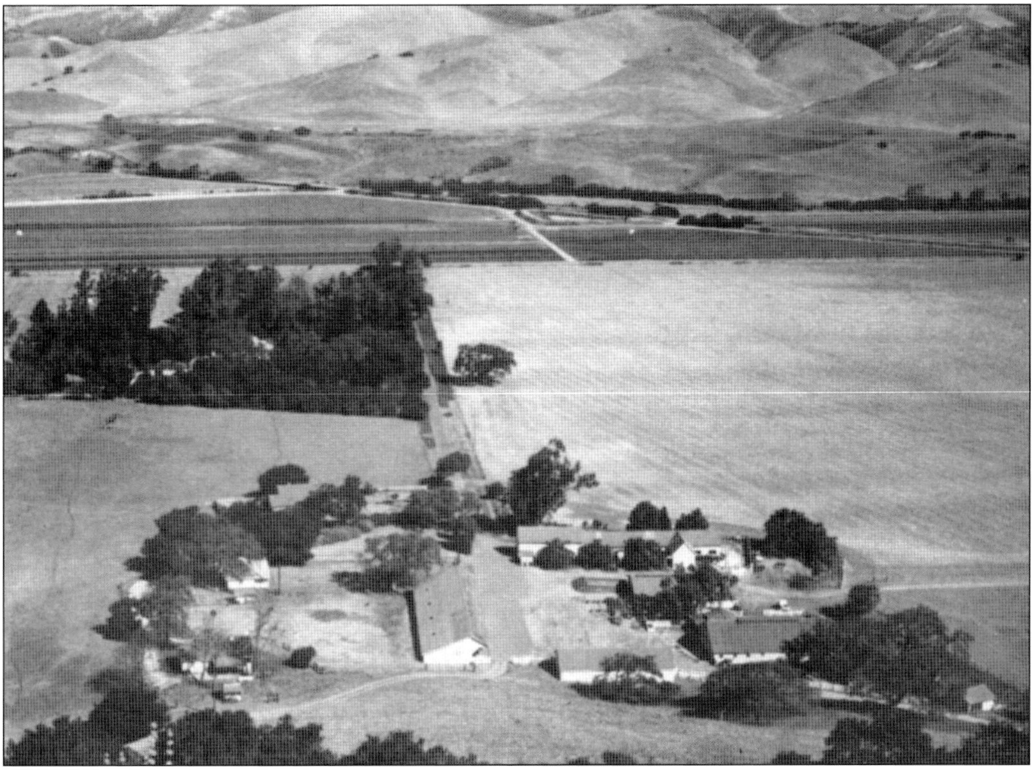

Rancho Los Alamos is seen from an airplane just north of the town of Los Alamos. Here, John Bell built his Victorian mansion (among the trees at upper left). The home later burned down. The ranch, about 3,500 acres, has been a cattle operation and agricultural business. A 1938 California ranch house is fitted as a guesthouse, with a vineyard and 25 acres full of redwood, oak, and cypress trees. (Courtesy of LAMC.)

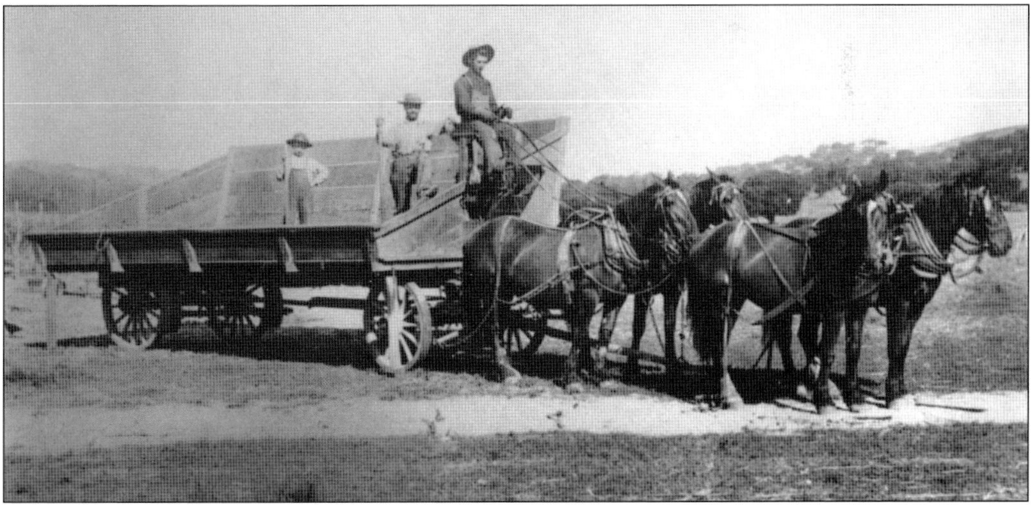

Frank (far left) and Charlie Tognazzi pause during their work for this photograph, taken on the Las Flores Ranch. A hired man drives the wagon, which is higher on one side to contain pitched hay. The Las Flores Ranch was largely dairy oriented until Charlie Tognazzi converted it to a cattle business. (Courtesy of Jeanette Sainz.)

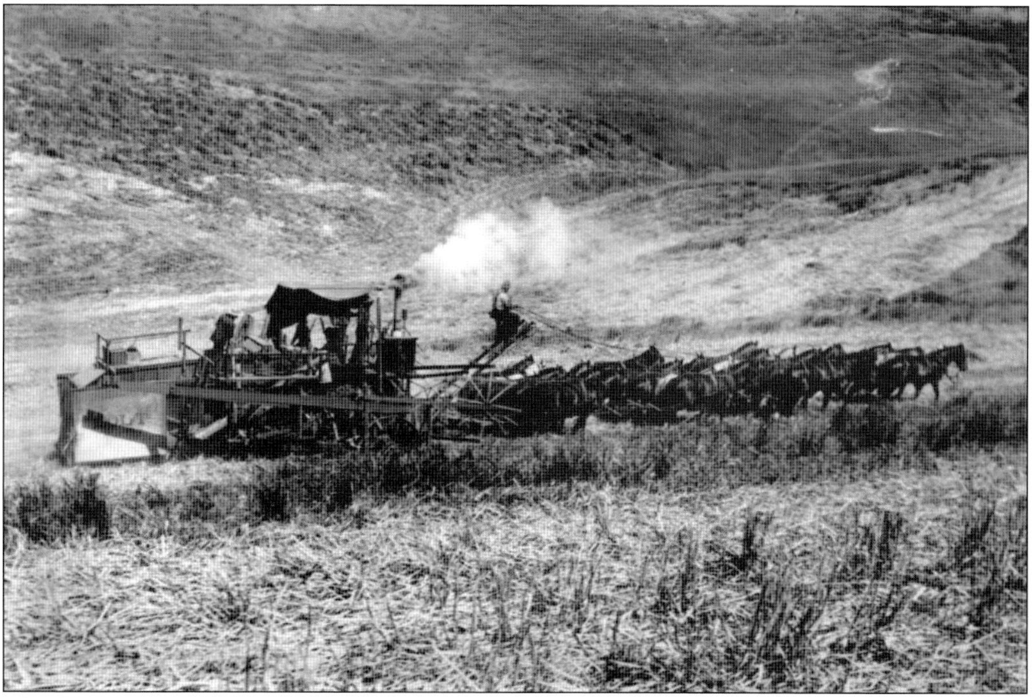

This horse-drawn thresher required a five-man crew and 16 horses to pull it. Here, it threshes grain on the Las Flores Ranch. It is being driven by Frank Tognazzi. Although a seat of sorts is rigged for the driver, operating the thresher required considerable driving skills. Some farms utilized stationary threshers, in which grain was fed into the machine, which was powered by horses on a treadmill. (Courtesy of Jeanette Sainz.)

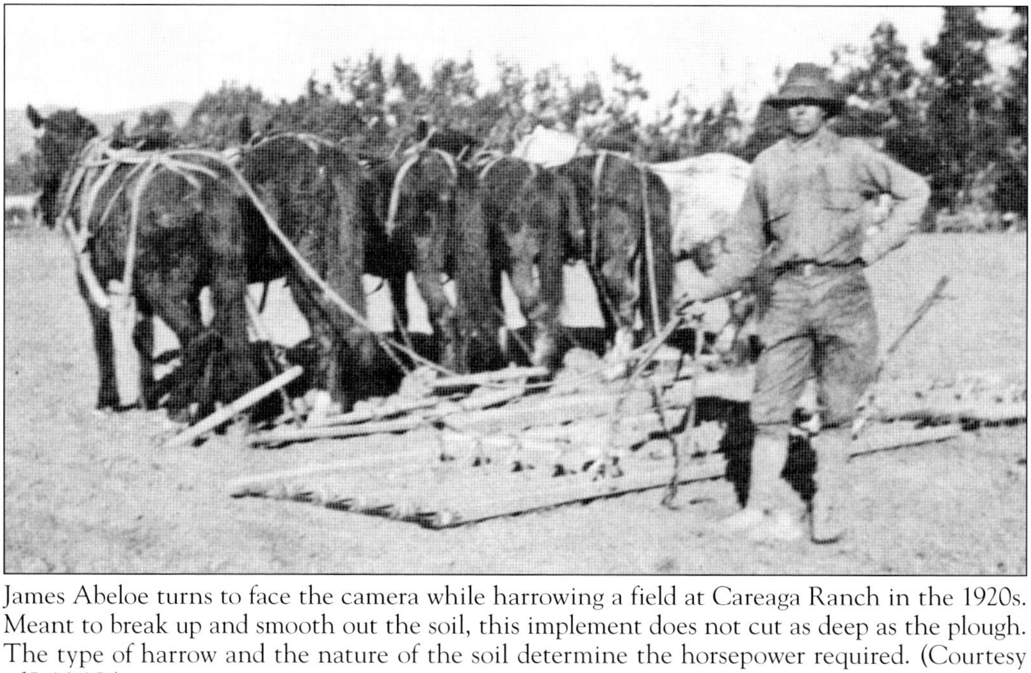

James Abeloe turns to face the camera while harrowing a field at Careaga Ranch in the 1920s. Meant to break up and smooth out the soil, this implement does not cut as deep as the plough. The type of harrow and the nature of the soil determine the horsepower required. (Courtesy of LAMC.)

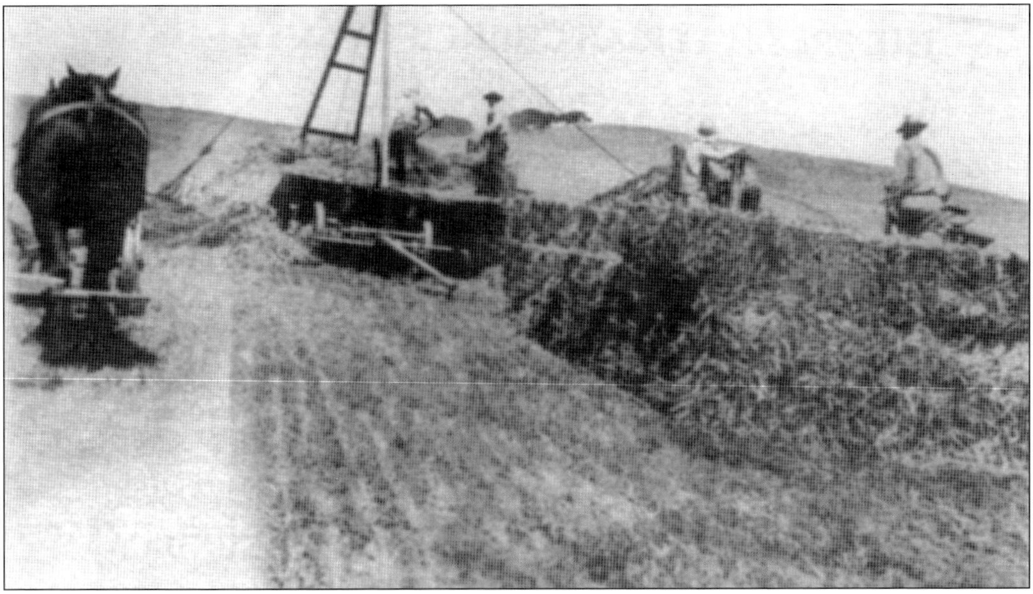

The Abeloe brothers, Carl and James, operated a stationary hay baler, and many young people in Los Alamos Valley worked on the crew. The positions were wire tie, feeder, bale buck, hay buck, buck fork, and tractor. Some people who worked on the crew were Carl Abeloe, Edward Gardner, Butch Abeloe, Frank Martinez, Jack Pritchard, Billy Evans, Johnny Bastanchury, Henry and Robert Parsons, and John Carr.

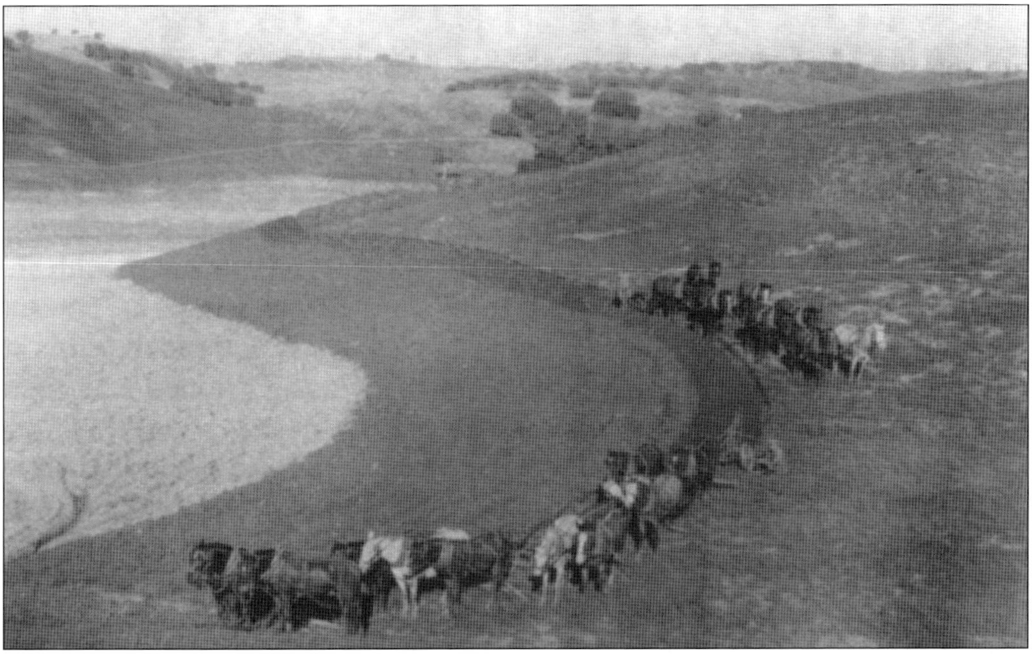

Seen here in the 1920s, two plow teams of 12 horses each work somewhere in the vicinity of Route 135. The second team waits patiently while the front team makes an adjustment to an implement. These two teams are plowing, but similar teams might be used for road building. Softly rolling contours and shallow sod made it possible for large horse teams to construct roads by hauling scoops. (Courtesy of LAMC.)

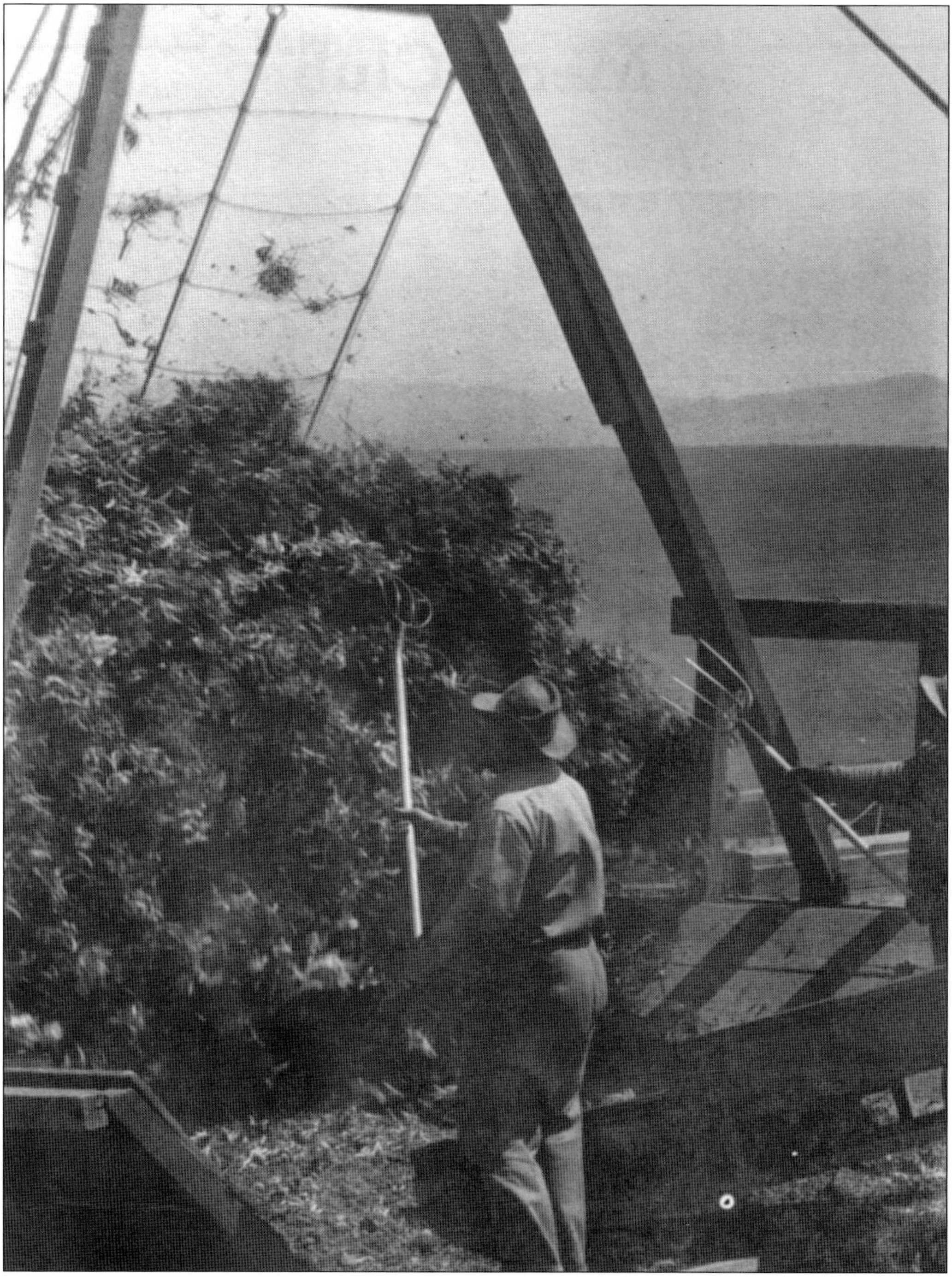

Carl Abeloe (center) and Edward Chick Gardner thrash beans on a Los Alamos Valley farm. While most varieties of beans did not thrash well, the soybean was an exception. Because the soybean can be grown in a wide variety of soil conditions, it is likely the bean the men are thrashing in this photograph. (Courtesy of LAMC.)

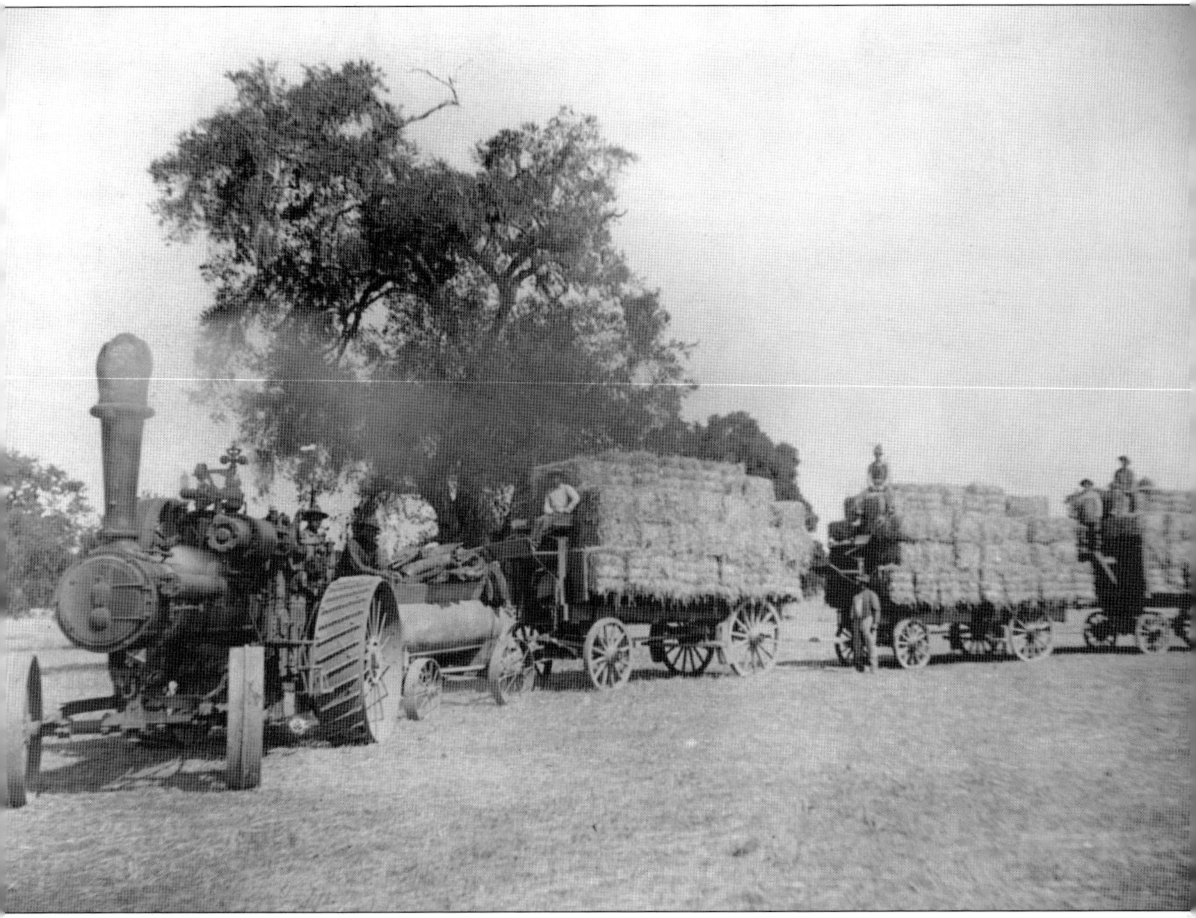

Steam tractors, while not easily maneuverable, had tremendous power for pulling loads and for plowing. This steam tractor, seen at an unknown location, easily pulls three full wagonloads of wheat. The engines could also be used to power nonmobile farming equipment. Steam tractors would have been useful mostly in the flatter areas of Los Alamos Valley.

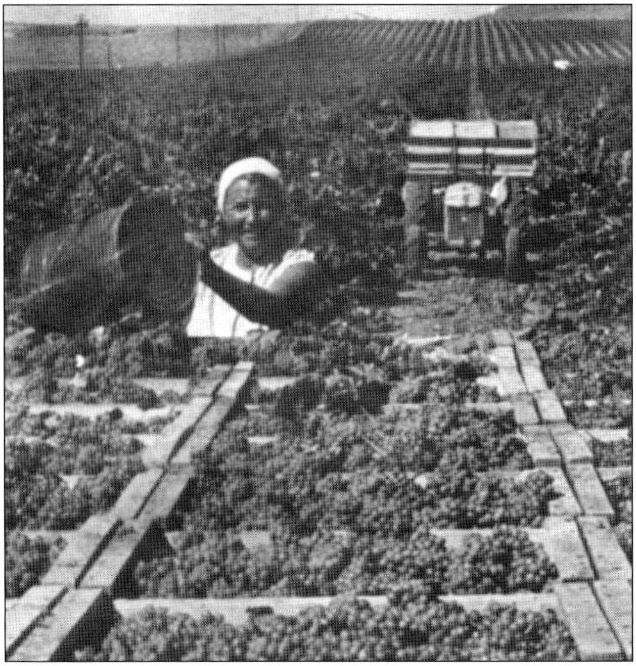

The Los Alamos Valley is adorned with vineyards and wineries. Wine grapes are not just an economically powerful product but are also a boost to tourism and a growing crop in itself. Several wine trails pass close by Los Alamos, and tourists arrive every weekend for tastings in the several tasting rooms in town. Large producers, such as Lucas & Lewellen, grow grapes in the valley. (Courtesy of LAMC.)

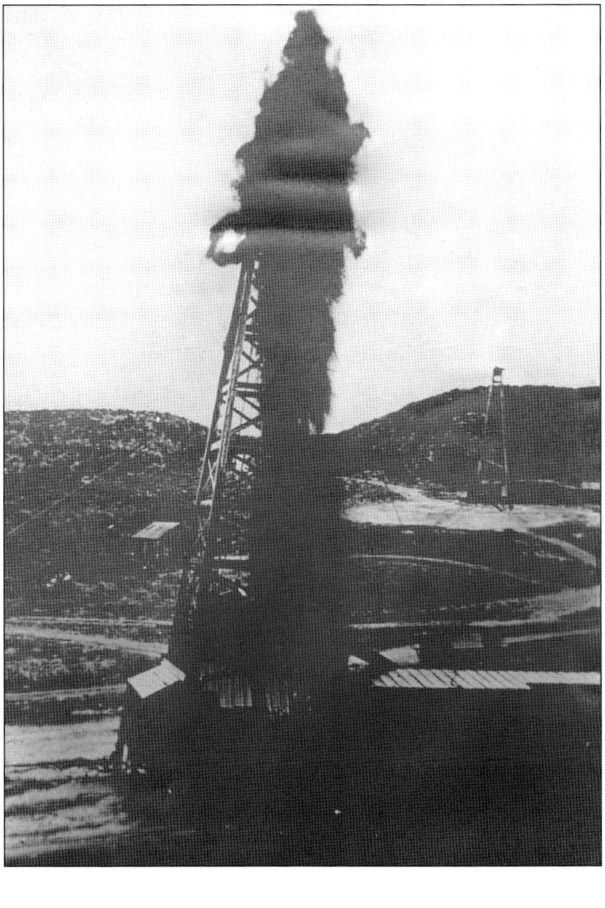

This is the iconic photograph of Old Maud blowing her top in the first heady days of oil discovery in Orcutt Oil Field, at the north end of Los Alamos Valley. The Union Oil Hartnell No. 1 ultimately produced 3 million barrels of oil. Darwin Sainz's grandfather was on the scene and took this picture. (Courtesy of Jeanette Sainz.)

Oil exploration was well under way all over the valley when Old Maude blew, and the discovery of oil fields such as Cat Canyon and Careaga Oil Field soon followed. Oil crews, such as this group of unidentified men, found plenty of work in the region. Of this photograph, Darwin Sainz used to comment that the one in the middle was the brains of the outfit. (Courtesy of Jeanette Sainz.)

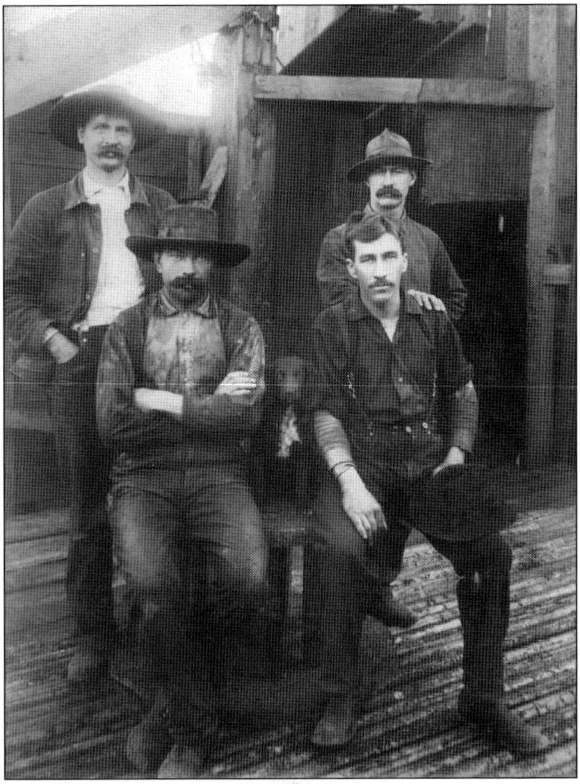

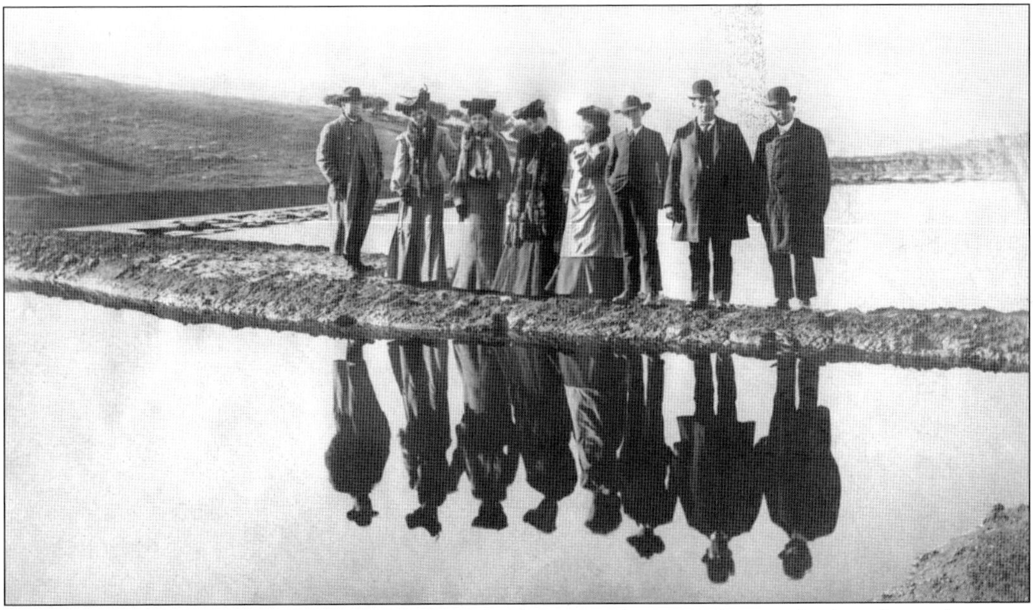

When Old Maude blew, eyewitnesses described a roar, then a column of oil and gas shooting 150 feet into the air. Oil poured down gullies and creek beds. With no way to cap the flow, the oilmen scraped up a series of earth dams, which collected pools of crude for miles. Here, the Hartnell family gathers in their finery for a photograph between two collection pools. (Courtesy of Jeanette Sainz.)

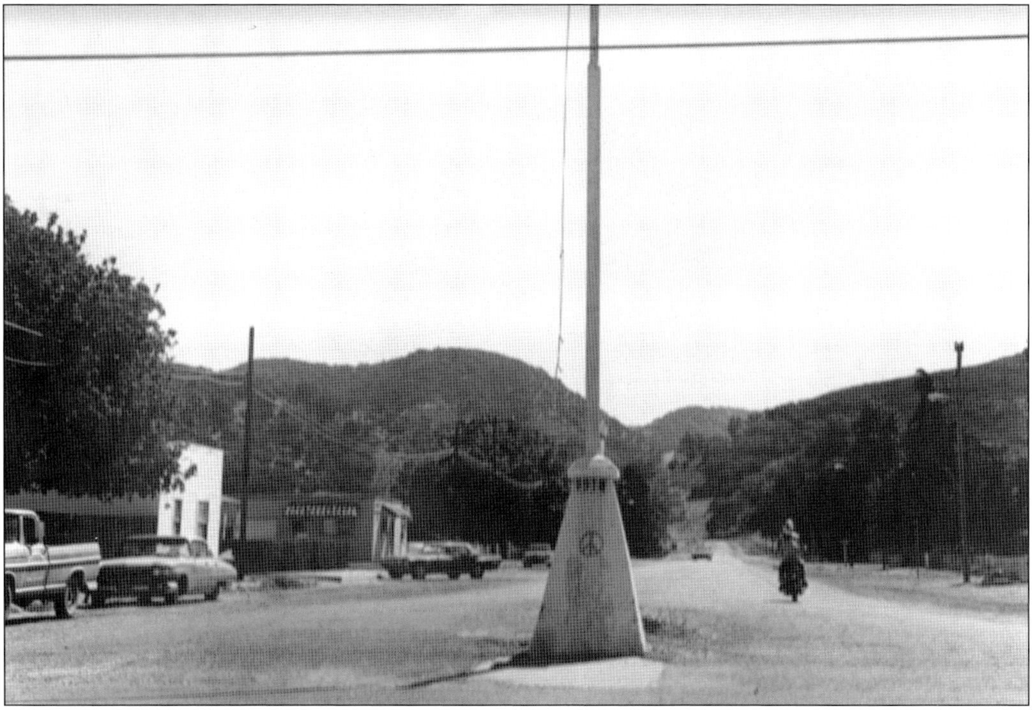

The Los Alamos flagpole was erected in Bell Street and dedicated on October 4, 1918. It was gifted to the town of Los Alamos for exceeding its quota of Liberty Bonds sales. Charles H. Pearson led the successful drive. The flagpole was later moved to Centennial Street. For years, George Shaw raised, lowered, and maintained the flag. (Courtesy of Olga Reed School.)

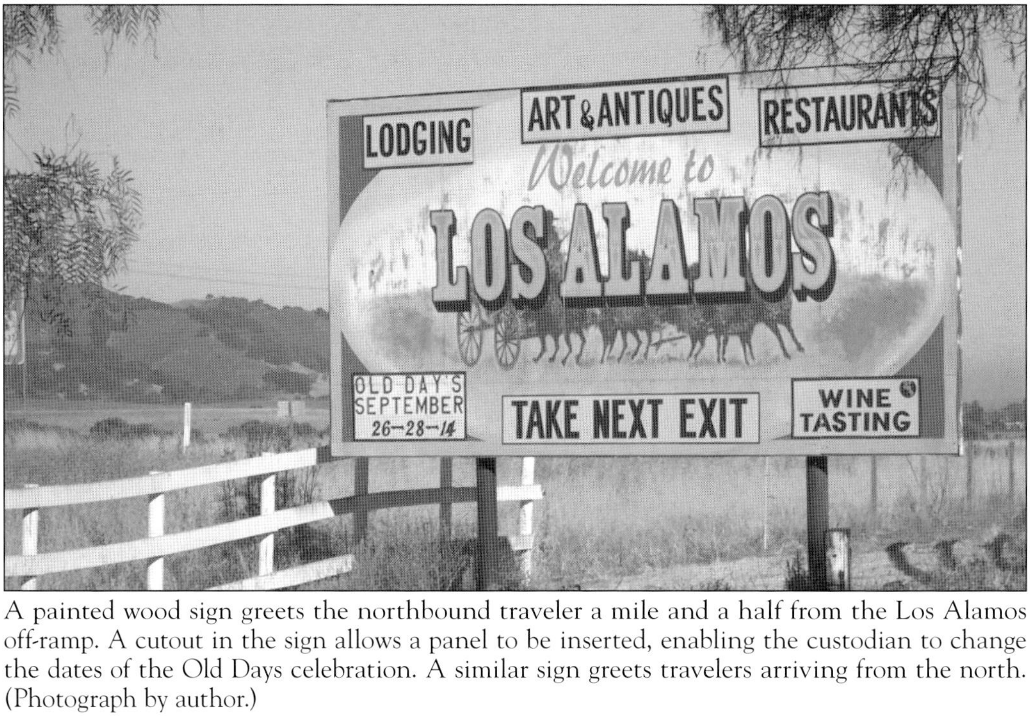

A painted wood sign greets the northbound traveler a mile and a half from the Los Alamos off-ramp. A cutout in the sign allows a panel to be inserted, enabling the custodian to change the dates of the Old Days celebration. A similar sign greets travelers arriving from the north. (Photograph by author.)

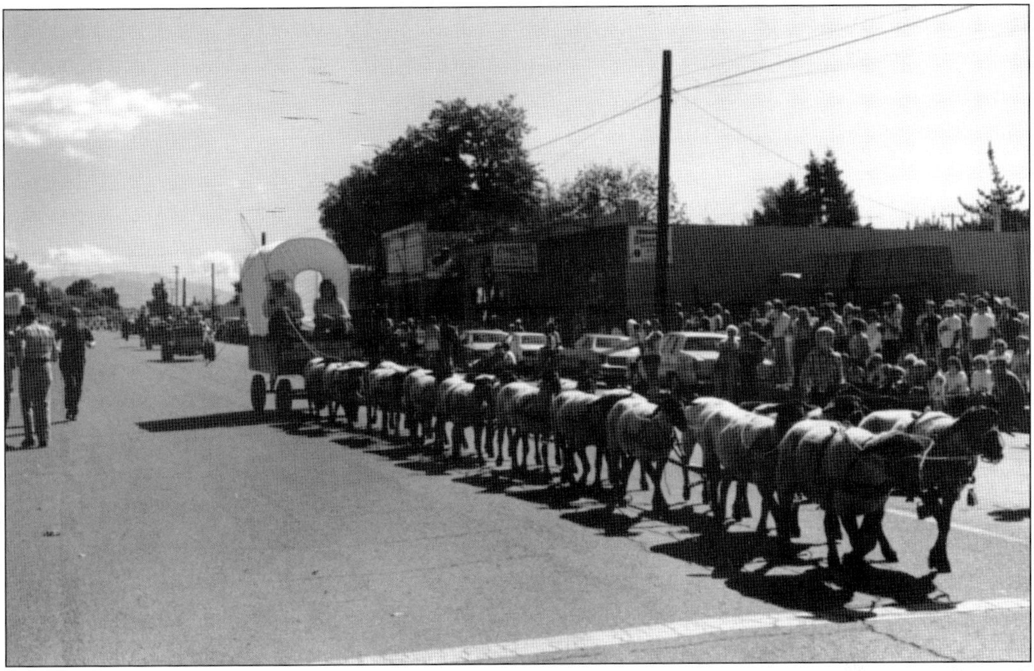

Los Alamos Old Days is always celebrated in the last weekend in September. Friday through Sunday, the town is packed with spectators, performers, vendors, and townspeople. The parade is a great attraction on Sunday. Participants range from skilled horsemen and -women to antique tractors, mariachi bands, and even this team of 18 sheep pulling a covered wagon. The parade route is usually crowded with spectators. (Courtesy of Charlie Gonzales.)

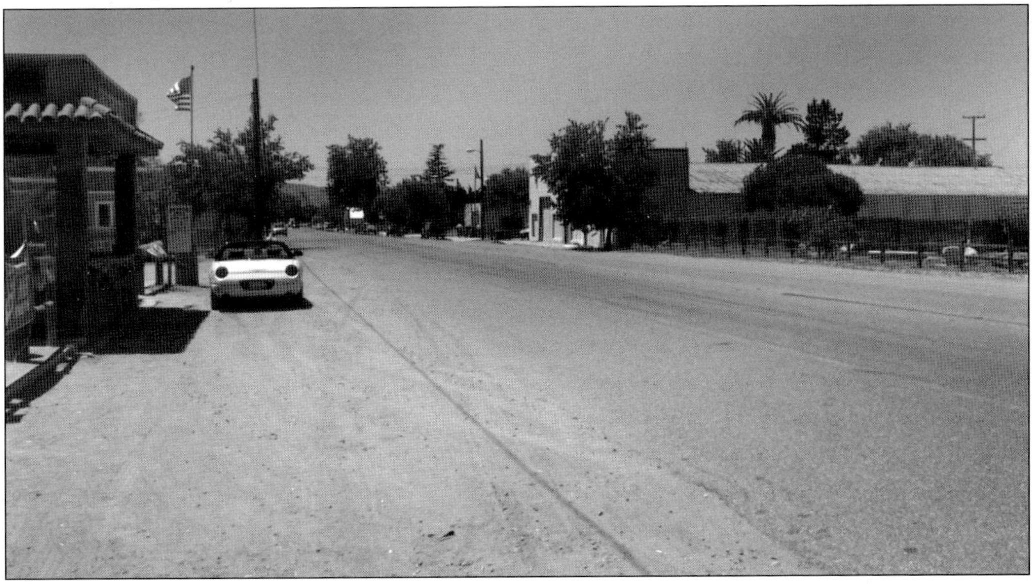

This relatively recent photograph looks west on Bell Street. It was taken after the current post office building was erected in 1966. It stands at center in the distance. At a later date, the Ghostriders Tavern moved into the building that the post office had vacated, across the street (second building from left). The flag seen at left is not on the town flagpole but on one that had been erected for the post office.

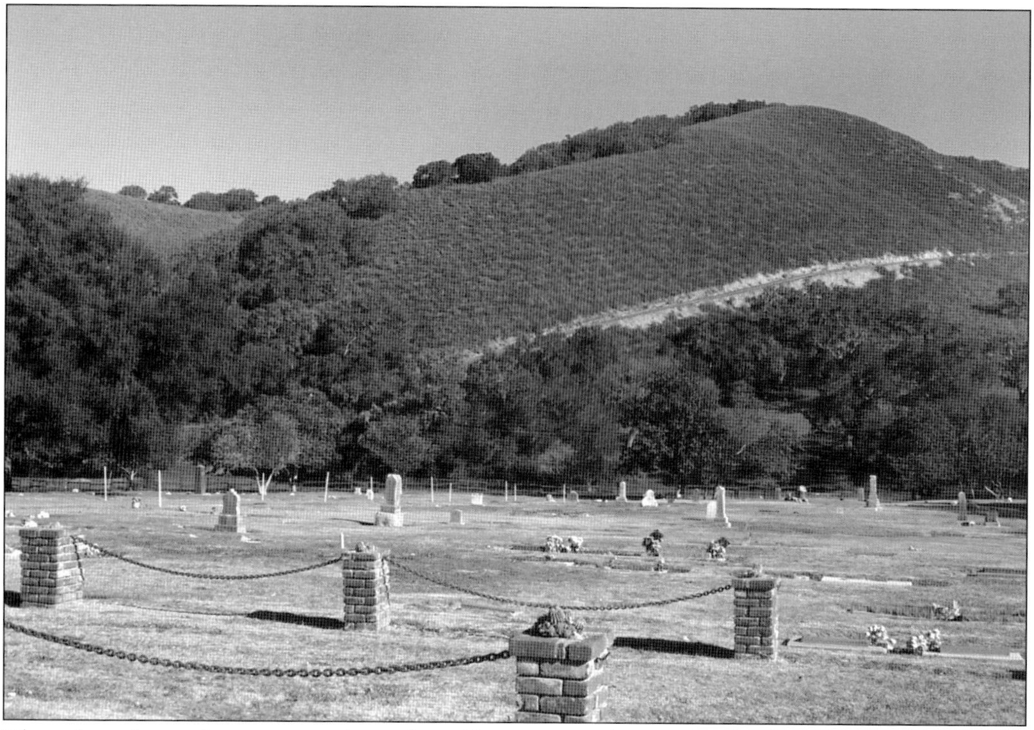

There have been three cemeteries in Los Alamos over the years. The first was located against the hills south of Foxen Lane in 1867. It was a private cemetery. There being no other, it was borrowed by other settlers until room ran out. A second cemetery was hastily established at the north end of St. Joseph Street. A cemetery committee was formed, and a permanent cemetery (pictured) was located on Drum Canyon Road. (Photograph by author.)

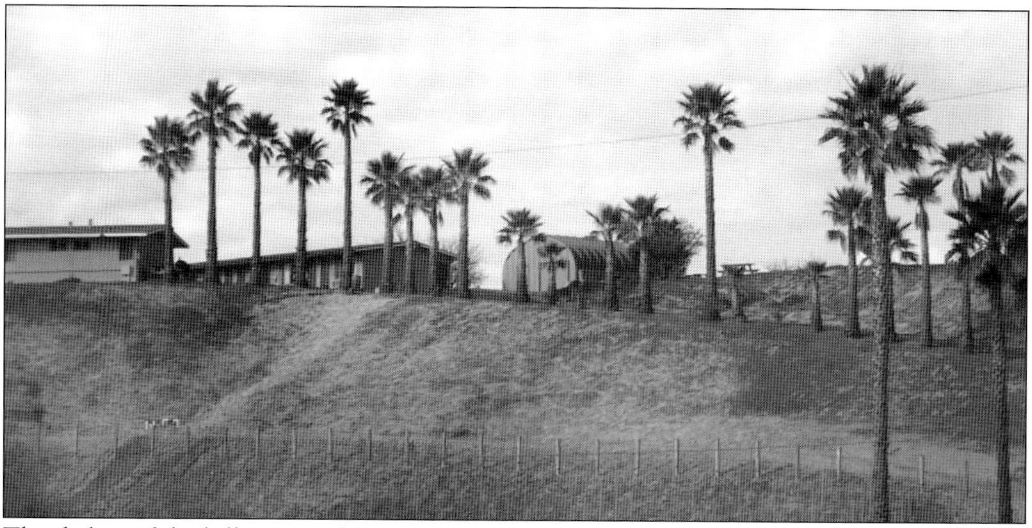

The skyline of the hills approaching Los Alamos was changed with the construction of the Sky View Motel in the late 1950s. Today, the palm-lined and graciously curving drive leading to the motel buildings perched on the hilltop near the off-ramp is part of the identity of Los Alamos. At night from far away, the lights from the motel shine for motorists like a beacon. (Photograph by author.)

Five

Getting There
A Catalyst for Growth

At each stage in the history of the growth of Los Alamos, the development of new modes of transportation was a catalyst, along with the foresight and dedicated effort of its citizens to draw these conveyors of people and goods to the valley. The stagecoach line that traveled through Foxen Canyon to the north shifted to run through Los Alamos Valley in 1874 to better reach the growing towns of Graciosa and Guadalupe. This necessitated a stable and a dining establishment for travelers in the valley. J.B. Shaw and Thomas Bell were quick to see the potential for growth brought by this change, and they set aside portions of their ranches for a town and land to offer to settlers. In 1876, they hired surveyors and platted a town. In 1882, the Pacific Coast Railway laid narrow-gauge track south to Los Alamos, connecting the town to the port of Point Harford. Consequently, Los Alamos became a major shipping point for the area's agricultural goods. With the discovery of oil in the valley and environs, the railroad adapted to meet the needs of the oil producers. By the second decade of the new century, the automobile was changing the landscape in California, and travelers needed gasoline, food, and rest stops. Again, Los Alamos was well situated. In 1927, town leaders convinced Sacramento to direct Highway 101 through Los Alamos. Service stations and restaurants blossomed in the town.

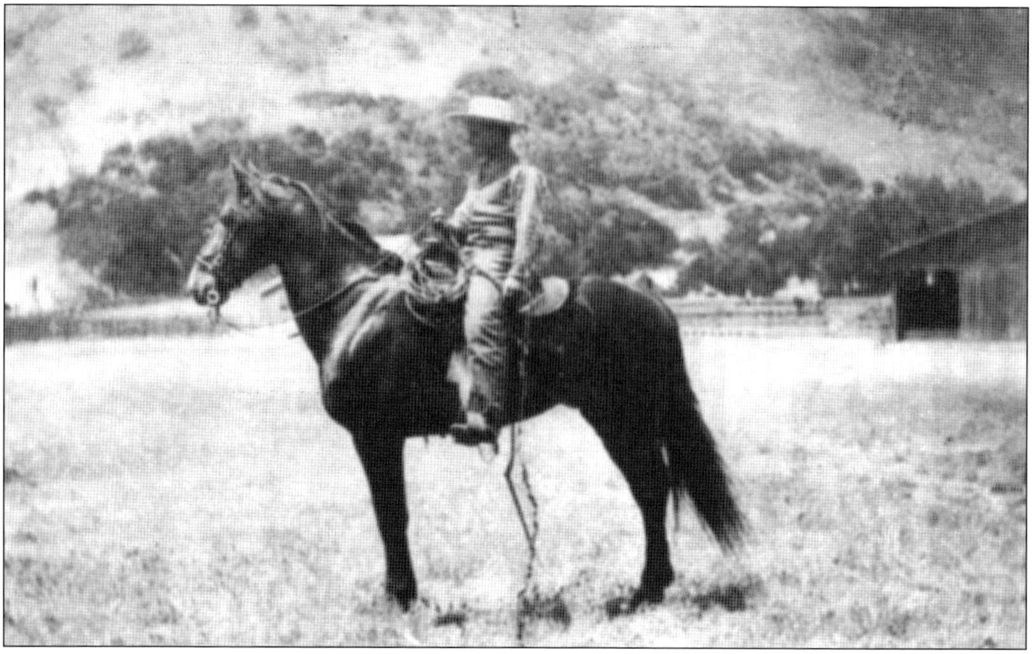

Alfredo Gutierrez, 24, is ready for work at the El Roblar Ranch in 1888. Gutierrez was born on the Zaca Rancho, then an extension of the Rancho La Laguna. A noted horseman, he trained polo ponies, with many winners. One of the last of the California vaqueros of the era of the great ranchos, Alfredo is descended from Octaviano Gutierrez, the original grantee of Rancho La Laguna. (Courtesy of the LAMC.)

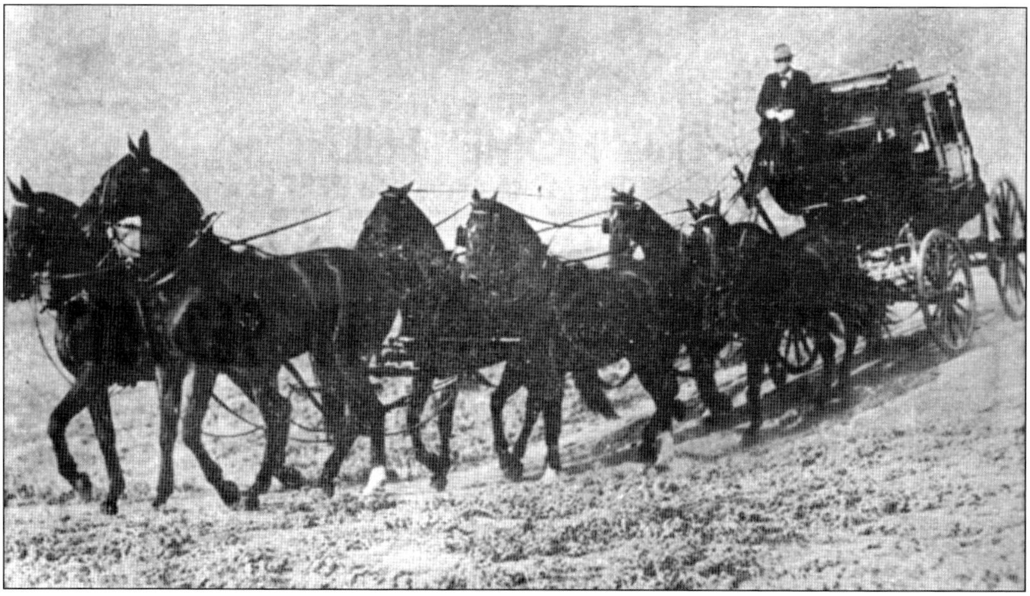

"Whispering" George Cooper drives a Concord coach and six in the Los Alamos Valley. His nickname came from his famously bellowing voice. It was said that, once, when Cooper broke a singletree, he killed a five-foot rattlesnake to use in lieu of baling wire to make a temporary repair. Among the other pioneer drivers were John Waugh, John Coleman, Ben Butterfield, Tom Edgar, Big Joe Sampson, and Billy Balch. (Courtesy of LAMC.)

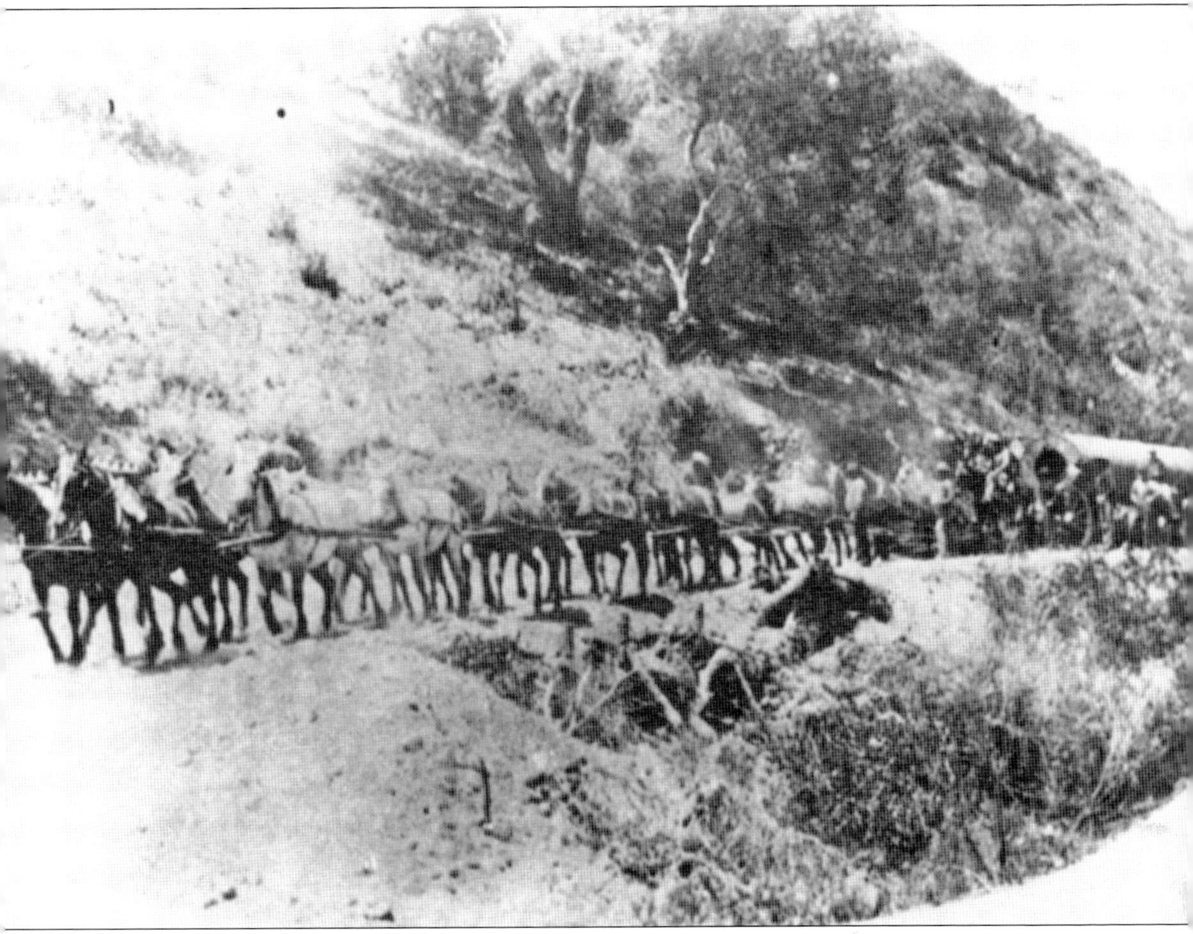

The 20-mule team in this photograph is hauling a boiler from the Santa Maria Railroad depot to the Sisquoc Asphaltum Mines, located on the Sisquoc Ranch east of Los Alamos. Dick Holland is the driver. The team was rented from a San Francisco drayman. The only way to transport oversized and heavy items along the narrow, winding roads of the Los Alamos region was by teams of horses. (Courtesy of LAMC.)

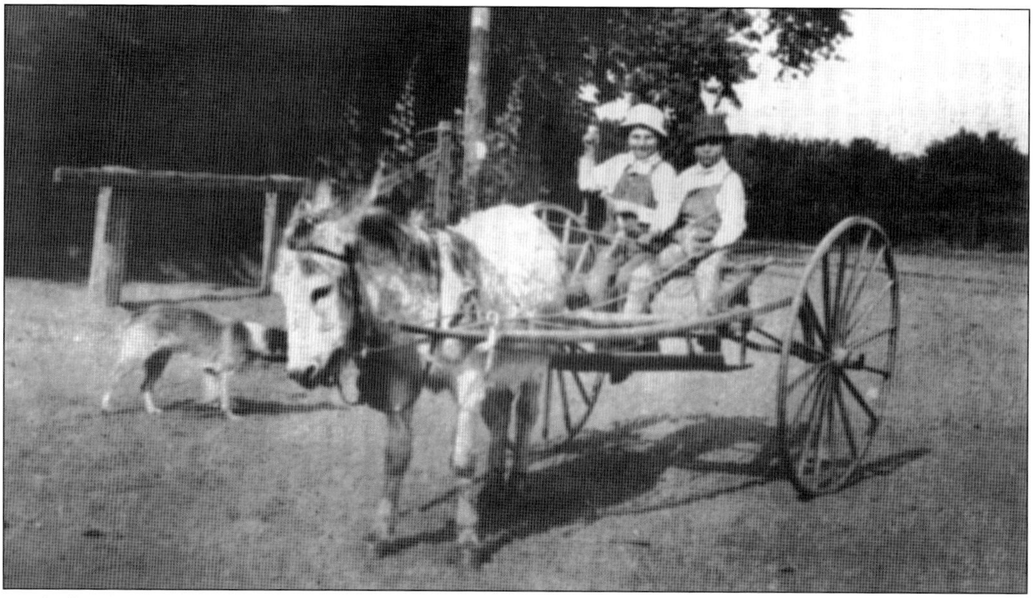

Link (left) and Dutch Wilson demonstrate how to drive a burro-drawn sulky. In the earliest days, light two-wheel carts were of the greatest utility for their maneuverability. They could be pulled by animals ranging from dogs and goats to ponies and mules. In the early valley, when roads were mostly cow paths, the cart was the most efficient way to transport goods or people. (Courtesy of LAMC.)

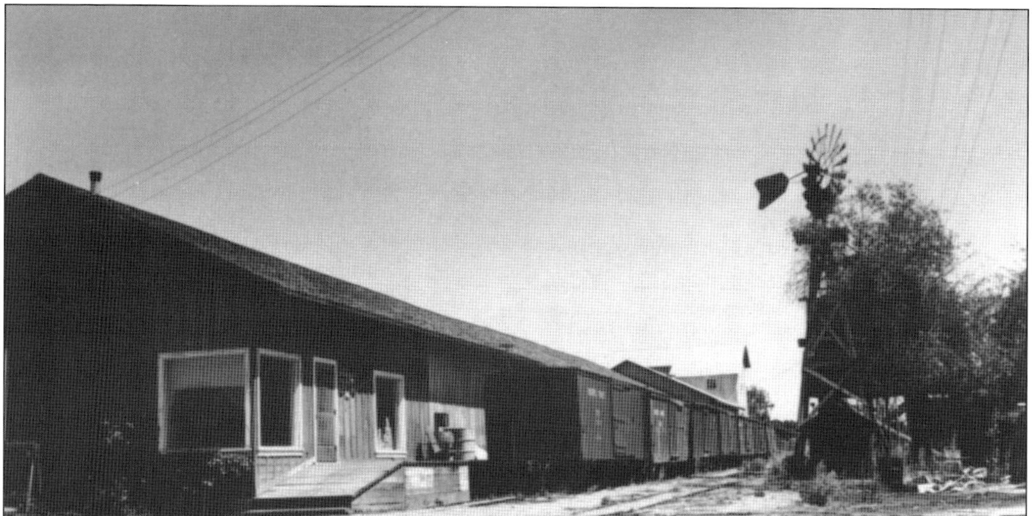

Several freight cars are lined up at the Los Alamos depot. Their wait may be long, as the overgrown appearance of the tracks and the lack of signage suggests the Pacific Coast Railway may have passed out of existence at the time of this photograph. The cars are on the siding. The main track passed to the right of them. (Courtesy of Madeleine Jex.)

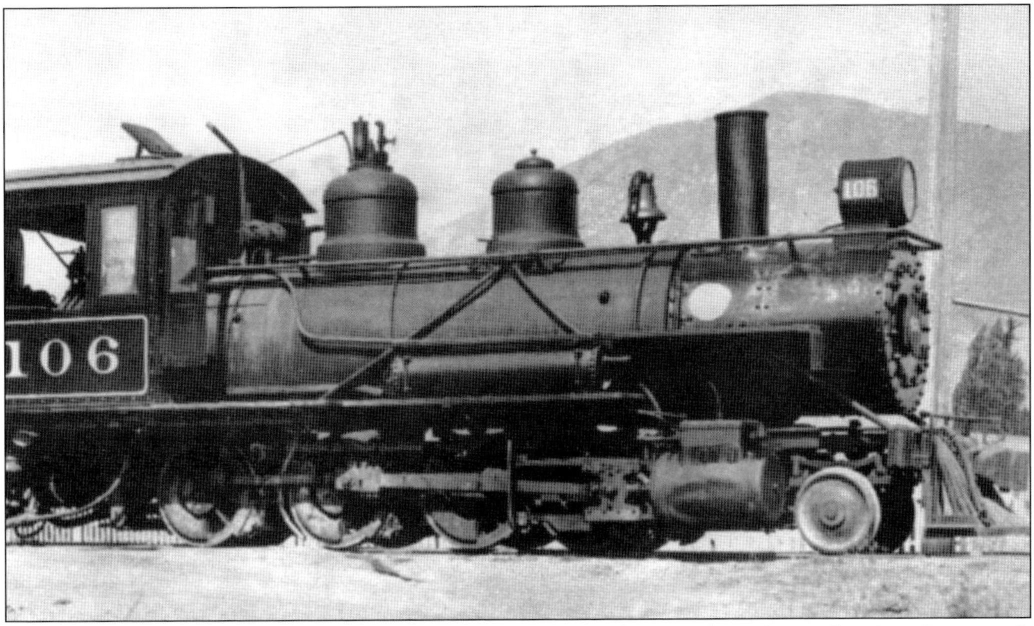

Engine No. 106 would meet its end in a collision with a gasoline truck not long after this photograph was taken. The train was knocked on its side, the gasoline ignited, and a spectacular fire burned the truck and the electric wires, rendering Los Alamos powerless. The engine's bell currently hangs in the courtyard of the Santa Ynez Valley Historical Museum. (Courtesy of LAMC.)

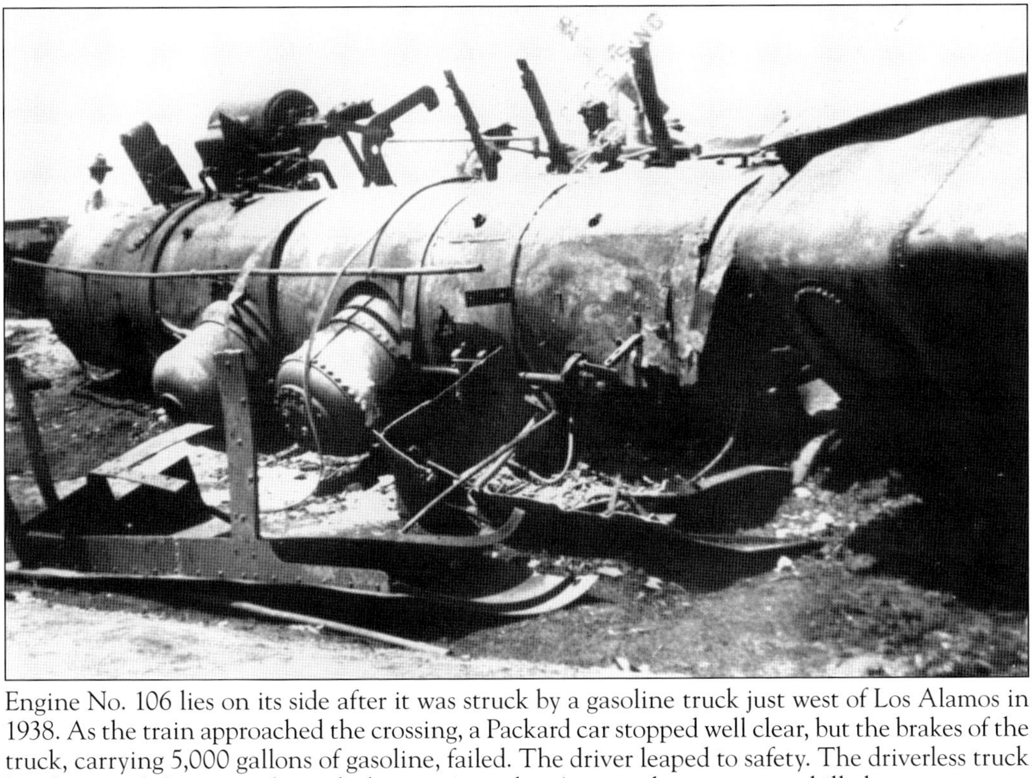

Engine No. 106 lies on its side after it was struck by a gasoline truck just west of Los Alamos in 1938. As the train approached the crossing, a Packard car stopped well clear, but the brakes of the truck, carrying 5,000 gallons of gasoline, failed. The driver leaped to safety. The driverless truck barely missed the car and struck the train's tender. Amazingly, no one was killed.

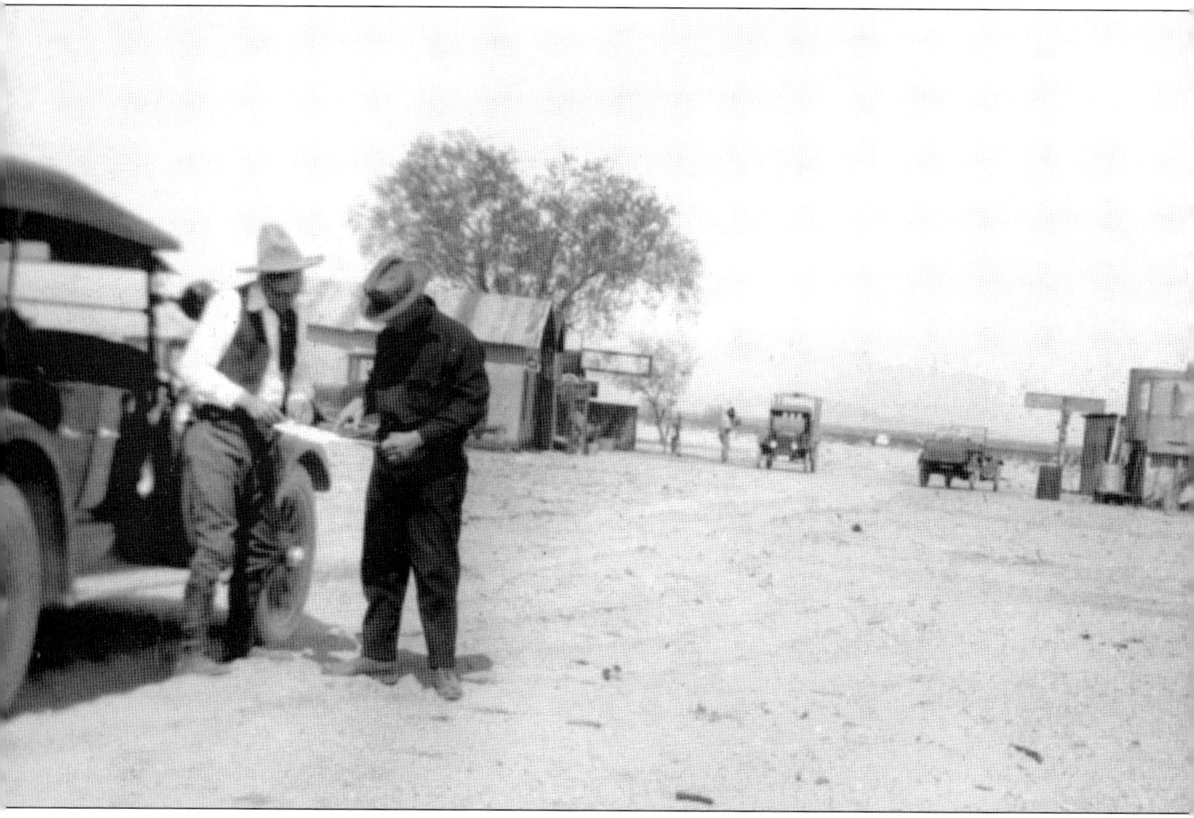

A driver huddled over a map receives directions in a scene that would become very familiar with the increased proliferation of the automobile. The photograph, taken early in the 20th century, likely shows the area west of Los Alamos, perhaps near the Santa Rosa Road turnoff. Water from the tanks (right) would have been a valuable commodity at the time.

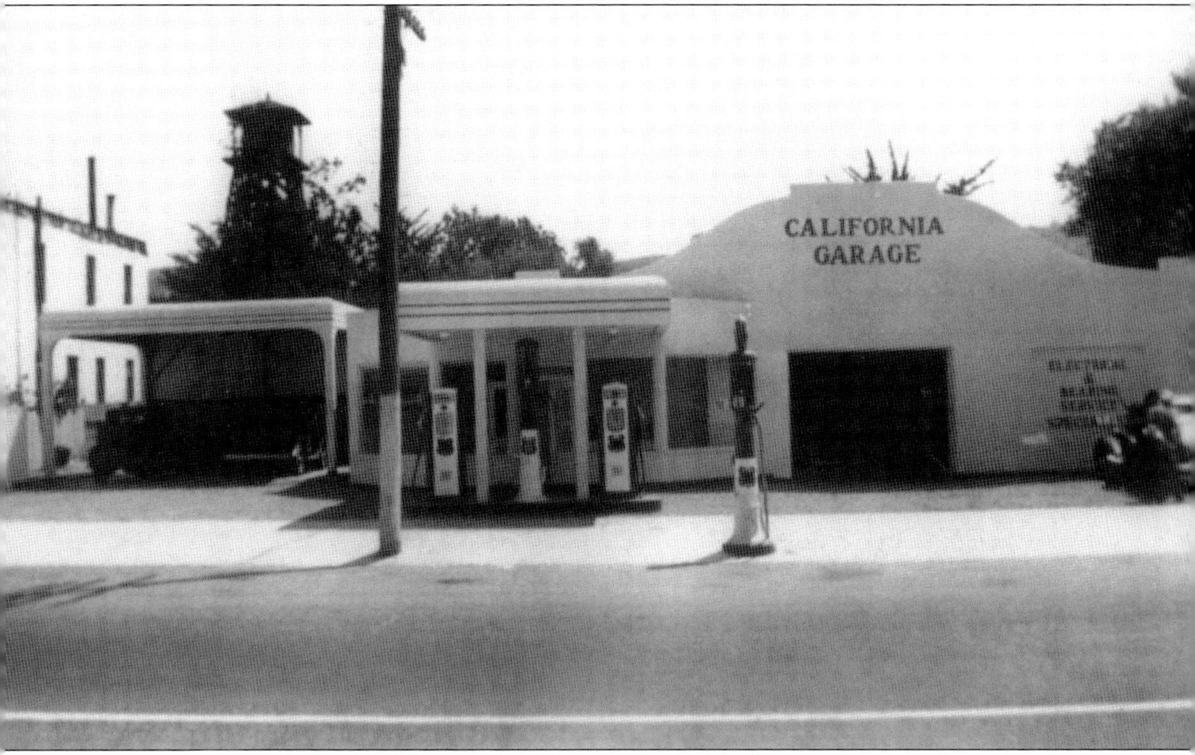

This photograph of Al Scolari's California Garage shows the graceful lines and attractive canopies the Scolari brothers built into it. The single old pump in the foreground has been replaced by two modern ones under the center canopy. At far left is the Hotel Los Alamos.

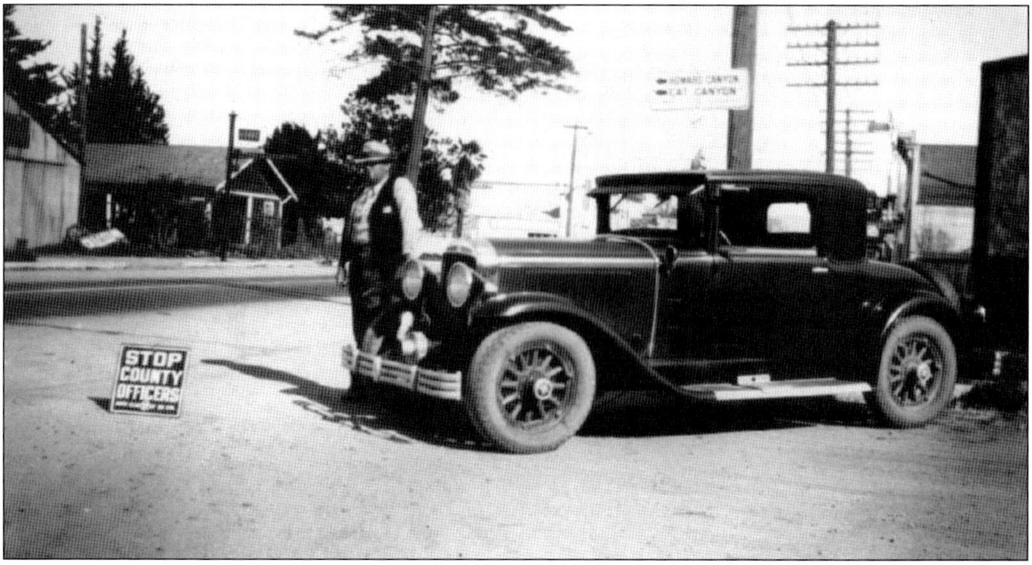

Constable Ed Robbins waits at an automobile road stop. He stands next to his chase car, which is poised for pursuit. Robbins stands across the street from the Wurtz Blacksmith Shop on Bell Street. He has taken his stance just before the turnoff for Cat Canyon (or Howard Canyon). The purpose of the roadblock is unknown.

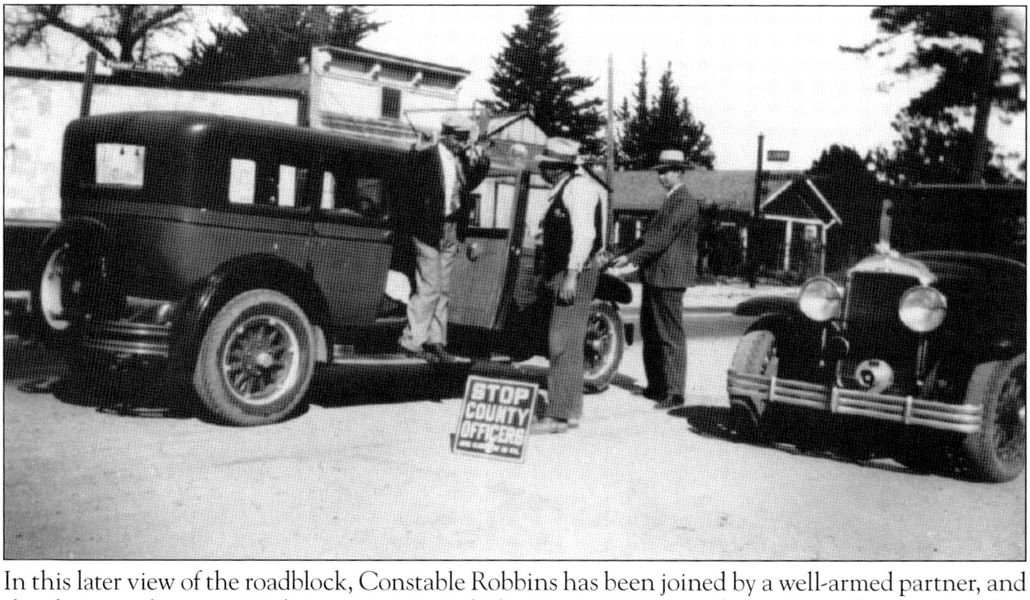

In this later view of the roadblock, Constable Robbins has been joined by a well-armed partner, and they have made a stop. Both men appear ready for action. However, the smile on the apprehended man's face, and the perhaps simulated bullet holes in the side of his vehicle, suggest this might be drama rather than reality. A large siren is visible on the chase car just above the bumper.

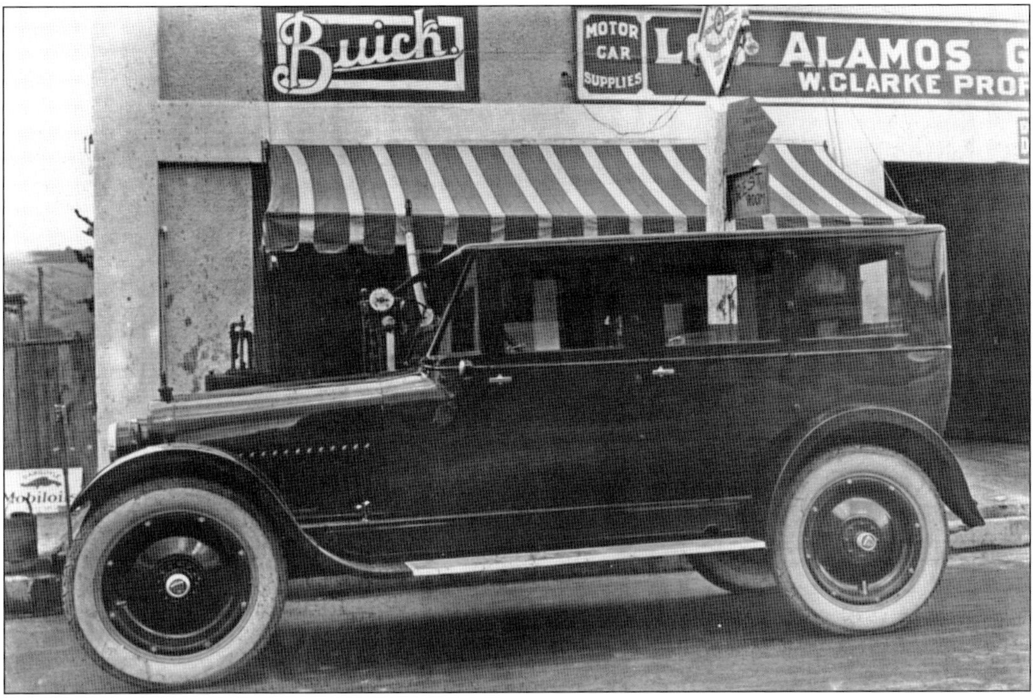

What appears to be a new 1930s Buick business coupe rests appropriately under the Buick sign in front of the Los Alamos Garage on the north side of Bell Street. Sidewalk gas pumps and oil pumps can be seen directly behind the car. There is even a sidewalk water faucet and a bucket, presumably for the windshield. Walter Clarke was the proprietor of the Los Alamos Garage. He married Beth Pearson.

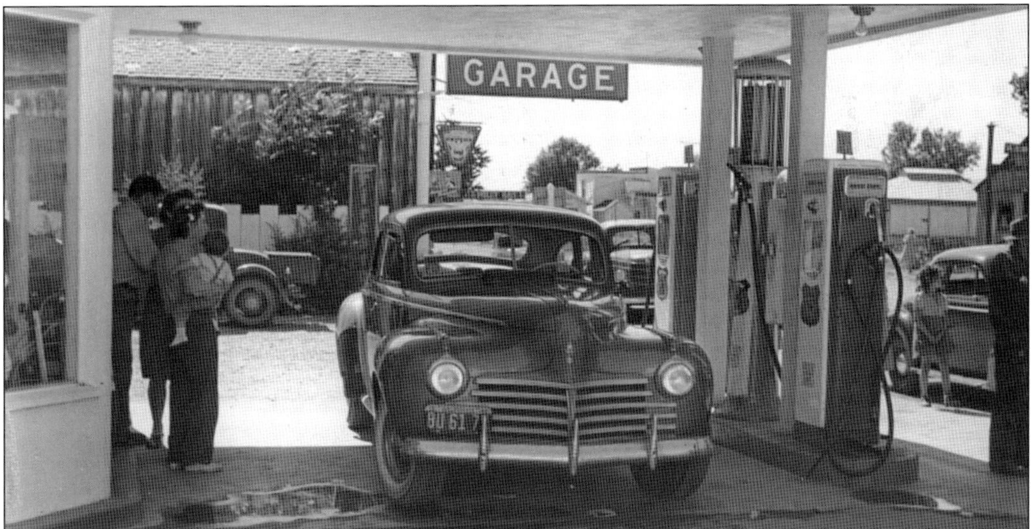

Travelers in the doorway of the 76 station appear to be consulting a map in the late 1940s. The blacksmith shop of A.B. Wurtz is directly across the street. The postwar era was a boon to Los Alamos, with the influx of newly mobilized Americans hitting the roads of California. A little girl (far right) stands beside an early import Volkswagen.

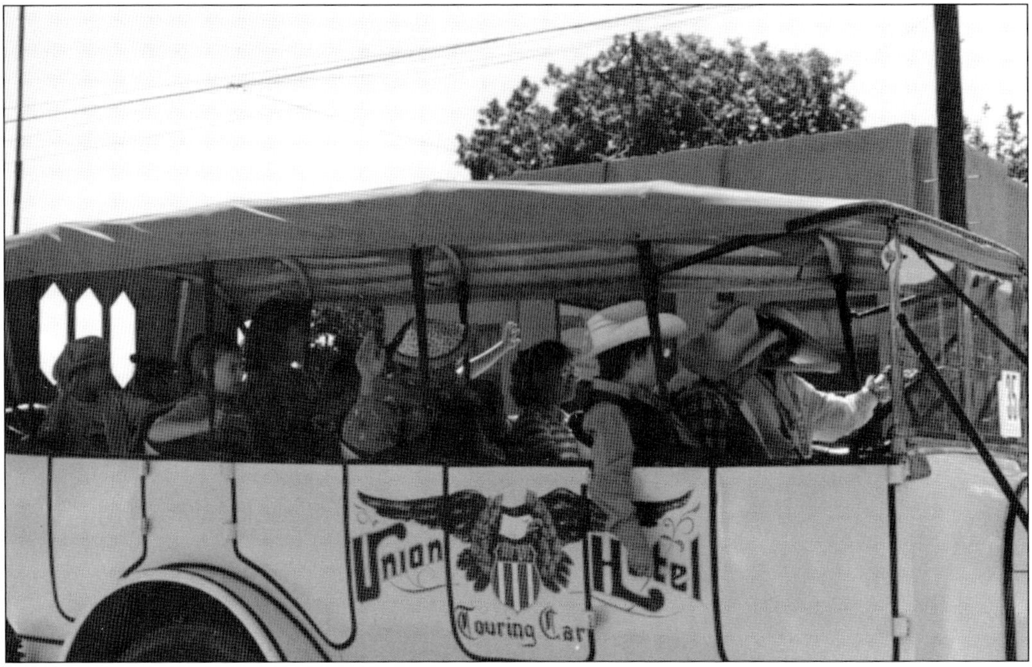

Tourists enjoy a trip in the Union Hotel Touring Car. When the freeway was routed by Los Alamos rather than through it, businesses in the town found it necessary to work harder to draw tourists and travelers. None was more imaginative than Dick Langdon, who returned the Union Hotel to period style and added the Victorian Mansion Bed and Breakfast in 1979.

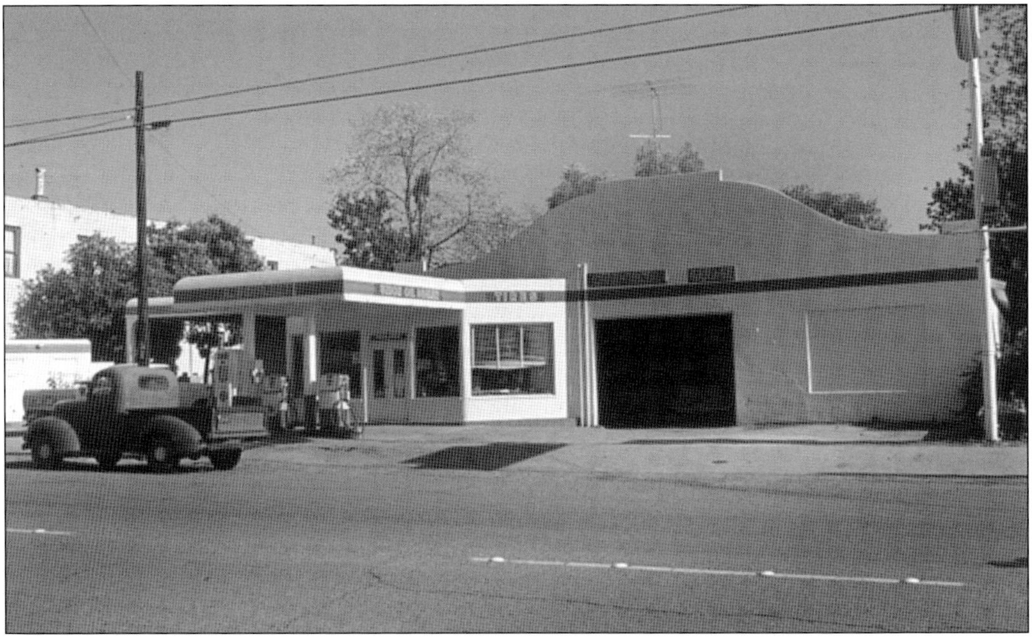

Business is slow in this photograph of Al Scolari's California Garage in later years. The establishment closed for good in the early 1980s. It sat dormant for a number of years as various owners considered plans for the building. It has now been remodeled for special events and is sought after for weddings and similar large occasions.

Six

Faces and Places
The True Town

The following pages are dedicated to the heart and soul of the Los Alamos Valley: the people who imprinted upon it. The history, growth, appearance, legends, and stories that characterize this place emerge from a fragile, interwoven fabric of diverse perspectives, races, and cultures gathered within the Los Alamos community. The Chumash were here first, and their heritage is lasting in place names and in skills and adaptations later borrowed by the Europeans. The Spanish came next, and then the Mexicans, many already of mixed lineage. Some Americans came early, joined the Catholic Church, married Spanish wives, and learned their language. Other Americans came after the Mexican-American War, a result of American expansionism. As the town of Los Alamos grew, the cultures of the world became represented here, for, in addition to the Spanish, Mexicans, and Americans, came Scots, English, Swiss, Italians, Canadians, and others. All of them influenced the town and valley in their own way and together became the faces of the people who loved, laughed, and lived here. By their industry, perseverance, and will, they made their mark upon the valley.

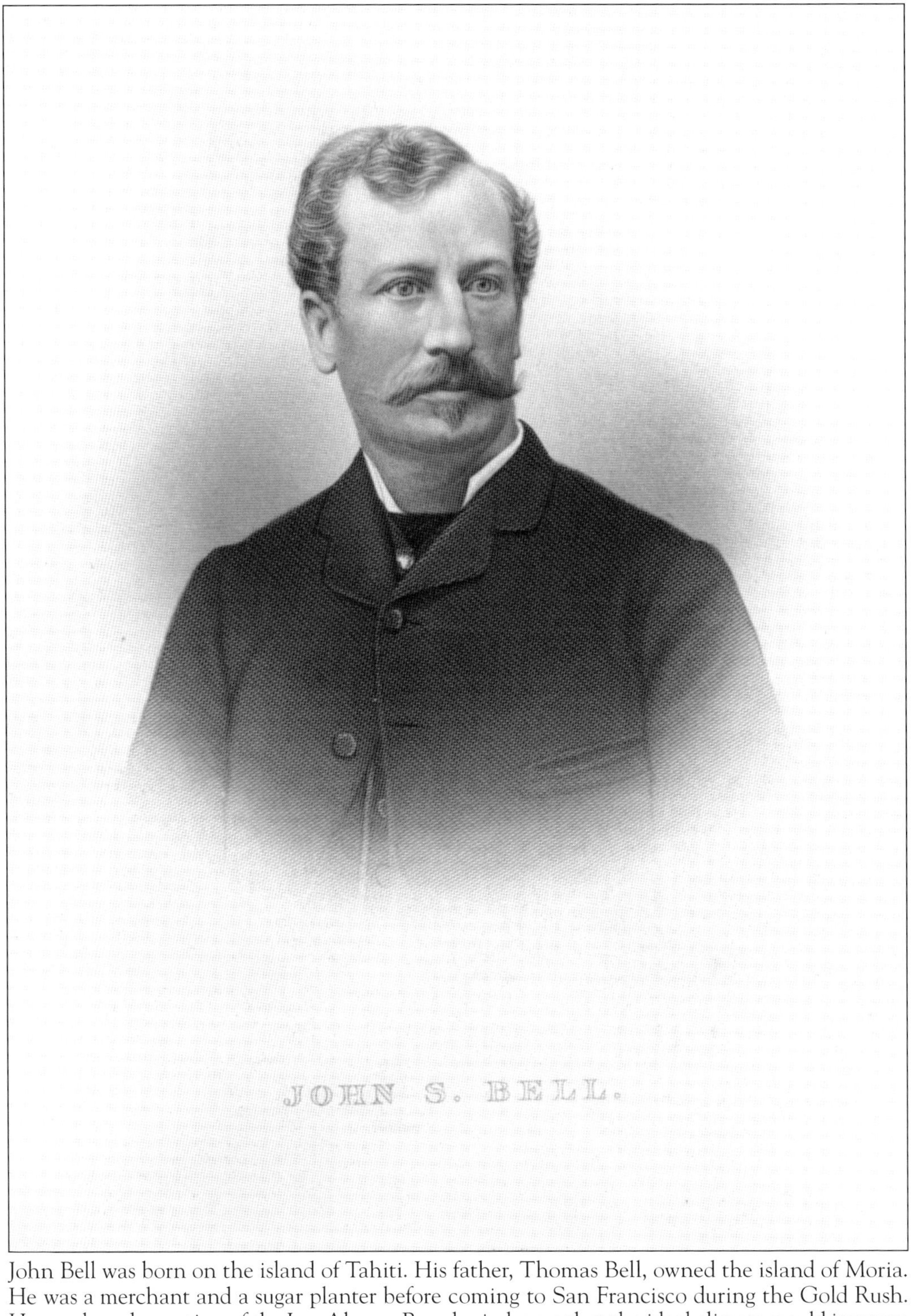

John Bell was born on the island of Tahiti. His father, Thomas Bell, owned the island of Moria. He was a merchant and a sugar planter before coming to San Francisco during the Gold Rush. He purchased a portion of the Los Alamos Rancho in hopes that the ideal climate would improve John's health. John was a pioneer in growing grain in the valley and built the first flourmill.

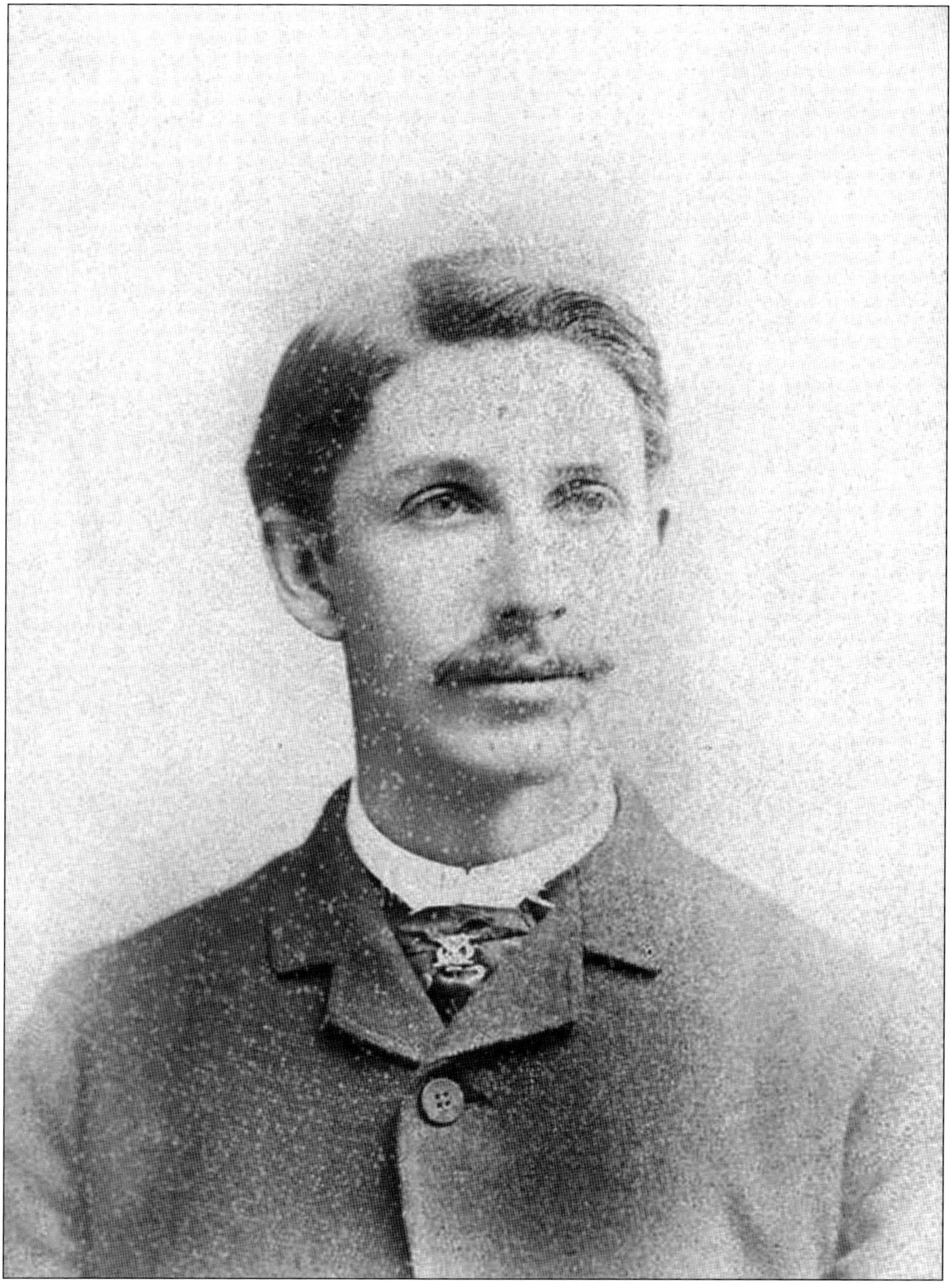

Dr. J.B. Shaw came from England in the 1860s to manage Santa Cruz Island, then owned by a British syndicate. He helped bring the Southern Pacific Railroad to Santa Barbara in 1887 and facilitated the arrival of the Pacific Coast Railway to Los Alamos. Dr. Shaw purchased a portion of the old Rancho La Laguna, cofounded the town of Los Alamos, and helped attract settlers to the region.

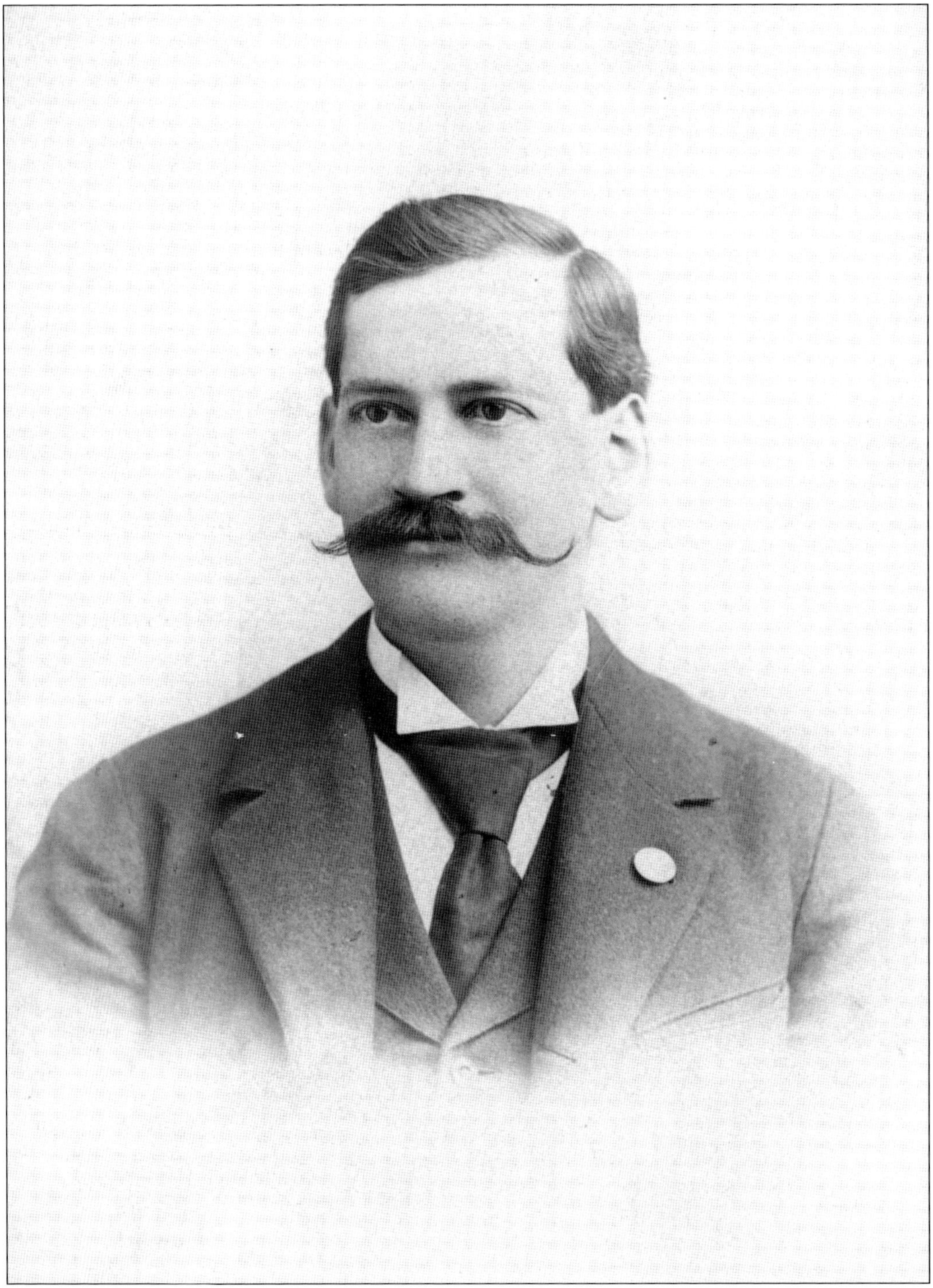

This portrait of James Barron Shaw Jr. was taken at Thors Portraits, 14 Grant Avenue, San Francisco. James's father, Dr. Shaw, stocked his Rancho La Laguna with sheep and, later, with cattle. He left the actual management of the ranch to James Jr. and moved to Santa Barbara to practice medicine. James Shaw Jr. eventually inherited the holdings.

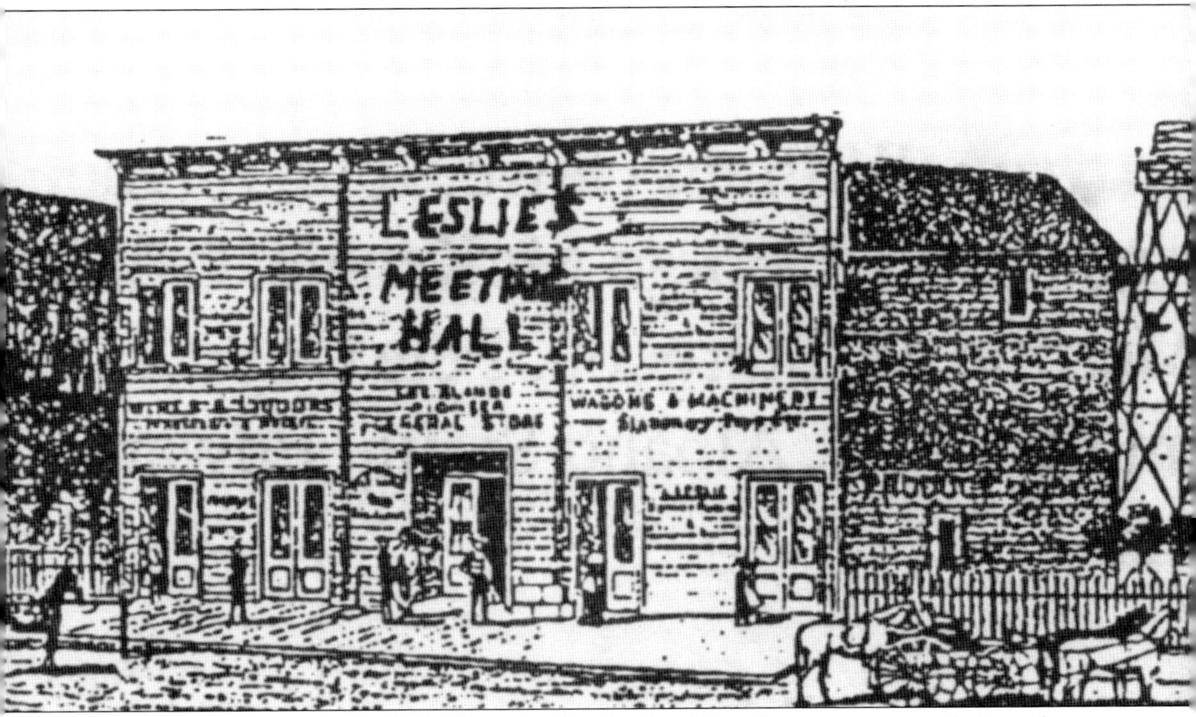

Alexander Leslie was born in the highlands of Scotland in 1847. He was postmaster for Los Alamos even before the town was platted. His buildings were among the first in Los Alamos, including this two-story structure that housed three stores and a meeting hall. He built a large home for his family. It still stands today on Bell Street. (Courtesy of LAMC.)

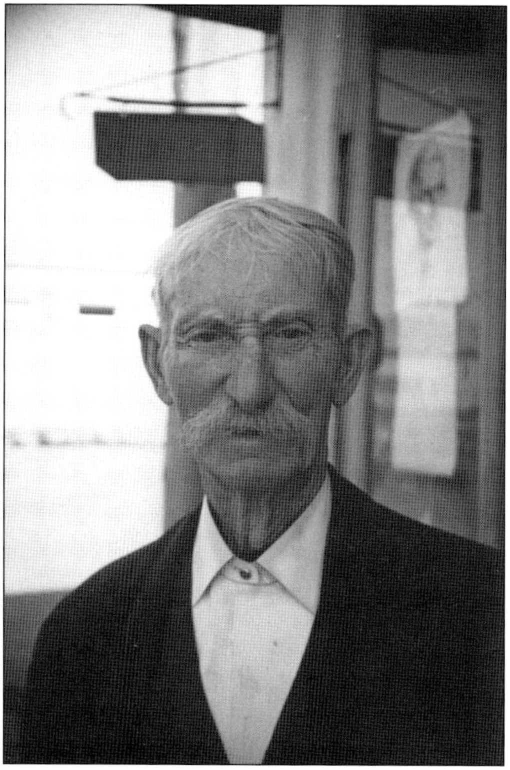

C.H. Pearson, born in 1852 in Canada, came to Los Alamos in 1879 and became a blacksmith. He sold his business in 1883 and became bookkeeper for the Laughlin Brothers Store before opening his own. Pearson owned three ranches and farmed and raised cattle. He served as coroner, deputy sheriff, and clerk of the school board. Pearson suffered a heart attack and died in 1942.

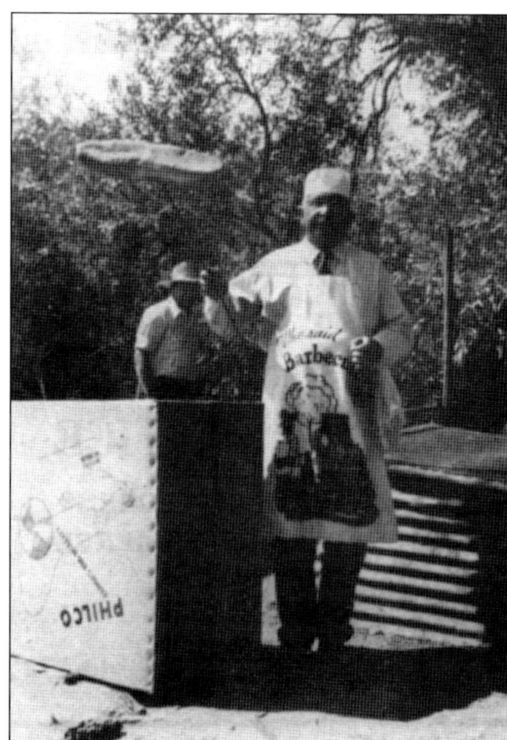

Joe Pico was the faithful barbecue chef for Los Alamos Old Days every year. Here in 1947, he is ready to prepare his toasted French bread in the old pit at the Los Alamos Valley Men's Club. Born in Los Alamos in 1883, Pico worked as a teamster on the ranches of John S. Bell, E.T. Fields, and Jack Rickard. John Bell built a small house for his vaquero on his ranch. (Courtesy of LAMC.)

Henry Gewe was born in Los Alamos in 1884, the son of Mr. and Mrs. William Gewe. He was the local postmaster for many years, always whistling a tune and known as the "walking history book." He served as trustee for the Los Alamos Cemetery District, the fire district, and the service district. He and his family are highly respected for all they have done for the town.

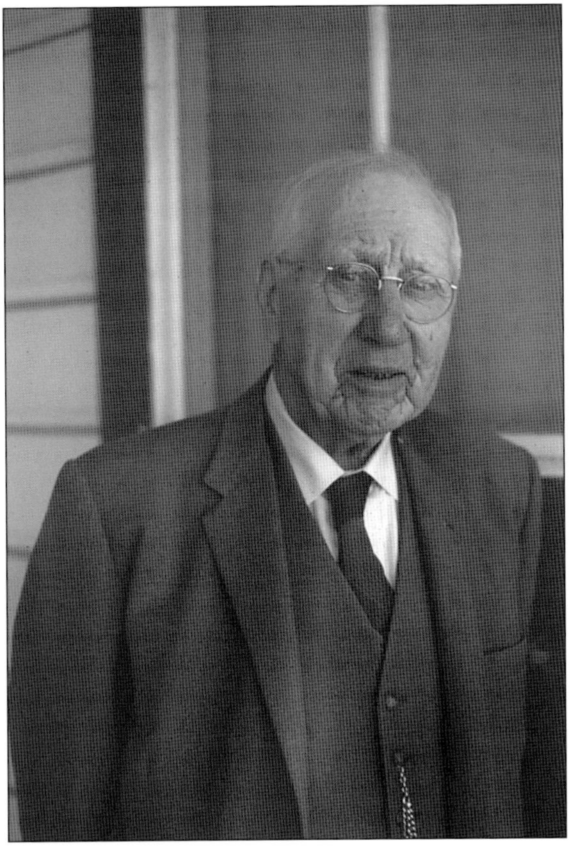

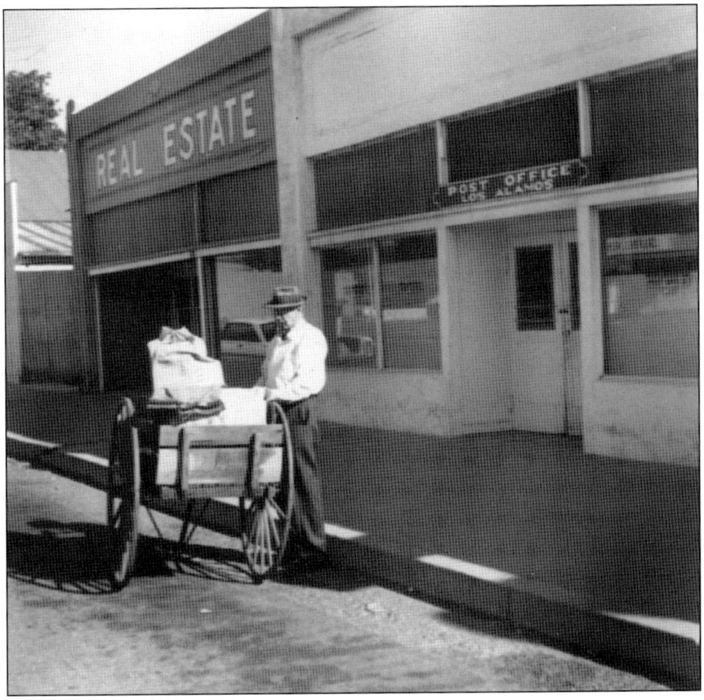

Henry Gewe, shown here with his cart and his pipe, was postmaster of Los Alamos from 1915 to 1949. Gewe owned the cart and used it to haul the mail from the narrow-gauge railroad station to the post office. This post office was located at 448 Bell Street, where Bedford Winery is now.

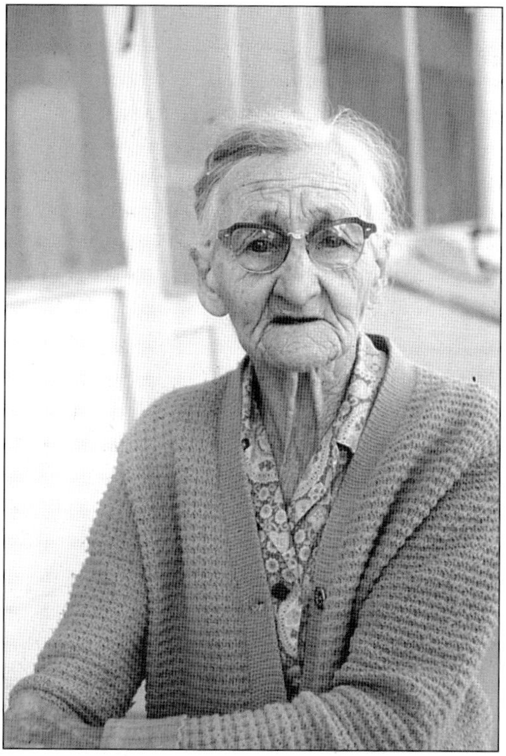

Hattie Mae Gewe Robbins was born in Los Alamos on May 19, 1885, the daughter of Mr. and Mrs. William Gewe. She married Ernest Robbins, who served as town constable. He built a filling station on the location of the Wurtz Blacksmith shop in 1923. The business was passed on to her son, Alvin.

On July 1, 1948, Ernest and Hattie Mae Robbins enjoy a surprise party at the Los Alamos Men's Club on the occasion of Ernest's retirement as constable and deputy sheriff in Los Alamos after 36 years. Ernest was able to perform his duties as constable while running his gas station full time. Attorney John Rickard (right) presents the gift. (Courtesy of LAMC.)

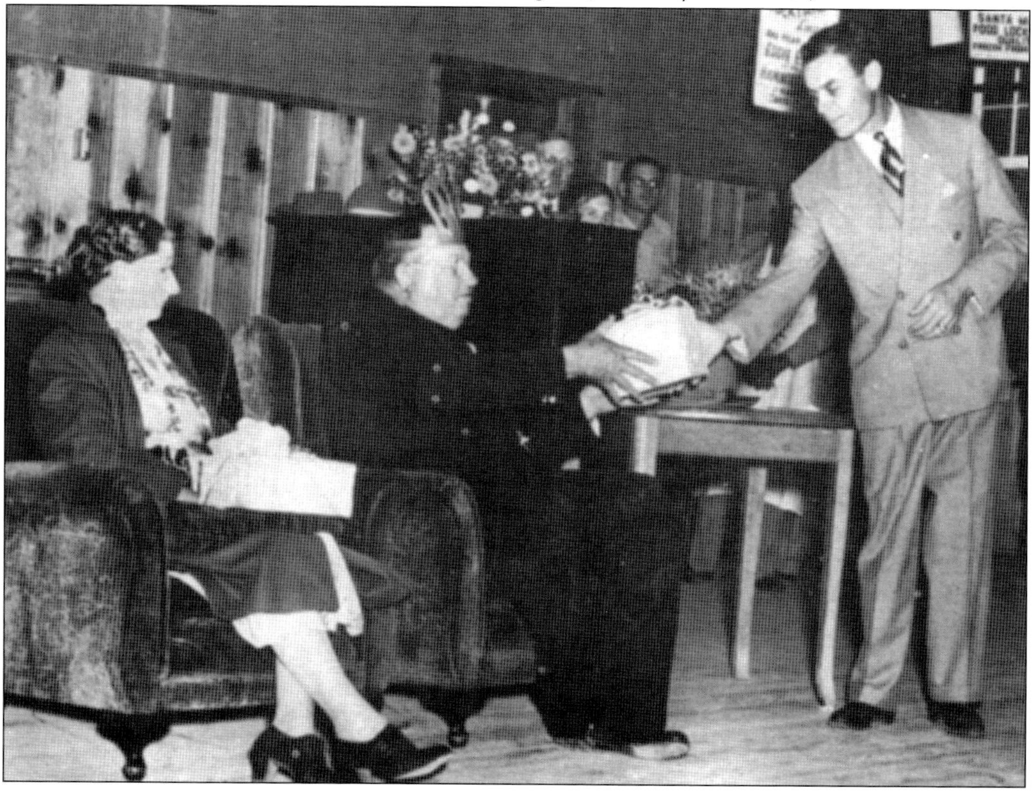

Shown here are, from left to right, Charlie, Charlotte, Helen, and Jeanette Tognazzi. Frank Tognazzi was born in 1892. Frank and his father, Victor, acquired the Las Flores Rancho in 1926 and began a dairy farm. Frank's son Charlie took over the operation at a young age and turned to raising cattle. Jeanette, his oldest child, was brought up to learn every aspect of the cattle business, and she acquired all the requisite skills. (Courtesy of Jeanette Sainz.)

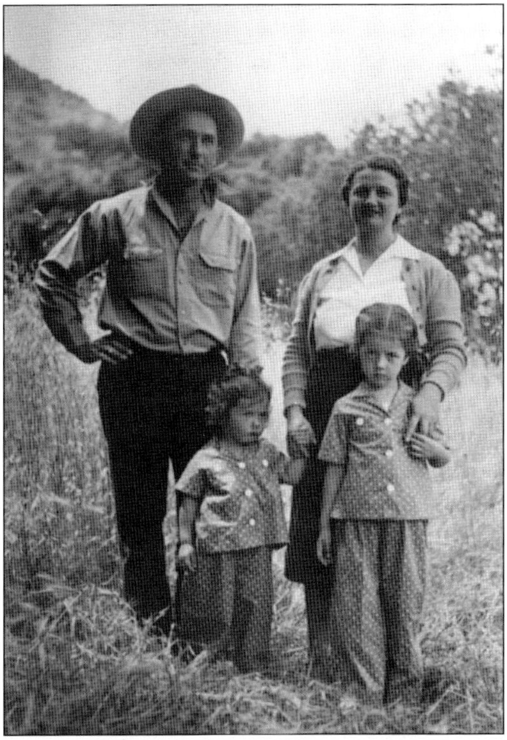

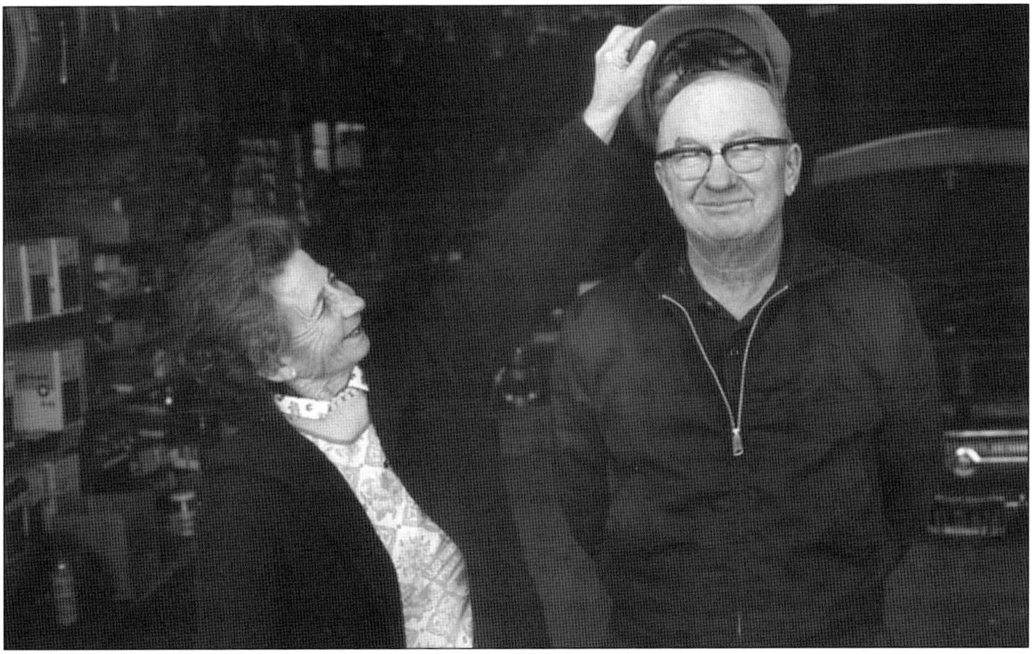

Both Alfonso and Dora Scolari's parents came from Switzerland in the late 1800s. Al was born on one of the Careaga ranches. When he grew up, he attended the National Automotive School. He opened the California Garage on Bell Street in the late 1920s. Dora was born in Lompoc and came to Los Alamos with her family as a child. Both Al and Dora were very active in Los Alamos affairs.

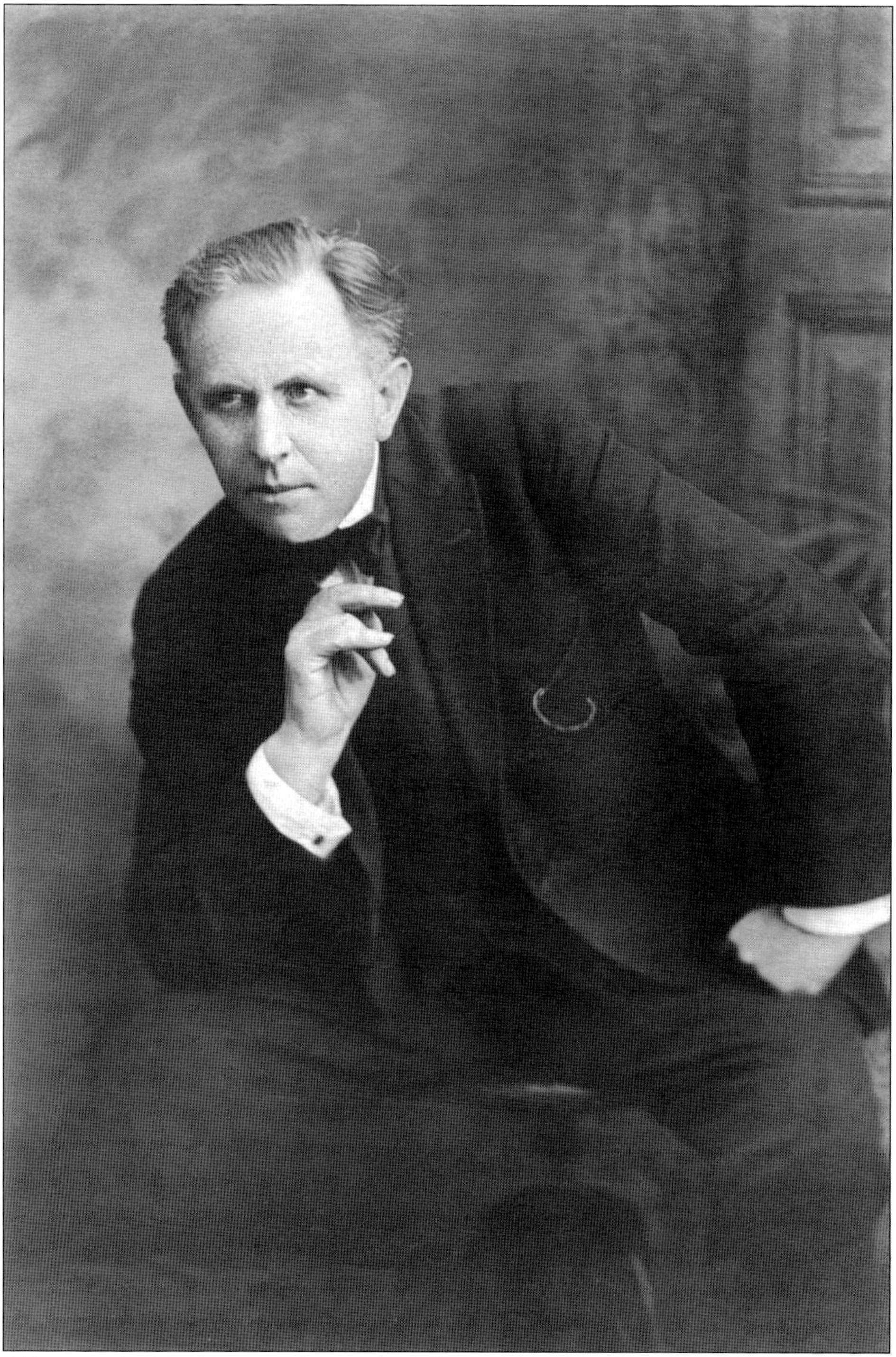

Max King purchased the general store from Alfred Newman in 1900. King named his store the Emporium, and his motto was, "We don't sell cheap goods, we sell good goods cheap." The general store had many owners over the years, but King may have been the most colorful, as his portrait reflects.

This photograph of a Mr. Smith and his daughter Florence was taken in 1905. Estella Smith came to Los Alamos in 1911 from Bakersfield with her husband and lived here 53 years. Gratie Smith came to Los Alamos with her husband in 1896 to become the society editor of the *Los Alamos Journal* newspaper, which later became the *Guadalupe Moon*. The author has been unable to connect the Smiths.

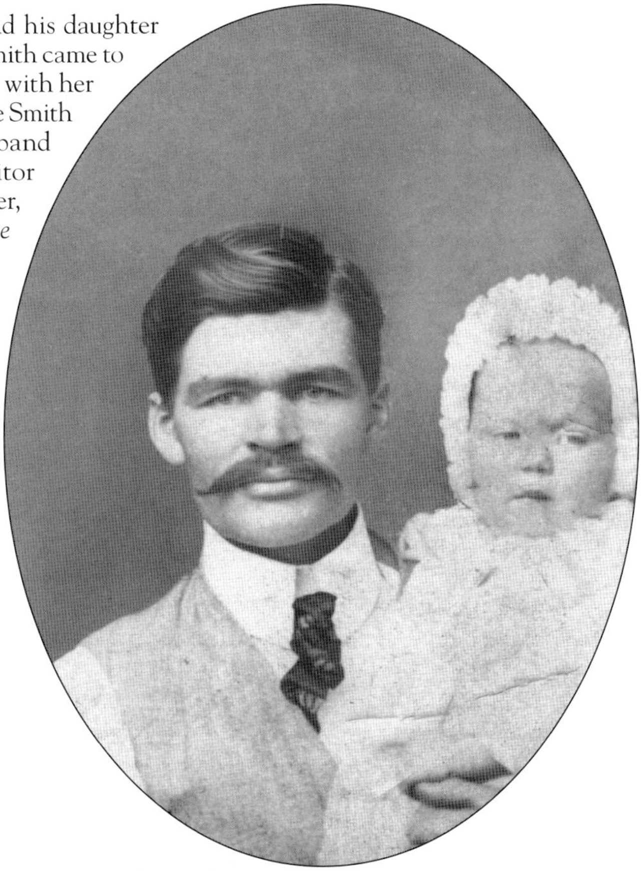

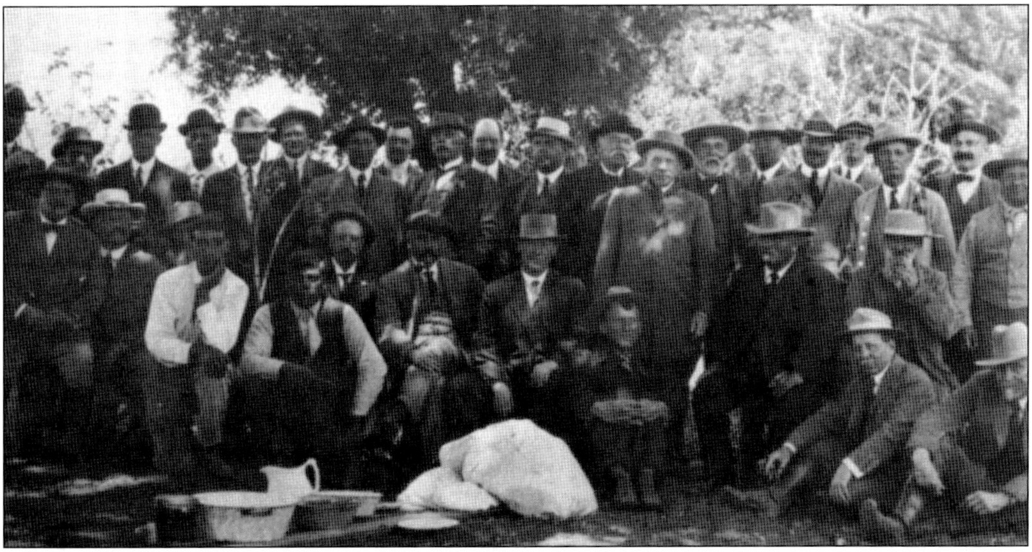

The Los Alamos Society consisted of ranchers who owned land west of the Santa Ynez Mountains. Owning a specific number of acres was required for membership. The organization is still active today, with 49 members throughout the United States. To join, one's name is placed on a waiting list, but no new member will be accepted until an old member passes away. (Courtesy of LAMC.)

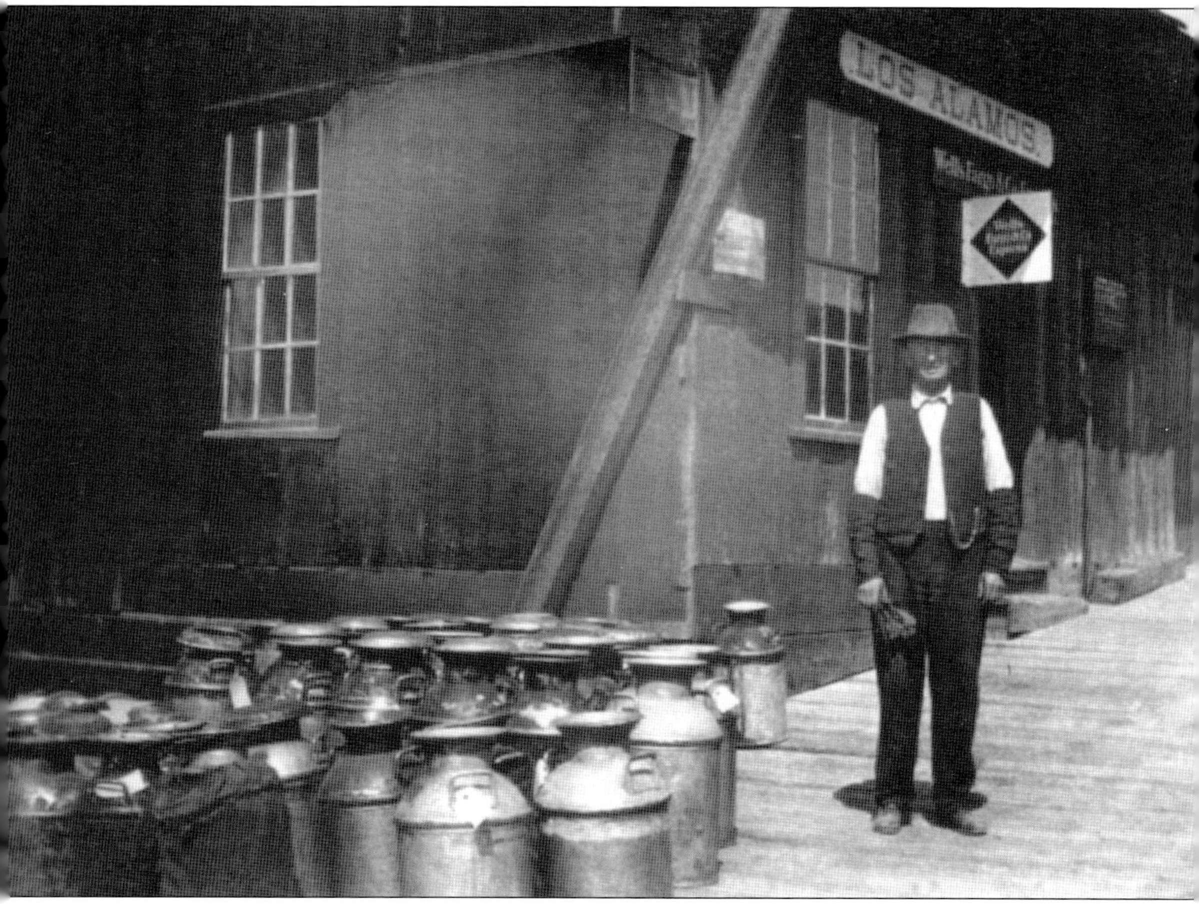

Stationmaster Fred Howard stands on the platform of the Los Alamos train depot. Behind him is the Wells Fargo Express Office. Milk pails, tagged for identification, stand ready to be shipped. At one time, Los Alamos had a large dairy industry. Depot buildings along the Central Pacific line were unpainted.

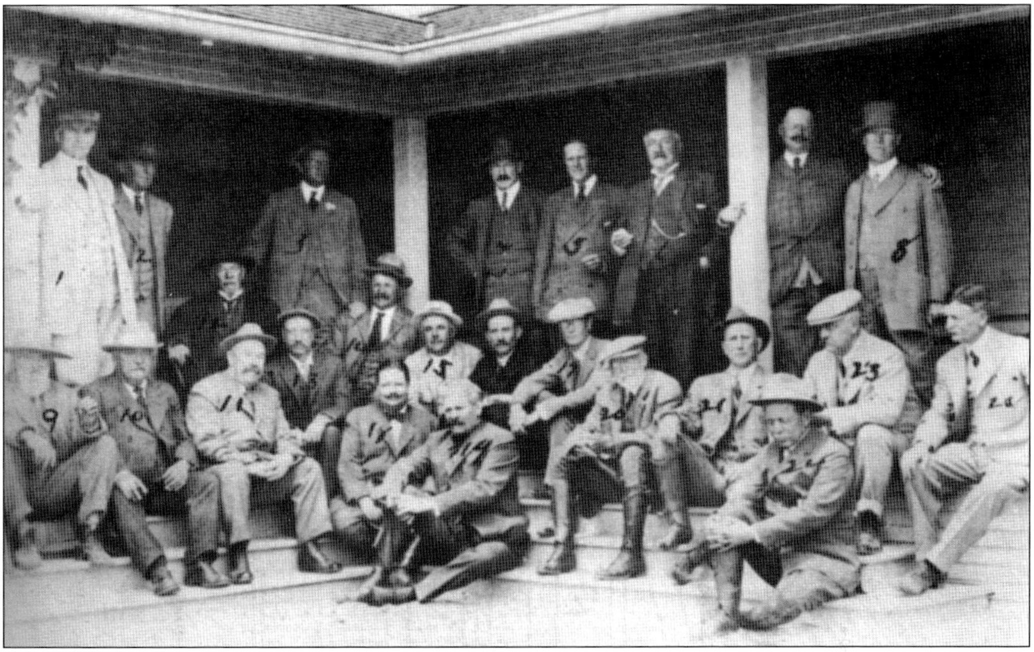

Early members of the Los Alamos Men's Club are, from left to right, as follows: (seated) John Waugh, Felix Mattei, Capt. Lawrence Harris, A. Leslie (behind Harris), John S. Bell, Samuel T. Coiner, Ernest Wickenden, T. Wilson Dibblee, Joel Fithian (center, second step), W.W. Burton (center, first step), Starbuck Masey, John McGillivray, A.M. Boyd, W. Campbell, and Ed Dela Cuesta (front); (standing) William T. Summers, Clifford Moore, Ed Schmiedell, Dr. Sidebottom, George Coles, John Conway, Francis T. Underhill, and Dario Orena. (Courtesy of LAMC.)

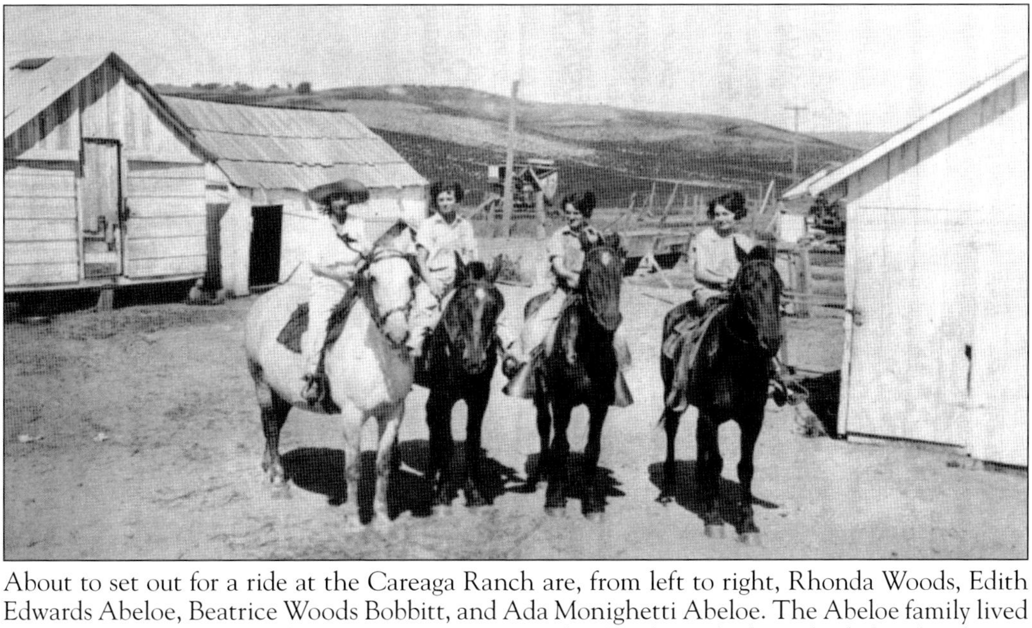

About to set out for a ride at the Careaga Ranch are, from left to right, Rhonda Woods, Edith Edwards Abeloe, Beatrice Woods Bobbitt, and Ada Monighetti Abeloe. The Abeloe family lived on the Careaga Ranch, where two generations of the family worked. Carl Abeloe, brother to Laura Abeloe, to whom this book is partially dedicated, can tell many stories of the town's past. (Courtesy of LAMC.)

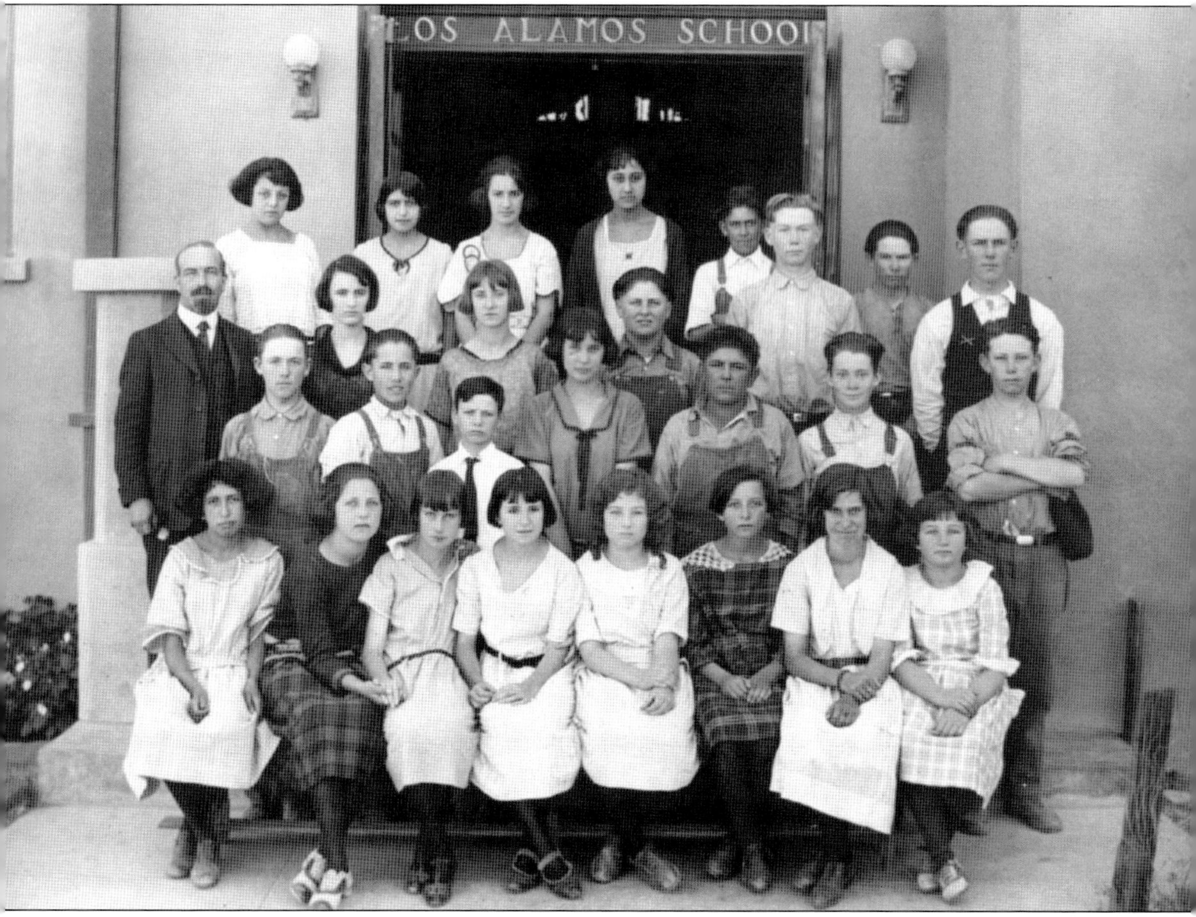

Proud students pose with their teacher, Mr. Bacon, for a photograph in 1919. From left to right are (first row) Virginia Calderon, Millie DeWitt, Anna DeRieux, Bernice Foster, Ellsie Guidolfi, Mable Medeiros, Marry Mellow, and Mary Guidolfi; (second row) unidentified, Manuel Costa, Joe Aguirre, unidentified, Carlos Delaguerra, Walter Marlett, and Dacus Phfitzner; (third row) Mr. Bacon, Jennie Sorando, Kathleen Bastanchury, and Anson Freitos; (fourth row) Mary Peters, unidentified Silva, unidentified Peters, Anna Martinez, Ed Delaguerra, Alvin Robbins, Alex Parker, and Everette Wurtz.

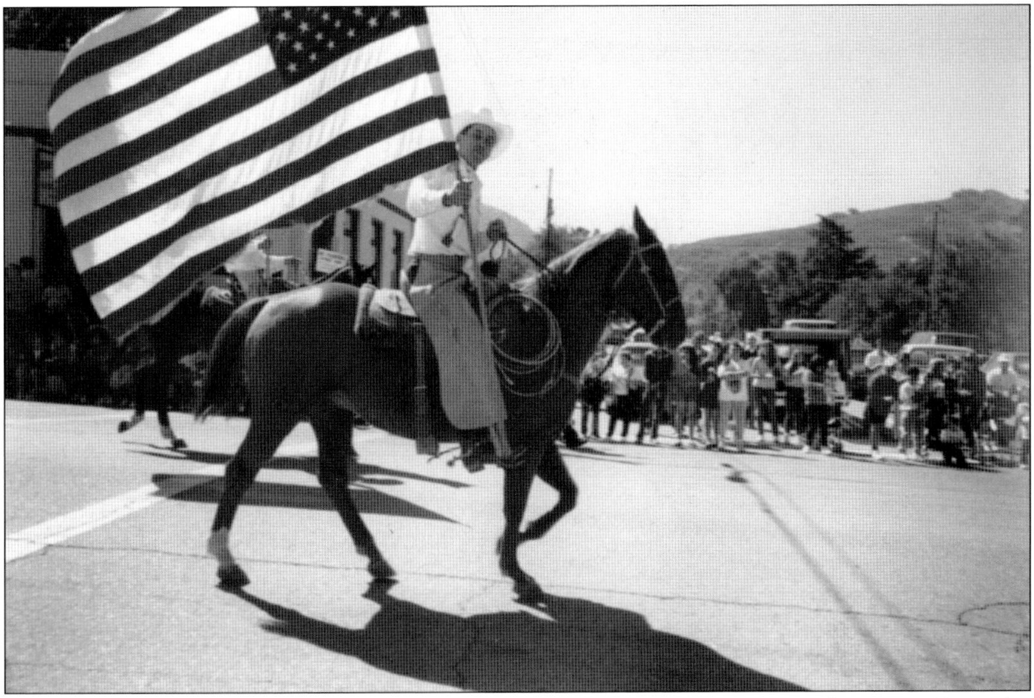

Brothers Bill (pictured) and Chuck King began a ranching operation together in 1965, in the footsteps of their ancestors. They grazed cattle and raised grains, hay, and garbanzo beans. The King brothers participated in the last cattle drive through Los Alamos, occasioned when they moved cattle they grazed in a pasture east of town to their home ranch on the opposite side. They participate every year in Los Alamos Old Days.

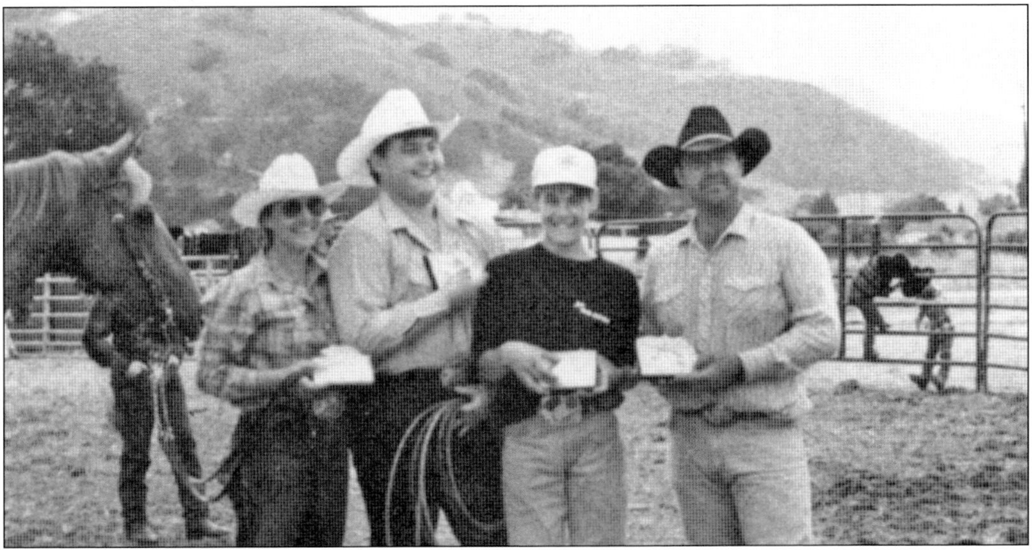

The ranching Branquinho family poses after winning the 1990 Ranch Competition at the Los Alamos Old Days Celebration. They are, from left to right, Brandy, Tony, Luke, and John. Young Luke would go on to become World Steer Wrestling Champion, a title he claimed repeatedly. Luke and his brothers come by their rodeo skills naturally, as descendants of old Californio families. (Courtesy of LAMC.)

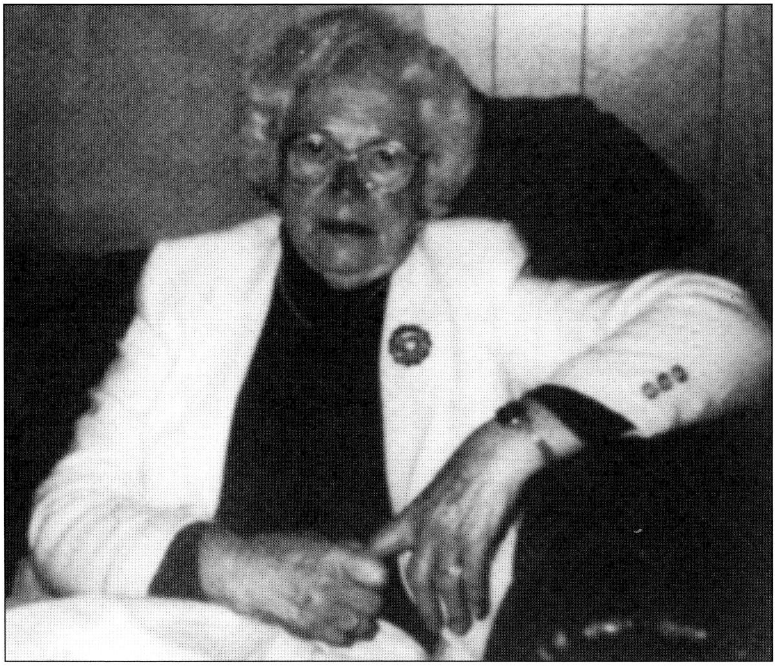

In 1977, Los Alamos School was renamed for Olga Reed (pictured). Born in Murphy, California, she was a graduate of Fresno State University. Her career in Los Alamos as a teacher and administrator spanned 43 years. She retired in 1972. The school has been fortunate in the quality of its staff of dedicated teachers. (Courtesy of LAMC.)

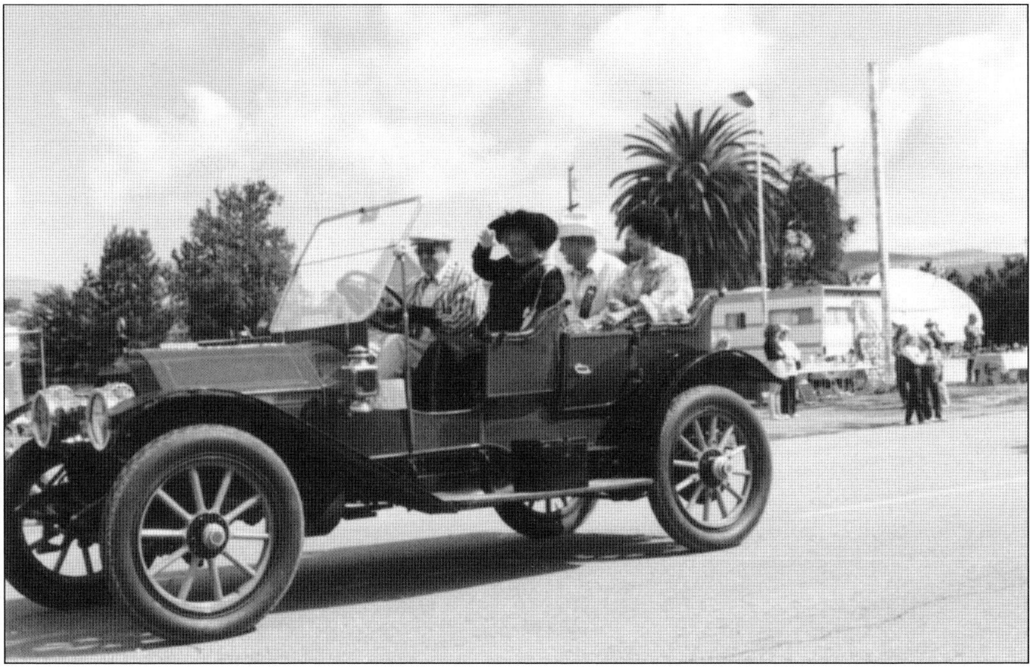

Jessie and Henry Gonzales (back seat) occupy the place of honor in the Old Days Parade. On an early trip through Los Alamos in his new Ford Model A, Henry Gonzales found himself stranded when the car broke down in the middle of town. Henry and Jessie decided to stay and opened a freezer/butcher business in town in 1957. Son Charlie owns Charlie's Place, a favorite restaurant in town. (Courtesy of Charlie Gonzales.)

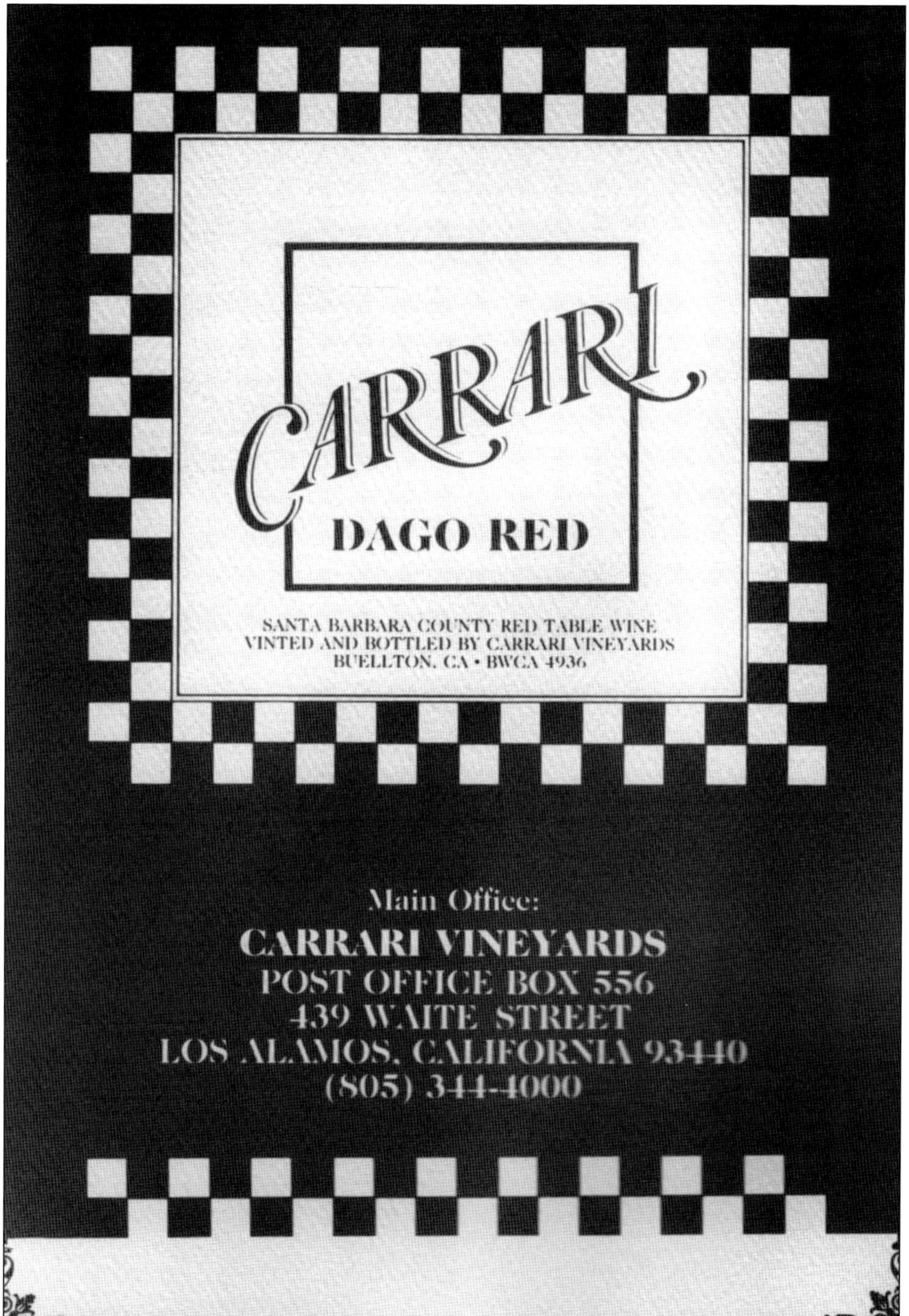

Joe Carrari first picked grapes when he was five years old. He came to Los Alamos from Soledad to manage the White Hills Vineyard. He soon purchased his own vineyard. When the market declined, he found himself with several varieties of grapes that would not sell. In a moment of frustration (or genius), he blended them all into one wine and named it Dago Red. It sold well. (Courtesy of LAMC.)

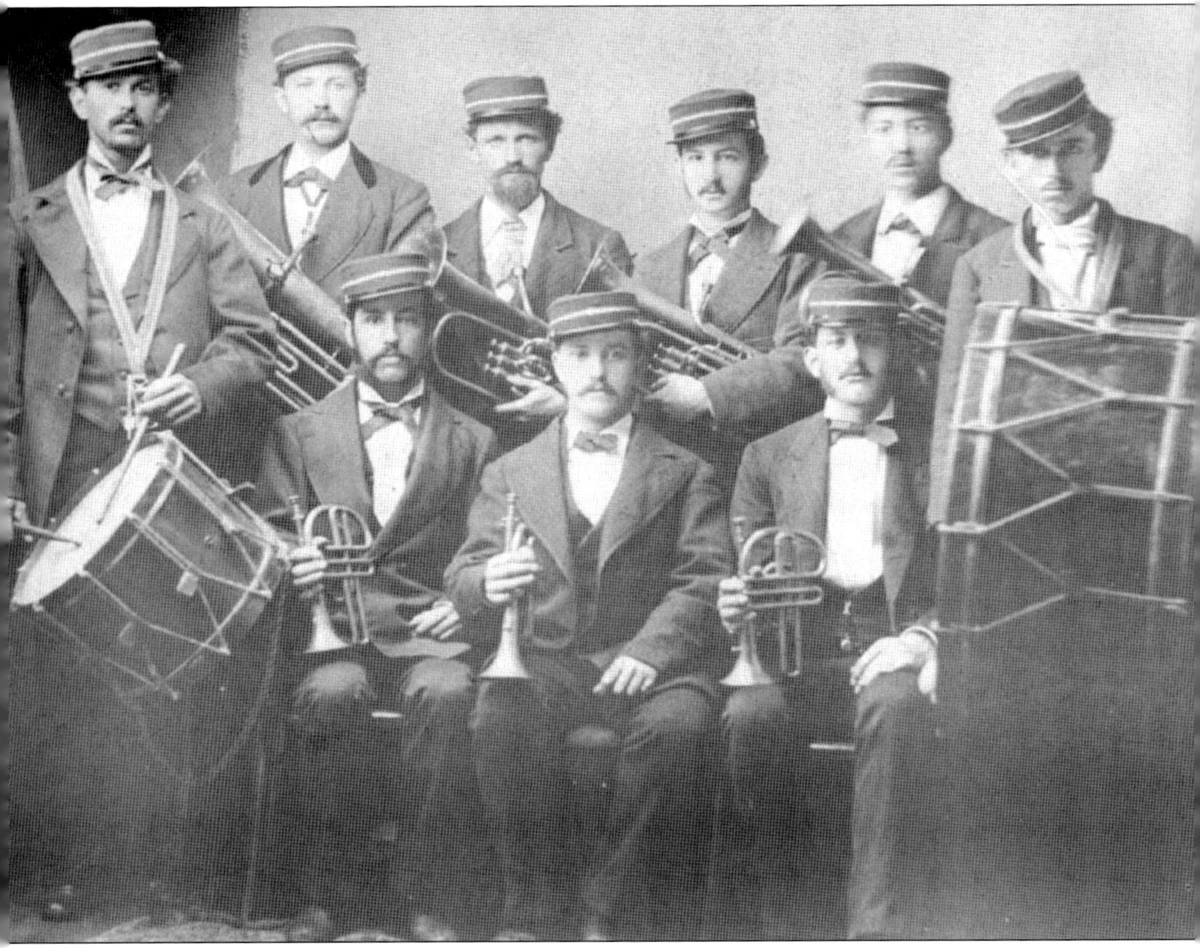

Prof. Joseph Green organized a brass band in Los Alamos in 1882 and dressed the members in these snappy uniforms. This photograph brings to mind Prof. Harold Hill from *The Music Man*, but Professor Green built an actual band. By 1900, marching bands had become thoroughly integrated into American society. They played at political rallies, minstrel and medicine shows, carnivals, picnics, dances, and every important occasion.

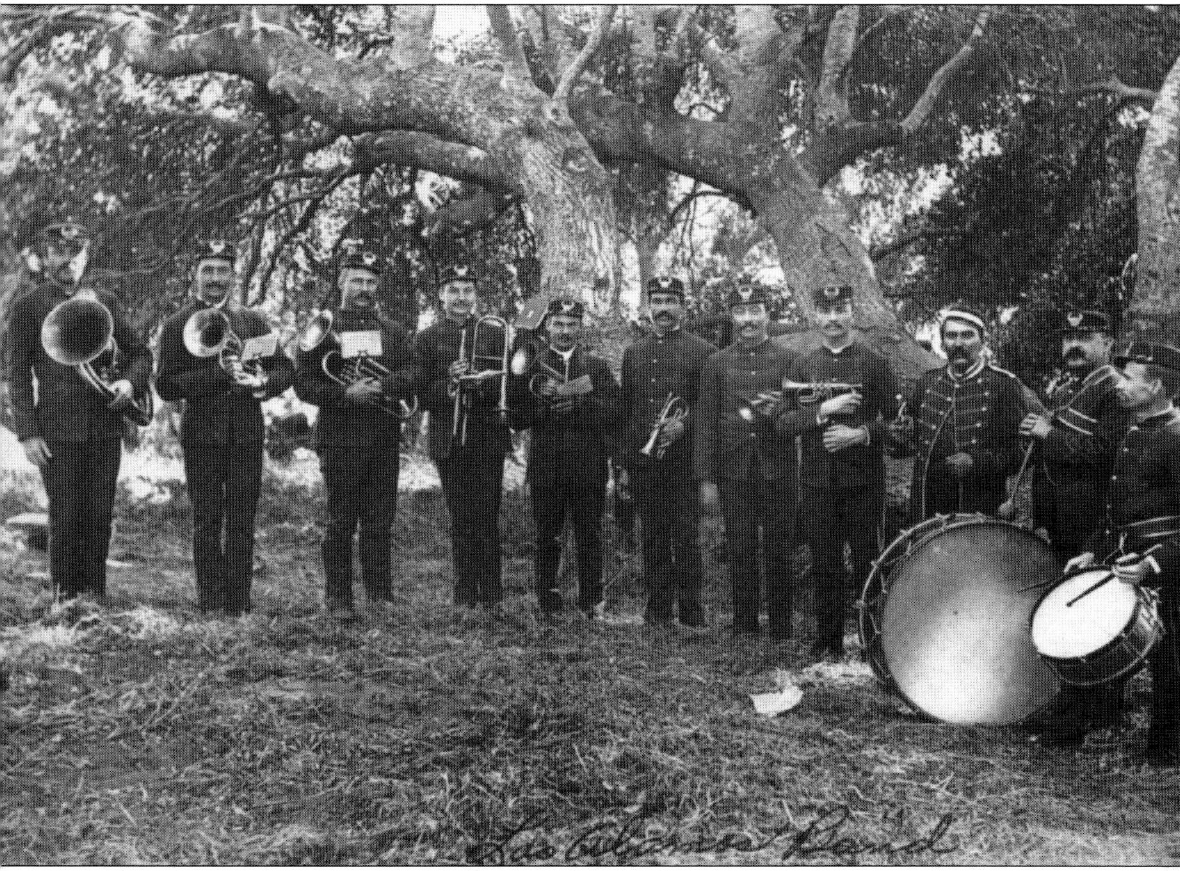

This is a later edition of the Los Alamos Band. The bands often had military-style uniforms, a reflection of their heritage from the American Civil War. Bands provided listeners with popular, light music while instilling patriotism. Such music was considered appropriate to almost any event. Bill Robbins is at the far left. (Courtesy of Jeanette Sainz.)

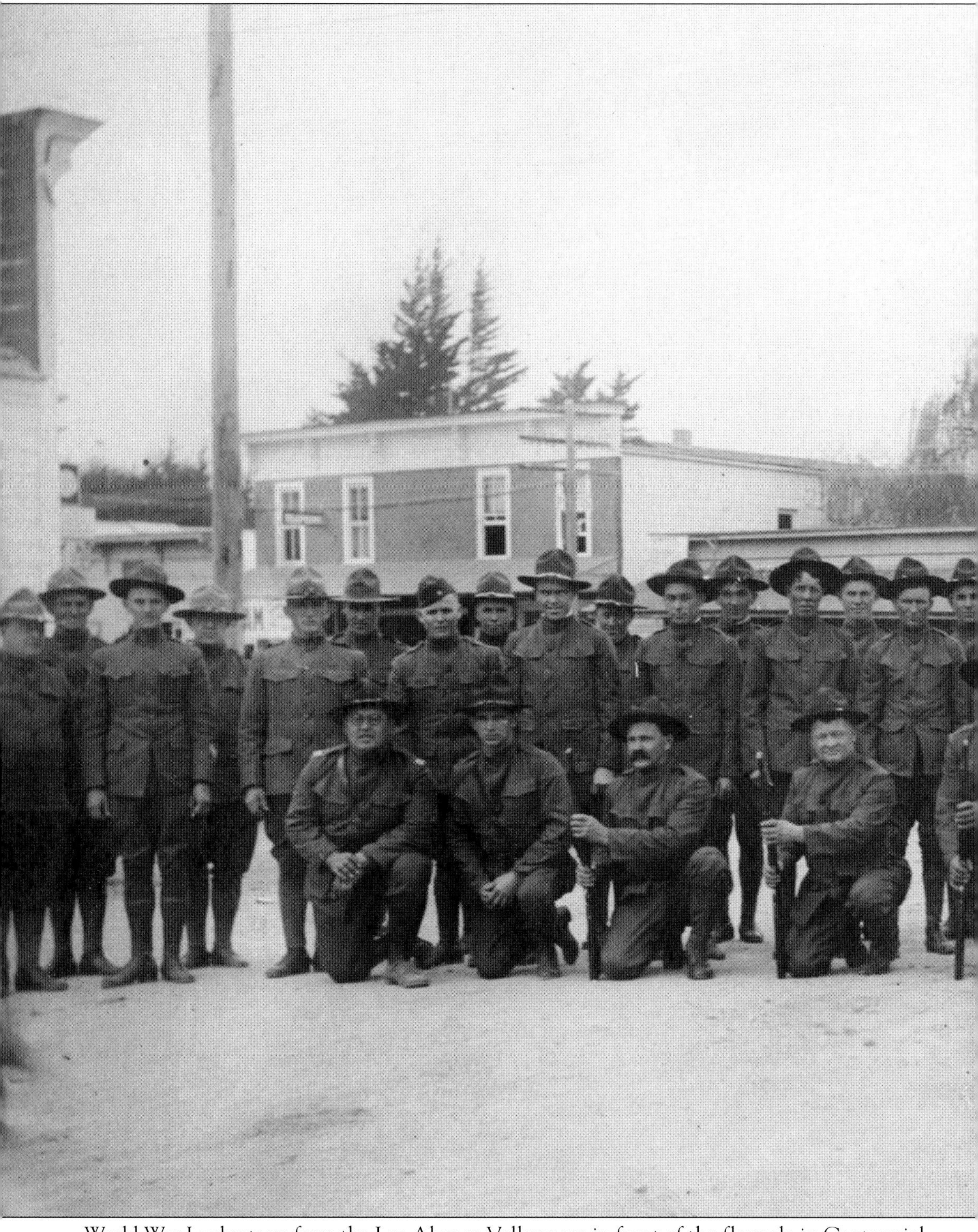

World War I volunteers from the Los Alamos Valley pose in front of the flagpole in Centennial Street. The flagpole was an award for a very successful Liberty Bond drive. It seems enlistment

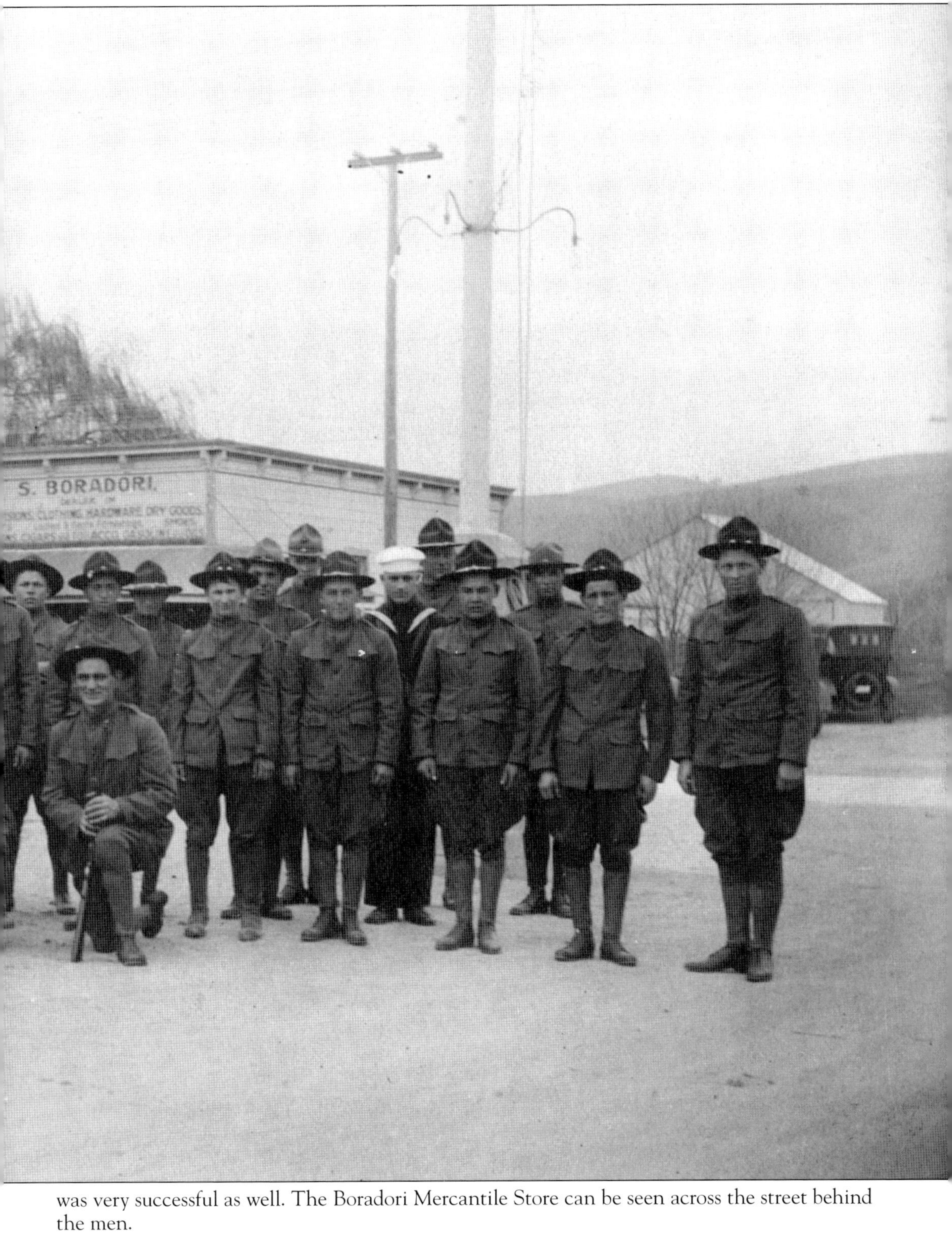

was very successful as well. The Boradori Mercantile Store can be seen across the street behind the men.

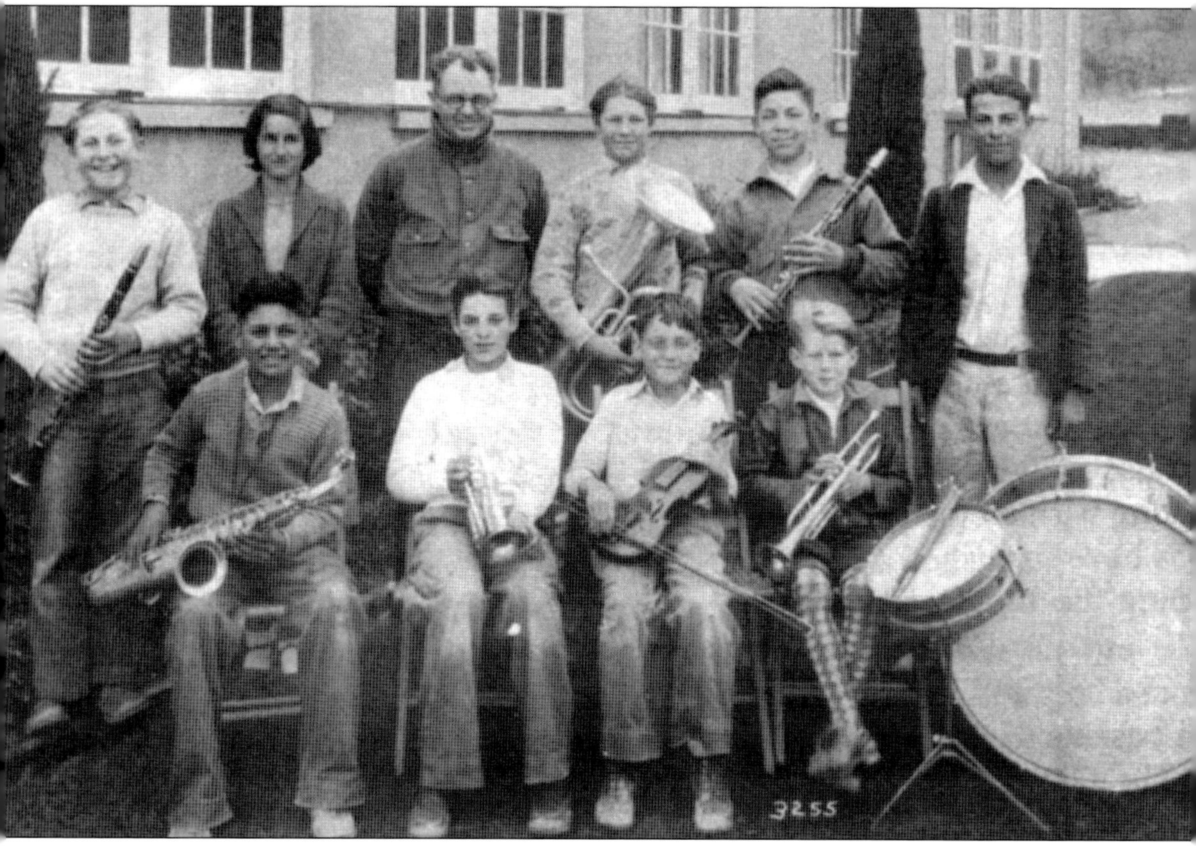

The Los Alamos Grammar School Band poses for a photograph in 1932. Shown are, from left to right, (first row) Billie Evens, Albert Rodrigues, Harold Holmes, and Dick Wade; (second row) Charles J. Eddy, Jean Boradori, teacher Henry Wide, Frank Drum, Henry Rono, and John Borges. Many of these young people grew up to become active members of the Los Alamos community. (Courtesy of LAMC.)

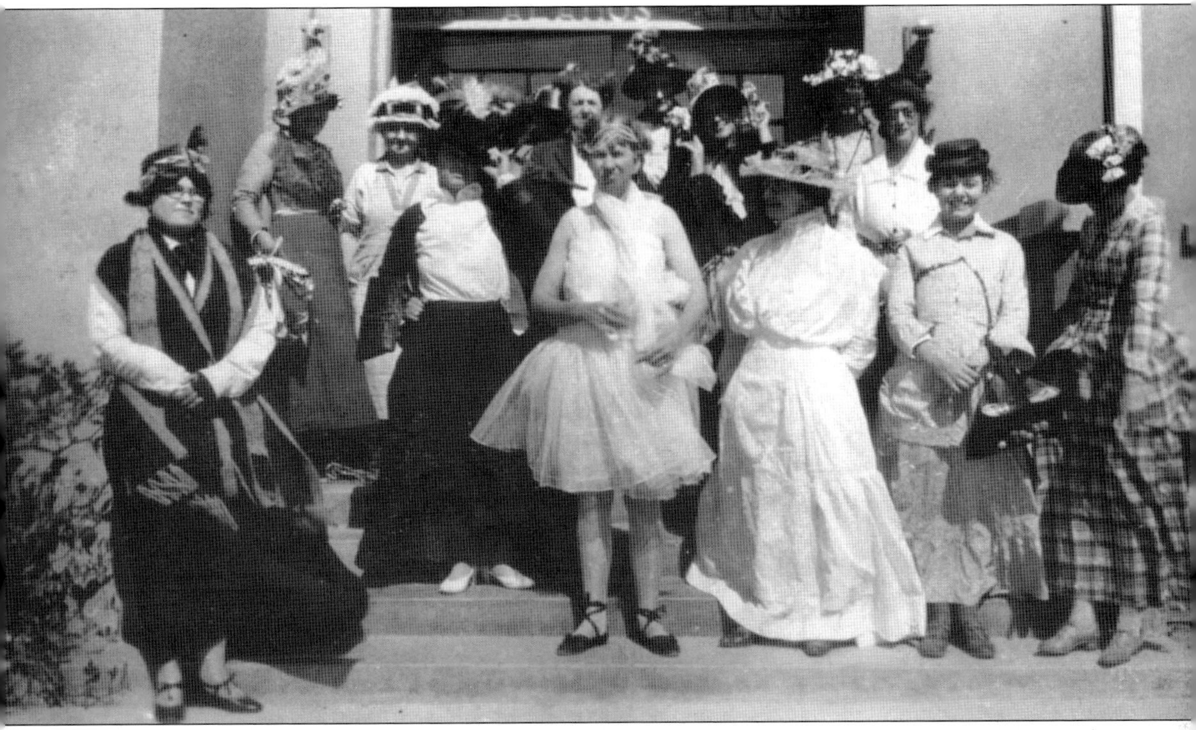

Young women gather for a dress-up affair on the steps of the Hotel Los Alamos. When Jake and Mary Stine owned the hotel, they named it the Gay Nineties Hotel. Possibly the guests here are dressing for an event about to take place. Even today, guests will sometimes dress to match the theme of their room in the Victorian Mansion Bed and Breakfast.

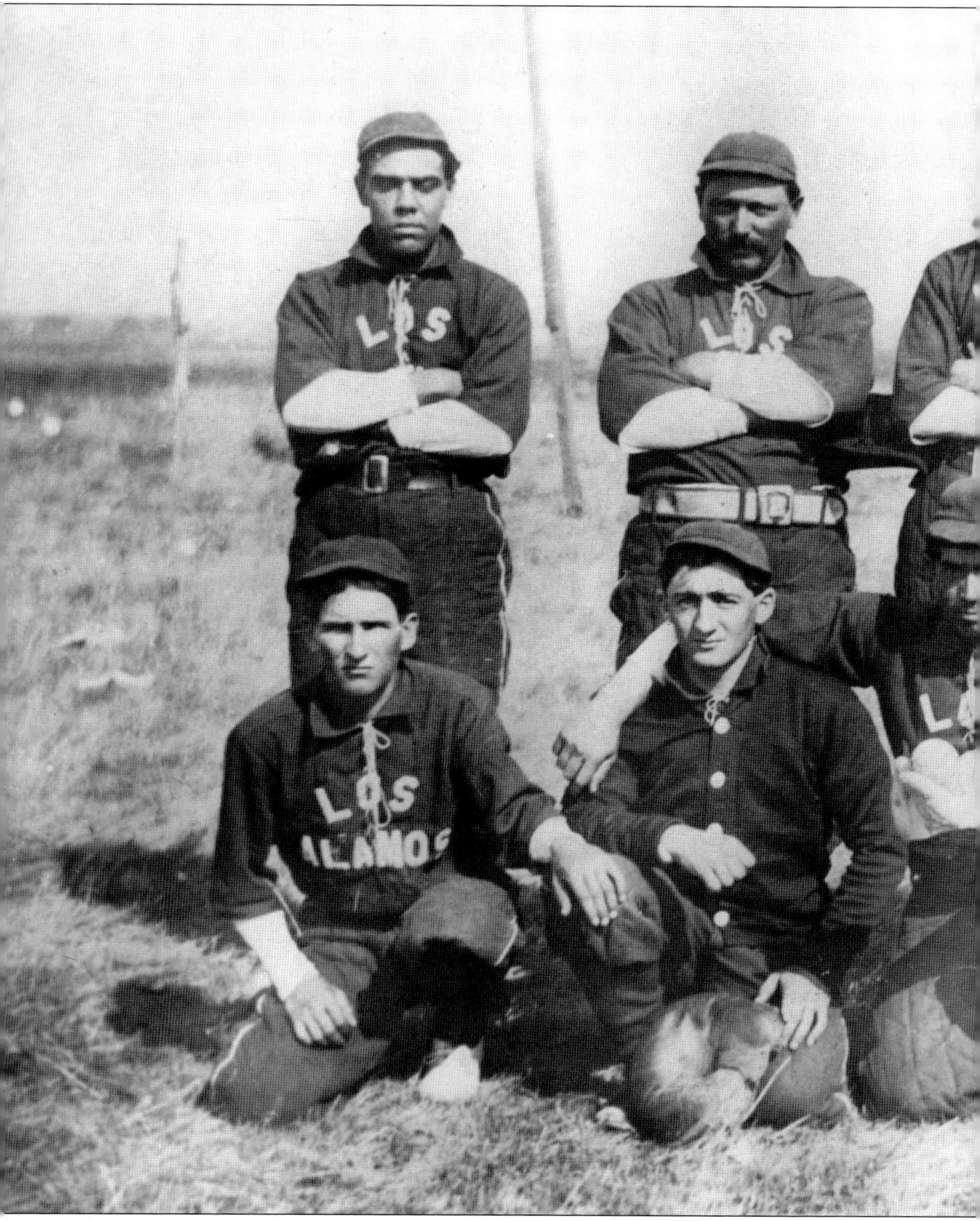

At one point in time, the town of Los Alamos supported a semipro baseball team, the Los Alamos Cowboys. The unwebbed baseball gloves they used would challenge even today's professional

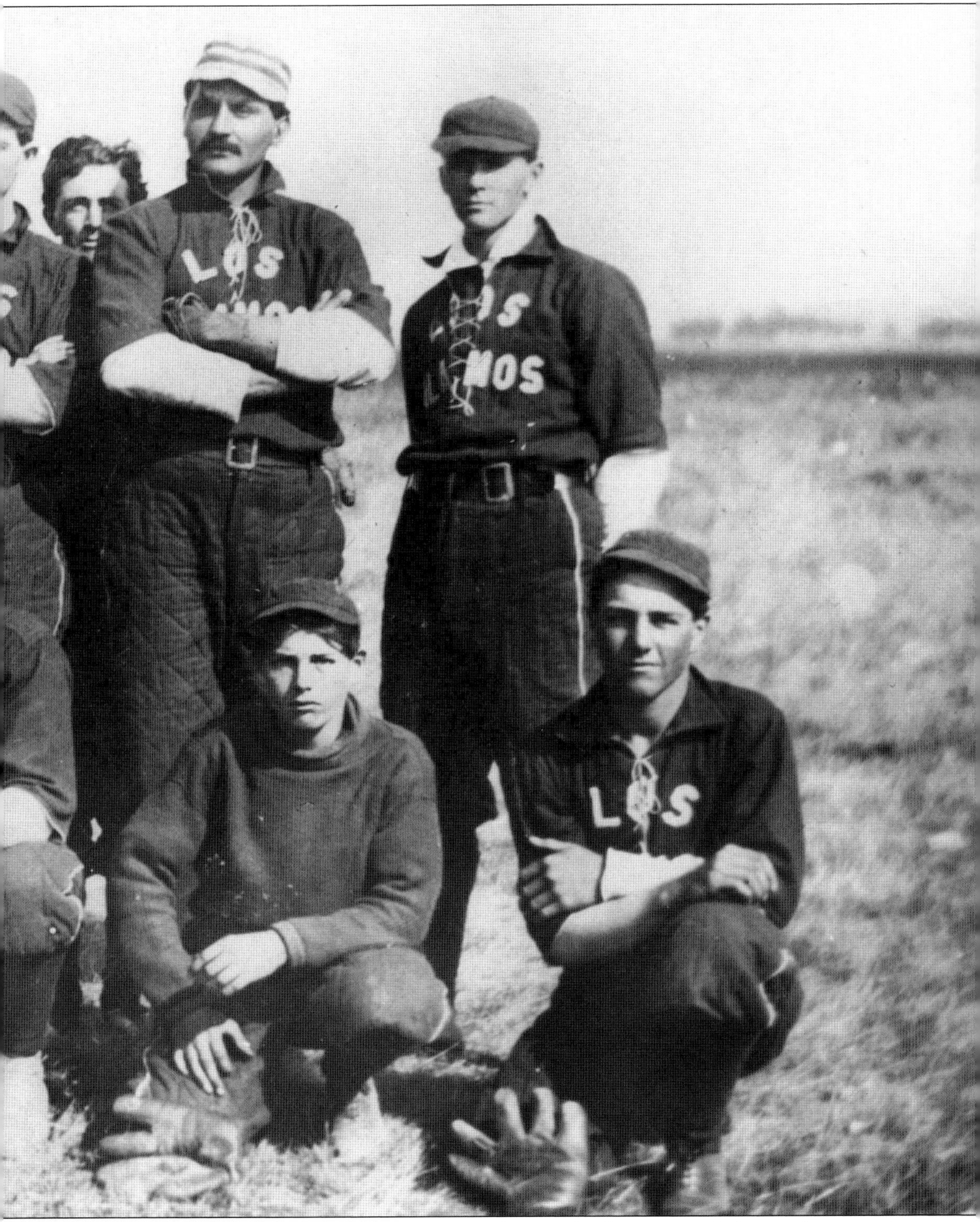

players. The pitching/catching tandem seems evident in the first row, and the coach is trying very hard not to be seen in the back.

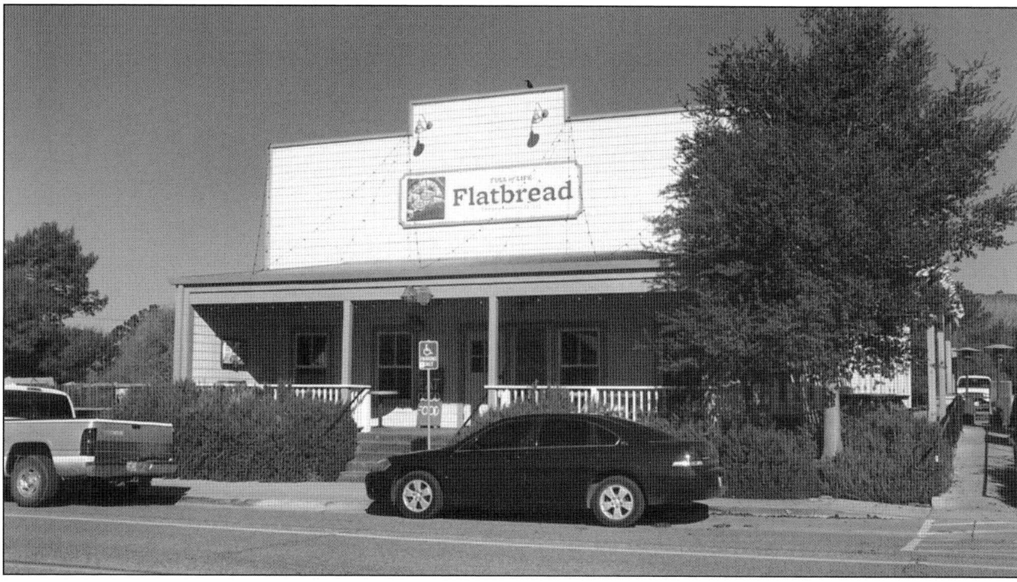

The Full of Life Flatbread Company opened in 2003, operating mainly as a wholesale business making frozen, organic flatbread. Former music business executive Clark Staub built a 20-ton stone oven modeled on a Quebec beehive oven, from which all his food emerges, except the salads. The attraction comes from the simple, healthful fare and the more than 90 wines offered. The restaurant draws great crowds every weekend. (Photograph by author.)

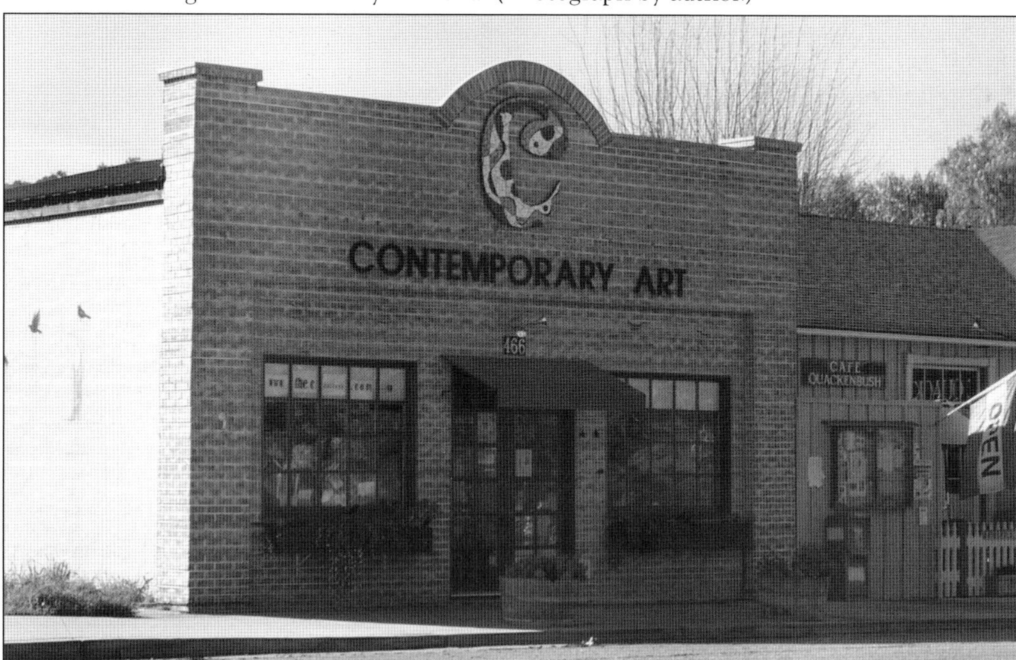

The C Gallery opened in 2008 as a space for contemporary art, with revolving exhibits of drawings, paintings, sculpture, and furniture accessories. The gallery offers small, intimate art classes for Los Alamos residents that combine beginning drawing skills and foundational art principles. Connie Rohde-Stanchfield owns the gallery and supports and encourages beginners as well as professionals. (Photograph by author.)

Jeanette Sainz met her husband, Darwin, in Santa Maria High School when she was Jeanette Tognazzi. Their marriage brought together three generations of oilmen and three generations of ranchers. Jeanette's home today is a museum of artifacts and documents pertaining to the history of both areas, passed down each family branch. Jeanette safeguards those documents and valued items. In recognition of her work, this book is dedicated to her. (Photograph by the author.)

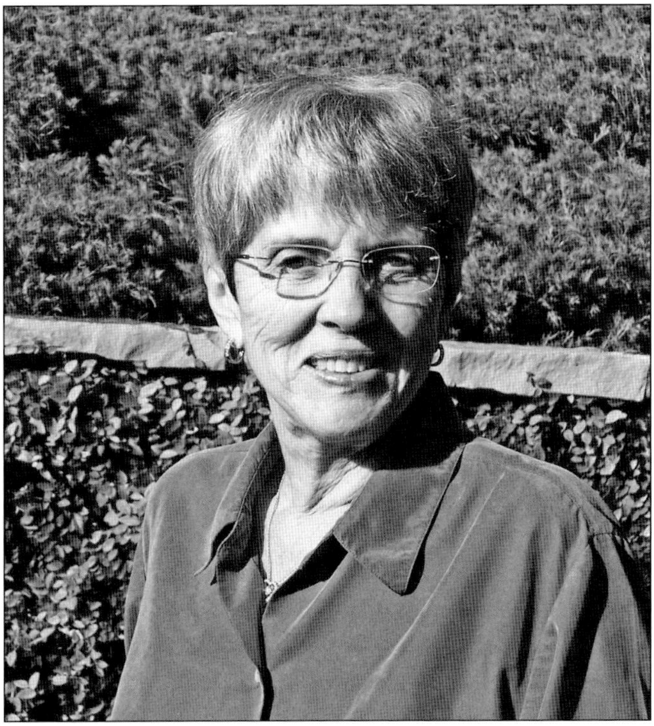

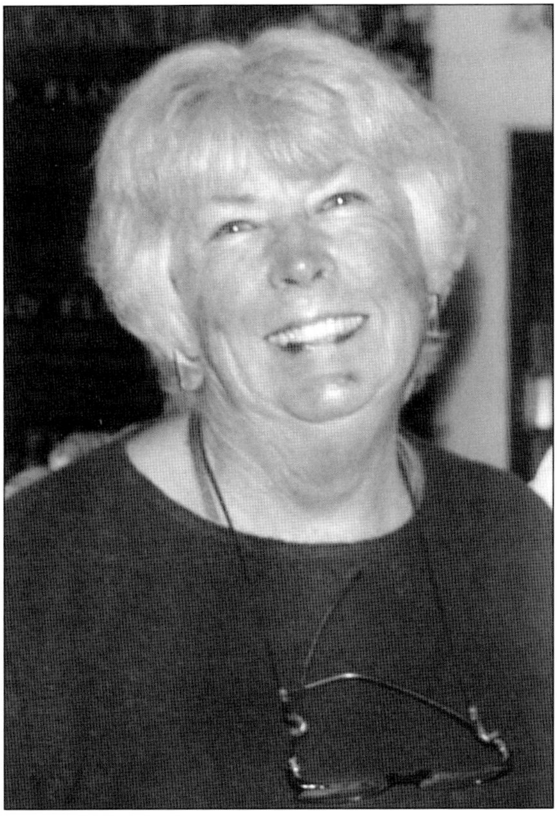

Laura C. Abeloe, to whom this book is also dedicated, was born and raised in Los Alamos and lived on the Abeloe property west of town. She worked for the General Telephone Company for 30 years. She developed her interest in Los Alamos history in the late 1980s and began to collect information from old newspapers and archives at Berkeley and elsewhere. Laura Abeloe passed away in 2009. (Courtesy of Carl Abeloe.)

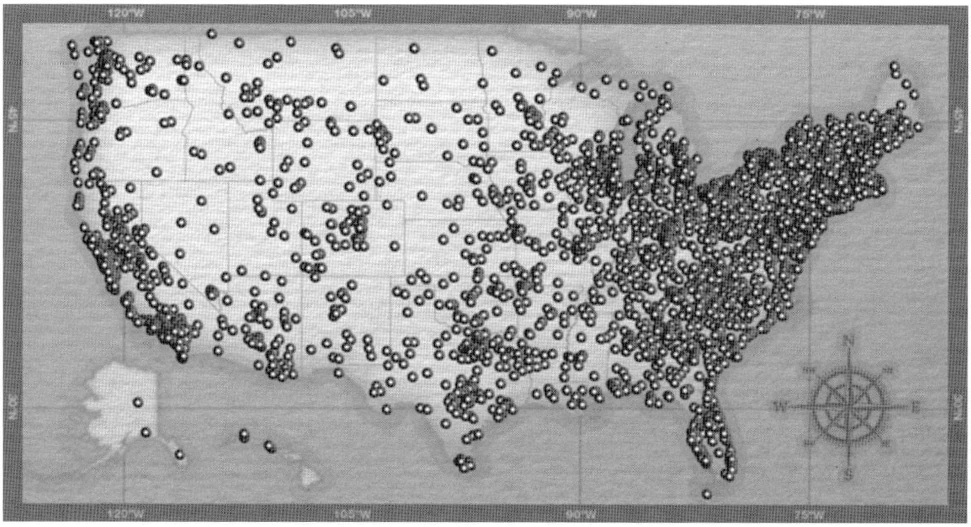